D0509497

GARDENING TECHNIQUES

Writer	Illustrator	Designer	Art Director
Lee Foster	April Funke	James Stockton	Karen Tucker

Ortho Books

Publisher
Robert L. Iacopi

Editorial Director
Min S. Yee

Managing Editors
Anne Coolman
Michael D. Smith

Production Manager
Ernie S. Tasaki

Senior Editor
Sally W. Smith

Editors
Jim Beley
Susan Lammers
Deni Stein

Design Coordinator
Darcie S. Furlan

System Managers
Mark Zielinski
Christopher Banks

Photographic Director
Alan Copeland

Photographers
Laurie A. Black
Richard A. Christman
Michael D. McKinley

Production Editors
Linda Bouchard
Alice Mace
Kate O'Keeffe

Asst. System Manager
William F. Yusavage

Photo Editors
Anne Dickson-Pederson
Pam Peirce

Production Assistant
Don Mosley

National Sales Manager
Garry P. Wellman

Sales Assistant
Susan B. Boyle

Operations Director
William T. Pletcher

Operations Assistant
Gail L. Davis

Administrative Assistant
Georgiann Wright

Address all inquiries to
Ortho Books
Chevron Chemical Company
Consumer Products Division
575 Market Street
San Francisco, CA 94105

Copyright © 1984
Chevron Chemical Company
All rights reserved under
international and Pan-American
copyright conventions.

First Printing in August, 1984

2 3 4 5 6 7 8 9
85 86 87 88 89

ISBN 0-89721-031-X

Library of Congress Catalog Card
Number 84-061503

Chevron Chemical Company
575 Market Street, San Francisco, CA 94105

ACKNOWLEDGMENTS

Photographs:
(Names of photographers are followed by page numbers on which their work appears. R = right, L = left, T = top, B = bottom.)

Ralph J. Adkins: 170
William C. Aplin: 8T
Laurie Black: Front cover, 94R
John Blaustein: 32
Ralph S. Byther: 169
Richard Christman: 60
Josephine Coatsworth: 9T, 92, 118, 131T
J. A. Crozier: 154TL,
B. Emerson: 143R
M. Keith Kennedy: 152, 171
Michael Landis: 10, 12, 33L, 63, 78, 87B, 81, 119B, 128, 140, Back cover: Top left, top right, bottom left
Michael McKinley: 8B, 13, 33R, 131B, 155R, 143L, 179
James K. McNair: 180
Ortho Photo Library: 178
J. Parker: 155L
Pamela Peirce: 142T, 142B
William Reasons: 181
Michael D. Smith: 80T, 154R
Tom Tracy: 154B, Back cover: Bottom right

Manuscript consultation:
Shirley Barker
Bob Cowden
Judith L. Donaghey
Harland J. Hand
M. Ali Haravandi
Raul Hernandez
Emile L. Labadie
Sharon Tracey

Special thanks to:
Kaye Wellman

No portion of this book may be reproduced without written permission from the publisher.

We are not responsible for unsolicited manuscripts, photographs, or illustrations.

Every effort has been made at the time of publication to guarantee the accuracy of the names and addresses of information sources and suppliers and in the technical data contained. However, the reader should check for his own assurance and must be responsible for selection and use of suppliers and supplies, plant materials and chemical products.

Front Cover:
The pleasures of gardening are open to a person who has the basic skills.

Back Cover:
Top left: A hose-end proportioner can be used to apply liquid fertilizers.

Top right: You can improve appearance and productivity by pruning fruit trees correctly.

Bottom left: Softwood cuttings of herbs can increase your supply. Remove lower leaves before burying the stem in a rooting medium.

Bottom right: Frequent watering is the most neglected step in planting a new tree. Create a soil basin to make watering easier in the important first weeks.

Title page: With careful attention to soil preparation, variety selection and planting dates, a backyard vegetable garden can produce a surprisingly large harvest.

CONTENTS

WATERING 61

FEEDING 79

PRUNING 93

SUPPORTING PLANTS 117

HOW TO USE THIS BOOK

Gardeners are often led to believe that the key to a beautiful and productive garden lies in the number and variety of plants it contains. Much of the gardening world supports this view. Beautiful and exotic seed catalogs tempt us with pages of colorful, striking flowers in every shape and form, as well as an endless variety of flawless, grade A fruits and vegetables. A stroll through a well-stocked nursery will break the resolve of all but the most stalwart of gardeners. Row upon row of plants flush with promise of future bloom and lush growth have their effect; the selections are made. Yet, all too often, the intricately designed and newly planted garden resplendent with color and variety begins to look shabby and unkempt. Ultimately, the beauty, productivity, and success of any garden depends upon the health and vigor of the plants. Even the simplest of gardens can be appealing if the plants are well cared for. It is the understanding of how to care for plants, of good gardening techniques, that can make a success story out of a group of indoor plants in an entryway, a bed of flowers, a vegetable garden, or an extensive estate garden. This

The reward of good gardening—a chance to relax among thriving, productive plants.

book describes and illustrates those basic techniques so necessary to a healthy, vigorous garden.

How the chapters are organized

Each chapter in this book has two separate sections: an overview of the theory underlying the technique, and a practical how-to-do-it techniques section. The first section, the overview, provides the theory behind the practice, the explanation of what is involved in certain gardening techniques, and why they have a particular effect on the plant. The chapter introductions also describe the basics of soils, water, climate, and the other elements that are required for plant growth. The introductions provide additional background for the gardener who wishes to have an understanding of, for example, why flowering annuals need certain proportions of fertilizers, or why fruit trees must be pruned in a particular way.

For the gardener who is mainly interested in the practical, step-by-step gardening basics, in adding a new technique to his or her repertoire, or in brushing up on a half-forgotten technique, the practical techniques sections may be used exclusively. Within a chapter, all the gardening techniques contained in the practical techniques

section are related, but each technique is presented as a distinct, self-contained topic on separate sets of facing pages. For example, pages 68 and 69 tell you how to install a sprinkler system. All the information about that particular technique is contained on those pages. The description of each technique is accompanied by illustrations, and in many cases by lists or charts. The book is designed for quick reference. For example, if your newly planted maple tree just blew over, you can find out what to do immediately by looking up "Staking Newly Planted Trees" on page 120. Later, at your leisure, you can read through the overview section and the other techniques sections in the chapter to learn more about staking and supporting plants.

Good gardening techniques

In order for plants to grow well, indeed to grow at all, certain plant requirements must be met, including such basics as light, water, soil, and nutrients. Good gardening techniques are simply the methods that work best in supplying those needs. Of course, plants differ in their requirements. Some plants are quite adaptable and will tolerate a wide variety of growing conditions, such as sun or shade, or wet or dry soil. However, a number of plants have quite specific cultural requirements and will struggle along or die if their needs are not met. But fussy or not, all plants have their own unique requirements that, when met, will allow them to grow to their full potential. So there are many variations of the basic gardening techniques that have been developed in order to provide the right kind of care for different plants. However, once the basic technique is understood and practiced, it is usually a simple matter to change a technique slightly to accommodate various kinds of plants.

In the following pages you'll find the tried-and-true techniques that have been used successfully by most gardeners. Several different methods can usually be used to accomplish any given garden task; many of them use innovative methods or techniques that may work well for some gardeners but

Right: These epiphyllums are adapted to a jungle environment. They do well in a moist, shaded setting.

Below: A healthy lawn and attractive landscape plants are signs of a careful and informed gardener.

have not been in use long enough or practiced widely enough to qualify them as consistently reliable techniques. Although the techniques described in this book may be just some of the possible alternatives, they represent proven, mainstream methods that are worthwhile mastering.

Watering, feeding, pruning, and the other basic gardening techniques apply to most kinds of plants, so you'll find all the major plant groupings (flowers, vegetables, trees, shrubs, and houseplants) discussed in the following pages. A section titled "Surefire Plants," beginning on page 178, lists a variety of reliable plants for specific purposes.

Garden challenges

Even the most accomplished gardener must sometimes face the challenges of weeds, insects, animals, and plant diseases. Plant pests of one sort or another are present everywhere, and they may seem overwhelming to the new gardener. Although even the best-tended garden can suddenly be plagued with aphids or mildew, good gardening techniques will help reduce the damage caused by plant pests. This is because plants that are well cared for are healthy and vigorous and are better able to resist pests and diseases. Also, techniques such as weeding and garden cleanup eliminate the places where many plant pests breed, greatly reducing the likelihood of attack in the first place.

However, certain measures and techniques must be used to effectively combat some pests. For instance, a hungry rabbit will most likely be enticed, not deterred, by a healthy, carefully grown lettuce plant. And if you've planted roses susceptible to mildew in an area where mildew is severe, even the best of growing conditions will not prevent infection.

You will find a discussion of weeds, insect and animal pests, and diseases in Chapters 8, 9, and 10. Once you've learned about plant pests and the special techniques for controlling them, you'll be able to easily add them to your regular garden care routine.

Top: Digging in the flower bed can be a pleasure if the digging is done right (see page 20). The flowers in front are nasturtiums.

Bottom: You can start your own plants (see page 31) or make your own potting mix (see page 22).

MANAGING SOIL

The soil is the foundation of a plant's growth. Soil is a dynamic substance that we can alter and affect to help plants grow better.

Plants and soil are so interrelated that one would not exist without the other. Soil exists only in areas where plants grow or have grown. The development of this complex substance is the end result of plant life moving from the protected ocean environment to the harsher conditions of dry land. As the first primitive plants gradually inhabited the earth's surface, they began to change the nature of the rocky terrain on which they grew; the result was soil. Soil provides plants with water and nutrients. It is also a medium into which plants anchor their roots, giving them the stability to defy gravity and grow upward. Understanding and managing this precious substance properly is one of the most important aspects of growing plants. So much so, in fact, that many gardeners come to regard the soil as their most important gardening asset.

The components of soil

What is soil? It is a complex mixture of solids, water, and air A typical garden soil contains 50 percentsolids, 25 percent liquid, and 25 percent air. Soil solids are either mineral or organic in nature. The mineral portion accounts for most of the soil solids, usually about 45 percent. The organic solids make

This pine needle mulch not only protects the soil, it also protects the lettuce from splashing mud.

up a much smaller portion, 5 percent or less. The remaining constituents, water and air, are held on the surfaces of the soil solids or in the spaces between them.

Mineral solids. The mineral solids in the soil range from extremely small to very large particles. The particle size and the proportion of particle sizes in a soil determine its *texture*. The soil texture has a profound effect on the physical properties of the soil. Specific descriptions have been developed to describe soil texture. Sandy soils comprise one extreme of soil texture, and clay soils are the other. Each of these extremes has very different physical properties. The intermediate soil textures, such as the silts and loams, have properties of both.
1. Sandy soil has large particles, large enough so that individual grains can be seen and felt.
2. Silt soil has intermediate particle sizes, about the size of a plant cell.
3. Clay soil has small particles, the size of bacteria.
4. Loam soil has a mixture of all the particle sizes.

Sandy soils have large pores, or air spaces, between the soil particles. They drain quickly but do not have the capacity to hold as much water as soils with a finer texture. Because of their large pores, sandy soils contain a lot of air, which moves into and out of the soil

easily. Air heats up and cools off rapidly, so sandy soils warm up quickly in spring; they also lose heat rapidly when the weather cools in fall. Sandy soils are usually less fertile than finer-textured soils because nutrients are not held as tightly to these large particles and are easily washed away. Roots grow easily in sandy soils. Because the large particles in such soils do not cling tightly to each other, digging and tilling in sandy soils is relatively easy.

Clay soils, with their microscopic particles, contain very tiny air pores. These soils have a much greater capacity to hold water than sandy soils, but if not carefully managed they may become waterlogged. Clay soils heat up and cool off slowly. The nature of the tiny clay particles allows them to cling tightly to nutrients so that they are available in the soil where plant roots grow. Clay soils are naturally more fertile than sandy soils because of this quality, and fertilizers will not wash away as quickly. Because these soils are not as loose as sandy soils, they are more difficult to work. They should not be cultivated when wet because the small particles can compress to an adobe-like consistency, reducing water and oxygen flow through the soil. Plant roots will penetrate such compacted soil only with difficulty.

Organic solids. The organic portion of the soil consists of dead and living plant and animal matter in various stages of growth and decay. This portion makes up only 0.5 percent to 5 percent in most native soils, but well-amended garden soil may contain as much as 50 percent (or more) organic matter. Organic matter significantly increases the ability of the soil to hold water. As dead organic matter gradually decomposes in the soil, it forms humus. Humus helps the mineral particles stick together in larger groups, giving the soil a granulated, crumbly property. This property, the way in which soil particles group together to form larger aggregates, is known as soil structure. Soil structure greatly influences the soil workability, or *tilth*.

The living part of the organic portion of the soil includes some large and obvious creatures, such as earthworms and insects. Earthworms perform a valuable service by creating tunnels for air and water flow through the soil. An invisible world of soil bacteria, fungi, and algae are even more crucial. These microorganisms decompose organic matter, contributing to the humus that improves soil structure and water-holding qualities. Microbial activity also contributes to the chemical reactions that allow plants to use mineral nutrients.

Soil profile

If you dig deeply into your soil, making a vertical section, you'll see that there are several distinct layers. The types and sequence of soil layers is known as the soil *profile*. The appearance of the profile can tell you much about the soil's potential for gardening success. The top few inches of the profile might be a dark, loose soil of fine texture, high in organic material. This *topsoil* supports most plant growth.

Below the topsoil lies the *subsoil*. Its layers may be more or less impervious. If the subsoil is compacted clay, drainage will be poor. If the profile is quite sandy, nutrients in the soil may leach quickly through to the subsoils.

About the only thing you can do to improve your soil a foot or two

Soil cultivates best when it is at just the right moisture content. When wet, it is too sticky; and when dry, it is too hard.

below the surface is compensate near the surface with additional organic material to buffer any limitations. Grave problems with subsoils may encourage you to garden with raised beds in a surface soil you create.

Soil liquid

The pores between soil particles are occupied by water, air, or both. Soil water contains dissolved minerals. Plants can only take in their food (minerals) dissolved in water. Water is also necessary for the physiological and chemical processes of plant growth. Water adheres to soil particles until small rootlets of plants take it up.

Drainage is one of the key considerations when assessing your garden soil. How well will your soil drain? How well will it hold water? Water drains much more easily from large pores, with air entering

the vacated space. Small pores will tend to retain water. An ideal soil has a mix of large and small pores, so that the soil will hold both water and air.

Deep soils drain better than shallow soils because capillary action draws the water downward. Shallow soils, such as those in containers, stay saturated at their base longer, which is why potting soils need to have large pores to prevent roots from dying.

Soil air

Spaces not occupied by water will be occupied by air. Soil air is more humid than the air we breathe and has a higher carbon dioxide content. But the soil air will have some oxygen, which is vital to the root growth of plants. Air diffuses easily from the ground surface into the soil if the soil particles are large. Cultivating the soil allows air, as well as water, to enter the soil.

Soil pH

The soil pH refers to its acidity or alkalinity. Soil pH is measured on a scale from 0 (totally acid) to 14 (totally alkaline), but only the middle ranges of the scale, from 4 to 8, are of interest to gardeners.

Soil pH has many crucial effects on plants. Most plants grow well in the neutral to slightly acid range and do poorly at either extreme. Some plants, such as azaleas and blueberries, flourish at very acidic pH levels. The correct pH is essential for making plant nutrients available in a form that can be used by plants.

Whether your soil is acid, alkaline, or neutral may depend on your region. Soil pH depends on the amount of calcium present in the soil. In high-rainfall areas, calcium, which is slightly soluble, is leached out. Acid soils are characteristic of regions with heavy summer rainfall and soils high in organic material. If a soil test shows that your soil has become too acidic, the condition can be corrected by adding lime (calcium).

Alkaline soils are characteristic of regions where the rainfall is low or where the soil is high in calcium. The situation can be corrected by adding sulfur to the soil in the form of soil sulfur, iron sulfate, or aluminum sulfate, by using an acid-reacting fertilizer, or by incorporating into the soil acidic amendments such as ground bark, sawdust, or peat moss.

Soil salinity

Soils may be high in salts where soils are high in alkalinity, where rainfall is too low to wash away accumulated soil salts, or where the native soil is naturally high in salts. Irrigation water may also be high in soluble salts. Softened water that has gone through a home water softener is very high in salts. Other salt sources include chemical fertilizers and animal manures. Salt buildup in soil soil can reduce germination of seeds and stunt the growth of plants. Counter salt buildup by thoroughly leaching the soil with water that is salt-free. If your salt problem was caused by

With paved paths between the raised beds, this gardener can hand-water without getting muddy feet.

salty irrigation water, you can still use such water to correct the problem. Paradoxically, with deep soaking of the soil, even salty water can wash the salts to below the root zone. If your house water is softened, use an outdoor water tap for all your indoor plant watering.

Soil temperature

Temperature is another variable to be aware of in soil. Most plants simply stop growing at soil temperatures under 50°F. Plants have minimum and maximum ranges within which they survive. Temperature also affects the speed of chemical reactions. Higher temperatures provoke more rapid soil reactions, up to a point. For example, some organic fertilizers release nutrients only at relatively warm temperatures. On the other hand, the availability of chemical fertilizers is only slightly reduced at low soil temperatures. Beneficial effects of soil organisms will occur only if the soil is warm.

Mulches

Mulching amounts to putting a protective layer of material on top of the soil. A mulch prevents soil erosion and is an insulation and

buffer, moderating the effect of weather and temperature on soil. Mulch keeps the soil crumbly, preventing it from baking to a crust on the surface. Mulch also slows the flow of rainwater, letting it trickle into the soil and minimizing runoff. Mulch slows evaporation, reducing summer watering chores. Winter mulches act as an insulation against freezing cold that could damage less than hardy plants. Mulches prevent the alternate freezing-thawing that kills many plants. Winter mulches also protect bare ground from the erosive forces of water and wind.

Soil for raised beds and containers

Containers of all kinds have become increasingly popular with home gardeners. Choosing the proper soil for plants in containers is critical. The roots of container plants have only that small amount of soil as a reservoir for nutrients, air, and water. A good container soil drains well, holds water well, has ample nutrients, and allows good oxygen penetration. You can make container soil from various combinations of mineral and organic ingredients (see page 22).

EVALUATING AND TESTING SOIL

If an abundance of plants, even weeds, are already growing well in the area you wish to plant, your soil is probably in good condition and will need only added fertilizer.

A range of tests can help in further evaluating your soil. You can perform most of them yourself. More sophisticated tests may have to be done by a lab.

Evaluating texture: the touch test

One quick way to tell whether your soil has a lot of clay or sand or is mainly loam is to wet a handful of soil and knead it into a ball in your hand. If it contains clay, it will make a firm, sticky ball that retains the imprint of your fingers after you squeeze it. A smear of clay soil is smooth and shiny. Sand in the soil makes it feel gritty. If you can't form the soil into a ball, or if the ball shatters at a touch, the soil is very sandy. If the soil forms easily into a ball but can be broken by prodding at it with a finger, it is loam, a blend of clay, silt, and sand.

Evaluating texture: the settling-out test

You can use the fact that larger soil particles (sand) sink in water faster than smaller particles to find out what percentage of your soil is made of what size particles. Fill two-thirds of a quart jar with water and a tablespoon of a water softener, such as Calgon, to separate the soil particles. Then fill the jar almost to the top with dry, pulverized soil. Screw on the lid and shake the jar vigorously. Then set the jar down and watch the materials settle.

Measure the depth of the soil that has settled out after 20 seconds. This is sand. Then measure the depth of material that settles out between 20 seconds and 2 minutes after shaking. These are the intermediate-size particles, or silt.

The clay will settle out over the next 2 weeks. When the water is clear or almost clear, measure the total depth of soil and divide to find the percentages of sand, silt, and clay in the soil.

Soil that has a sand content of 80 percent or more is classified as sandy. Clay soil contains 60 percent or more clay, and silt soil contains 85 percent or more intermediate-size particles.

Evaluating drainage

To see if you are likely to have drainage problems, dig a hole 3 feet deep so you can see the composition, or *profile*, of your soil. Look at the layers of soil, called *horizons*, in the profile. Is the subsoil loose and porous, or is it tight and clayey? Drainage problems are caused by hard or impervious layers and by strongly contrasting layers. For instance, if your topsoil is a fine-textured clay and it sits on a sand or gravel subsoil, water will drain very slowly into the subsoil. If the entire profile is clay, the soil will drain more quickly than if it has layers of coarse-textured material.

Fill the hole with water and let it sit for a day. Then fill it again. How quickly does the water recede? If the water level drops more slowly than ¼ inch an hour, you have drainage problems. If it drops faster than 1 inch an hour, your soil has excellent drainage. Solutions for soil drainage problems are given on page 18.

If you strike a layer of very hard soil or rock, try to dig through it with a crowbar. If the layer is a few inches thick and looser soil is under it, you have *claypan*, a layer of extremely dense clay, or *hardpan*, which is like rock and is almost impervious to water. Some solutions to these problems are given on page 18.

Testing for pH

The pH value is a measure of the degree of acidity or alkalinity in the soil. (A more complete descrip-

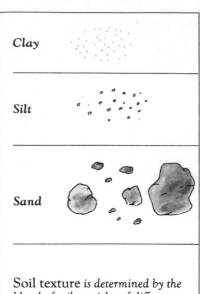

Soil texture *is determined by the blend of soil particles of different sizes. Clay, silt, and sand indicate particle sizes; loam is a mixture.*

Soil coring tool. *With this hollow rod, you can extract a soil sample without digging.*

Take a soil sample *by scraping the side of a hole you dig with a shovel.*

tion is given on page 12.) Home soil test kits give approximate, but useful, pH readings. Some tests use strips of paper that are pressed against wet soil; for others, a sample of soil is placed in a special liquid. In most cases, pH is read by comparing a color change with a chart. A soil test laboratory can make a more accurate test.

The pH Scale

Some common substances	Soils		
		3	
Lemon juice, vinegar	Peat moss		
Grapefruit juice	Best for azaleas,	4	
Apple juice	rhododendrons, blueberries		More acid
		5	
Coffee	Best for camellias, gardenias, heather		
		6	
	Good garden soil		
Distilled water		7	Neutral
		8	
Soap	Alkali soil		More alkaline
		9	

Acidity or alkalinity is measured on the pH scale. The pH of a few common substances is shown here for comparison with soils. Alkaline means a pH of more than 7; alkali is sodium-laden soil, usually with a pH higher than 8.2.

A Horizon: Topsoil

B Horizon: Subsoil

C Horizon: Parent rock

Soil profile. *The horizons may be similar or distinctly different.*

Testing for soil salts and plant nutrients

An electrical conductivity test will determine whether your soil has salt problems. Salt problems are common in irrigated areas of the West. This test is simple but it requires special equipment, so it should be done by a lab. Heavy irrigation may be required to leach salts from the soil if they are present in excessive amounts.

The levels of nutrients in the soil can be measured, but the measurements are tricky to make accurately. It is usually simpler and cheaper for the home gardener to add fertilizers routinely than to add them according the the needs of the soil, as farmers do.

What to do with the test results

Most labs provide information on how to correct the problems revealed by their soil tests. If you have made your own tests, you can make soil more alkaline by adding 5 pounds of ground limestone per 100 square feet of garden area and tilling it in well. Wait a week, then test again. Repeat the application if necessary. To make soil more acid, add the same quantity of soil sulfur or iron sulfate. The reaction is slower than that of lime, so wait a month before retesting.

Taking a soil sample

Whether you're using a home soil test kit or sending the sample to a lab, it's important that the sample be truly representative of your soil. If a lab will be doing the tests, ask whether there are special instructions on how to take the sample.

Here's one good method:
1. Determine the test area or areas. Take about five separate samples for each test area. These are the criteria for separating a garden into different test areas:

■ Are the soil types known to be different?

■ Will the areas have different uses? Make separate tests for lawns, vegetable gardens, flower beds, and any other special uses.
2. Using a clean shovel, dig a hole about 12 inches deep, exposing the zone where your plants' roots will grow.
3. From the side of the hole, take a ½-inch slice of soil along the full 12 inches. Discard the top ½ inch of the slice because it is probably atypical. (A coring tool is a handy device that allows you to take a soil sample without all the digging. You simply plunge the hollow cylinder into the soil and extract a core of soil.)
4. Put this soil slice into a clean bucket and remove any obvious rocks or litter.
5. Take at least five such samples from each area identified earlier.
6. Thoroughly mix all the samples for an area together in the bucket. This makes a sample that is average for the test area.
7. Put a pint of this mixture into an unbreakable container, such as a plastic bag within a box. Send this sample to the lab.

If a lab is doing your tests, send along with the sample any information you know about the history of your soil, especially whether it has been limed, fertilized, or amended in the past 5 years. Also indicate what you want to plant there.

Laboratory soil tests

State agricultural colleges usually do soil tests for home gardeners free or for a nominal charge. Contact your Cooperative Extension Agent for information. Commercial labs charge about $25 for tests of soil salts and pH and from $25 to $100 for tests to determine levels of soil nutrients. Private agricultural or soil testing labs can usually be located through a local nursery. If there is one in your area, it should be listed in the telephone book.

SOIL AMENDMENTS

Soil amendments are bulk materials that are incorporated into soil to improve drainage, structure, microbial activity, aeration, and other soil properties. They are usually relatively fine-textured decomposed organic materials, such as manure, ground bark, or sawdust. A mulch, by contrast, is a material placed on top of the soil for purposes such as reducing erosion, preventing soil crusting, and minimizing weeding. Many of the same materials are used for mulching as for amending. Indeed, mulches are often incorporated into the soil at the end of the gardening season, becoming amendments.

Kinds of soil amendments

Here are some of the main soil amendments and their characteristics.

Animal manures of all types have long been used as soil conditioners. All the commonly used manures have modest amounts of the major nutrients (nitrogen, phosphorus, and potassium). Chicken manure is the most potent, so use smaller amounts of it. All manures work better if they are composted first. Manure often carries weed seeds, depending on where the animals were grazing. The amount of salt the animal has eaten is another factor. Bagged steer manure is usually from feedlot steers, which are fed diets high in salt, so the manure is high in salt. Leach water through the manure in the garden to carry the dissolved salt into the subsoil.

Wood by-products, such as ground bark and sawdust, are widely sold. The wood by-product has often been fortified with nitrogen. The process of decomposition requires nitrogen; if organic materials are not already decomposed, the bacteria that decompose them will use nitrogen from the soil to aid in the process. If you use raw sawdust as a soil conditioner, add a nitrogen supplement as well. For

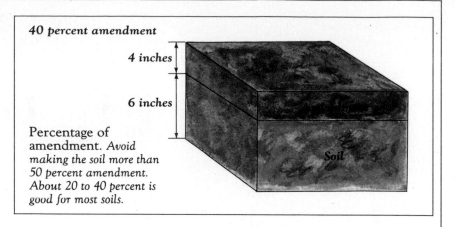

40 percent amendment

4 inches

6 inches

Percentage of amendment. *Avoid making the soil more than 50 percent amendment. About 20 to 40 percent is good for most soils.*

Soil

each 100 pounds of sawdust, add 1 pound of actual nitrogen. If you're putting 2 inches of sawdust onto a 100-square-foot area, add ½ pound of nitrogen. Page 82 tells how to calculate the amount of actual nitrogen in a fertilizer.

Lawn clippings are both plentiful and free, if you have a lawn. Moderate amounts of lawn clippings can be worked directly into the soil without composting. But if your grass has gone to seed or if it is a variety that grows from its stems, such as Bermudagrass, don't use it in your garden as an amendment without composting it first.

Compost, either made in your own yard or purchased, is an excellent soil amendment. When properly managed, the high heat of decomposition (160°F) will kill most weed seeds, insects, and disease organisms. See page 24 for a description of how to make compost for your garden.

Leaf mold, decomposed leaf material, is often sold commercially. This material may be acidic, depending on the leaves used, making it a favored amendment for acid-loving plants such as azaleas and blueberries. Make sure no poison oak or poison ivy has been included in the mix.

Agricultural by-products include a wide variety of materials, some of which may be available in your region. *Peanut hulls* are an excellent amendment. *Tobacco stems*

work well but should be kept away from plants in the same family (tomatoes, potatoes, peppers, nicotiana) because of virus problems. *Cottonseed meal* has fairly high levels of plant nutrients. *Cocoa bean hulls* hold water well, have a pleasing appearance (and aroma) as an amendment or mulch, and are acidic. *Rice hulls* are sometimes available in the West. *Bagasse* is a sugar-cane by-product used an an amendment and mulch in the South. *Apple* and *grape pomace*— the leftover skins, seeds, and stems of these fruits after processing— has been used with good results. *Ground corncobs* are available in the Midwest. *Straw,* a traditional soil amendment and mulch, must be supplemented with nitrogen when worked directly into the soil; it often has weed or grain seeds.

Peat moss (from ancient swamps) is commonly available at nurseries. It is peat made from moss and is an excellent soil amendment. *Sphagnum moss* is sometimes confused with peat moss; it is dried, but not decomposed, moss. Sphagnum moss is used as a packing material, for making hanging baskets, and to cover the surface of pots; but it is not used as a soil amendment.

Peat moss is expensive; but it retains moisture well, drains superbly, and is lightweight. It has an acidic effect (a pH of 3.5 to 4.5) that may be desirable for certain plants, or you can neutralize this acidity by adding 5 pounds of lime per 100 square feet when peat moss is used 4 inches deep. Peat moss is the longest lasting of the organic mulches, minimizing

Turning in amendments. *Most amendments are fluffy enough that you will turn over about 6 inches of soil no matter how much amendment is on top of it.*

shrinkage of soil volume that would be caused by further decomposition. In some areas, other types of peat are available, such as *sedge peat*; but these other types are inferior to peat moss as an amendment in the garden.

Vermiculite and **perlite** are mineral pieces whose size has been expanded by a heating process. Vermiculite has a porous structure. It retains water and nutrients very well, but it is fragile and keeps its structure for only a few months in the soil. Perlite particles are impervious to water and don't retain water or nutrients. It lasts much longer in the soil than vermiculite.

Both perlite and vermiculite allow for good soil aeration and are lightweight, making them ideal for container soils, especially when a sterile soil rather than ordinary garden soil is desired. A sterile soil will reduce plant pathogen problems when seeds are germinating.

Sand is often added to heavy clay soil in an effort to improve drainage, but it may have the opposite effect. Unless you make the resulting blend more than 80 percent sand, the mix will have worse drainage than the clay alone. The clay fills in the spaces between the sand particles, acting like a cement. Sand, especially coarse sand, will improve drainage in a container mix that does not include any heavy soil.

Where to get soil amendments

When buying soil amendments, you can usually get a better price by purchasing in bulk rather than in bags. First determine the quantity you want, then consider your means of delivery or the fee charged for a nursery's delivery truck. A cubic yard of amendment material is slightly more than 13 hefty 2-cubic-foot bags.

Estimating how much you need

You will usually need to add about 1 to 4 inches of soil amendment to your garden. This chart will help you gauge the amount you need. A cubic foot of amendment will cover an area of 12 square feet to a depth of 1 inch. A cubic yard is 3×3×3 cubic feet.

AMENDMENT NEEDED	
Depth of amendment	Volume required to cover 1000 square feet
¼ inch	2 cubic feet
½ inch	4 cubic feet
1 inch	8 cubic feet
2 inches	17 cubic feet
3 inches	1 cubic yard
4 inches	1¼ cubic yards

Buying topsoil

Topsoil can also be used as a soil amendment. If you are adding an amendment to raise the level of your soil, you should use topsoil or some other mineral amendment (such as sand). Organic amendments will gradually decompose, causing the soil to return to its original level. Here are some points to consider if you are buying topsoil:

■ Topsoil has no legal definition. Before you buy, learn what you can about the history of the soil: where it came from, how it was processed, and what it may have been mixed with. Sometimes topsoil is sold mixed with various soil amendments, such as manure and ground bark.

■ Look at the topsoil offered to see if it is free of rocks and debris and has a soft or crumbly structure. Try to match the texture of the soil in your yard; if you have sandy soil, buy a sandy topsoil.

■ The topsoil should be free of weed seeds and toxins. If you have the time, grow a few radishes in a flat of the topsoil for 2 weeks. If the radishes grow well, there are no serious toxin problems. If weed seeds are present, the weeds will also show up within 2 weeks.

SOIL DRAINAGE

Good drainage is essential for a healthy garden. Plant roots need loose, well-aerated soil for survival; most can't live in soggy soil because it lacks oxygen. Fortunately, the most common drainage problems are easy to identify and fairly simple to correct.

Analyzing drainage problems

To determine what kind of drainage your garden soil has, first take a look around. Are there wet areas or a white crust on the soil in low spots? A white crust is caused by water evaporating from the surface of the soil.

Now dig one or more holes 18 inches deep. Were you able to dig the full 18 inches, or did you run into a hard layer that you couldn't break through? If you reached *bedrock*, the soil is so shallow that very little will grow there. Some bedrock (sandstone, for instance) is soft enough that it is tempting to dig holes in it and plant in the holes. But because the holes won't drain, plants growing in them won't do well. The best solution is to do your gardening in containers or to raise the soil level by adding topsoil.

If you hit a hard layer that you were able to break through, on the other hand, you have *hardpan*. It's not quite as impossible as bedrock, but it does require special treatment. You can plant in containers or raised beds, as you would if you had a shallow soil, or you can break through it under each plant. If you're planting only a few trees or shrubs, break through the hardpan under each plant with a crowbar; if you are setting out many small plants, break the hardpan at 2-foot intervals. If you have a lot of hardpan to break up, a rented backhoe does the job most easily. *Claypan* is similar to hardpan but is made of packed clay. Claypan doesn't drain any better than hardpan, but you can dig through it with a soil auger.

Did you find radically different soil textures in layers as you dug?

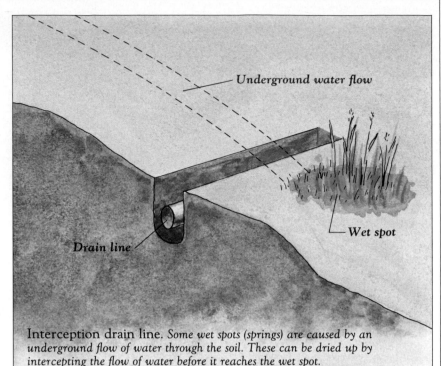

Interception drain line. *Some wet spots (springs) are caused by an underground flow of water through the soil. These can be dried up by intercepting the flow of water before it reaches the wet spot.*

Sudden changes in soil texture—from clay to sand or from sand to clay—block drainage through the soil. To make the soil more homogeneous, till through the layers to break them up and mix the different soils.

If water filled the hole as you dug it, you have a high water table. Lay drain tile or pipe to carry away the water from the area you want to use for planting.

If the hole remained dry, fill it with water, let it drain, and fill it again. Take note of how long it takes the water to drain away the second time. A rate of ¼ inch per hour or faster is acceptable drainage. If this hole was dug in a wet spot, the problem is not in the soil structure but in the soil surface, which is probably either compacted or crusted. In either case, add organic matter and till it into the top few inches. See page 16 for instructions.

Did the water stay at the same level for several hours? If so, your drainage problem is caused by heavy soil. You can add organic matter to improve its texture. Or use surface drainage, such as shaping the soil surface to control water runoff and retention, to retard the amount of water that gets into the soil. Planting in raised beds is another solution.

Raised beds *can be used with any type of drainage problem. Trees need 1½ to 3 feet of soil.*

Mounds *are similar to raised beds, but require more soil and look more natural.*

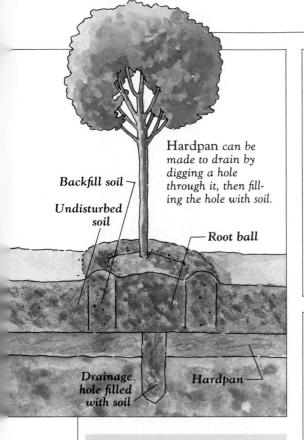

Hardpan *can be made to drain by digging a hole through it, then filling the hole with soil.*

Backfill soil

Undisturbed soil

Root ball

Drainage hole filled with soil

Hardpan

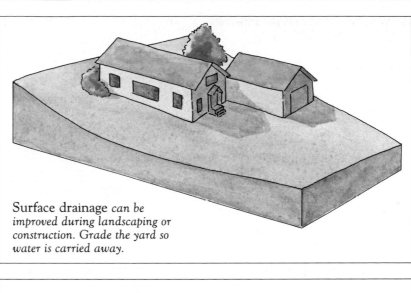

Surface drainage *can be improved during landscaping or construction. Grade the yard so water is carried away.*

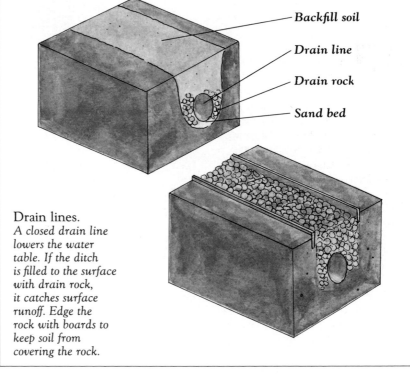

Backfill soil

Drain line

Drain rock

Sand bed

Drain lines.
A closed drain line lowers the water table. If the ditch is filled to the surface with drain rock, it catches surface runoff. Edge the rock with boards to keep soil from covering the rock.

LAYING A DRAIN LINE

1. A slight slope (at least 1 foot drop for each 100 lateral feet) is necessary for the water to drain. First decide where the water will leave the drain line. This place is called the *outfall*. Now plan backward, toward the area that needs draining, to see how deep you can make the drain line. The elevation of the outfall often limits the depth of the drain line. Because the water table cannot rise higher than the drain line (the water drains away as it reaches the level of the pipe), install the drain line as deep as you want the water table to be. Most trees need at least 4 feet of drained soil, but a lawn needs only about 2 feet.

2. Dig a trench from the outfall to the area you wish to drain. The steeper the pitch, the less likely it will be to fill with silt and plug up later. Line the bottom with a couple of inches of sand, and lay the drain line in it. The flexible, corrugated type of drain line is easiest to work with. The holes in the pipe go down.

3. Cover the line with 4 inches of drain rock, then backfill the ditch with soil. To drain a large area, run several parallel lines about 6 feet apart.

Solutions to drainage problems

Here are some solutions to the most common drainage problems:

■ Create fast-draining mounds for landscape trees.

■ Plant in raised beds or containers (see page 28).

■ Add organic soil amendments (see page 16) to aid aeration and drainage. Till these materials in as deeply as possible, into the top 12 inches of soil if you can.

■ Construct a dry well, or *sump*, by excavating an area and filling it with porous gravel or rock. You can make a simple sump with a posthole digger. Direct drainage water into the sump.

■ Install a system of drain lines under your garden area or along retaining walls.

CULTIVATING THE SOIL

Cultivating the soil allows you to increase aeration, mix in amendments, and control weeds.

Cultivation and soil moisture

Do not attempt to cultivate soil that is either too wet or too dry. Moisture content is an important consideration in all but the sandiest soils, but it is especially important in clay soils. When clay soils are too wet, cultivating can compact the particles and destroy the soil's structure. The hard clods that form as the clay dries won't break down easily. To test the soil, turn over a shovelful and try to break the clod. If it breaks easily, it's ready to work. If it's too sticky to break, wait a few more days.

Cultivating soil that is too dry can also be a problem. If your soil is dry and hard, soak it thoroughly and let it drain for a day or two, until a clod breaks easily, before cultivating.

Preparing a bed for planting

Whether you're using a rotary tiller or are tilling by hand, it is important to loosen the soil and be sure it's ready for planting. The first step in preparing an area for planting is to clean off any debris that you don't want to incorporate into the soil. Then spread soil amendments and fertilizer and mix them into the soil. (For instructions, see pages 16 and 84.) Break up clods with a hoe or cultivator, and rake the surface smooth.

Tilling with a shovel, spade, or fork. Dig one row at a time. Turn each shovelful of soil on its side, not upside down, so that any weeds are buried but don't make a layer in the soil. Forks are more effective in light soil and soil with good tilth. Spades work best in clay soil and soil that hasn't been cultivated before. Shovels are general tools that can be used in any situation. Both shovels and forks turn over about 6 inches of soil.

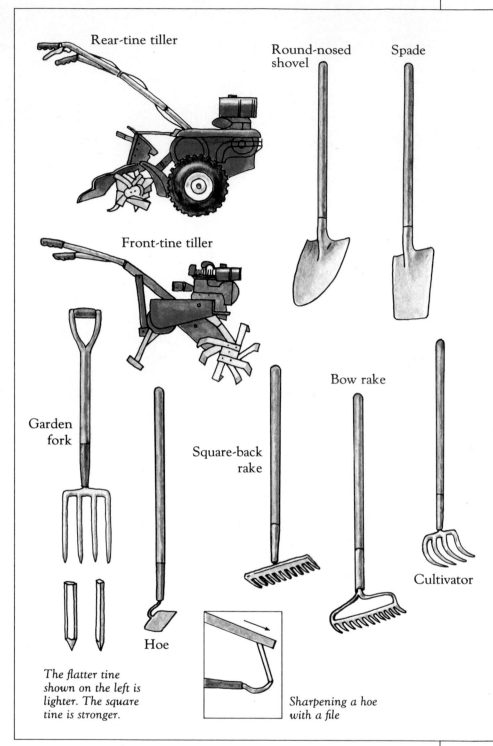

The flatter tine shown on the left is lighter. The square tine is stronger.

Sharpening a hoe with a file

With a spade, you can turn over 8 inches if you work hard.

Using a rotary tiller. If the soil is hard or dry, it may be necessary to make several passes across the garden, with each pass tilling a couple of inches deeper than the one before. Make these successive passes at right angles to one another.

Tillers don't get into corners well, so plan to finish off by hand. Unless the tiller is extra large, it will till about 6 inches deep.

Smoothing the bed. For a coarse, quick job, use a cultivator to smooth the surface. For a seedbed

When turning over soil with a spade or shovel, lift the soil only a couple of inches, then drop it back in the same spot on its side.

When double digging, remove soil from the first trench and loosen the soil at bottom of the trench.

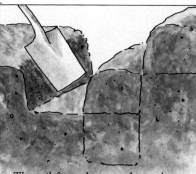

The soil from the second trench goes into first trench. Use soil from the first trench to fill the last one.

with more finely textured soil, use a garden rake. One quick way to dispose of the hard clods and rocks that you rake up is to dig a deep hole at the end of the garden bed and bury them. Bury them below tilling depth or you'll have to deal with the rocks again next year.

Cultivating for weed control

Cultivation is the method most frequently used to control weeds. A hoe is usually used around plants. A rotary tiller set at a shallow depth will control weeds in a large empty area or between rows of plants. Till whenever a new crop of weeds appears. If the weeds have perennial roots, kill them with a systemic herbicide first (see page 148) to prevent resprouting.

Hand tools

The tools you choose for cultivating will depend on your garden. Larger gardens will require more specialized tools.

Shovel. For most gardeners, the first tool to choose is an all-purpose round-nosed garden shovel. The angle between the wood handle and the blade is an important factor. The more pronounced the angle, the better the shovel will be for scooping without requiring you to bend over. A straighter angle will make it easier for you to dig deeply into the soil.

Spade. This tool can be useful when turning heavier soil deeply, when double digging beds, and when straight soil edging is desired for appearance. D-handle spades are ideal for working in close quarters.

Garden fork. A garden fork is helpful for digging up plants, cultivating loose soil, and turning compost piles. The sturdier forks have tines and base as one cast-iron unit. Square-tined English spading forks are heavier and sturdier than flat-tined forks, which sometimes bend out of shape under the stress of working in heavy soil.

Hoe. A hoe is useful for breaking up clods after turning the soil over with a spade or fork. The kind of hoe in which the handle is fitted into a solid socket is stronger for heavy cultivating.

Rake. There are two basic styles of rakes. The *bow rake* is sturdier and a little heavier than the *square-back rake*. You can turn either type over and use the back for finishing off a seedbed.

Cultivator. A cultivator is useful for light cultivation in well-tilled soil. It also helps to break up clods after turning the soil over with a spade or fork.

Rotary tiller

If you have a large, open garden, you may find a rotary tiller to be invaluable. This tool makes it possible to cultivate with relative ease areas that would take many tedious hours to spade. Tillers are especially good at mixing soil amendments and fertilizer evenly into the top 6 inches of soil.

Some rotary tillers have the tines in the front and others have the tines in the back. Front-end models tend to be best for light jobs; rear-end tillers usually work better for heavy-duty tasks.

DOUBLE DIGGING

Double digging can improve a vegetable garden by incorporating air and organic material deep into the root zones. Most herbs and ornamental plants don't need double-dug beds.

1. Using a spade, make a trench 1 foot wide and one spade deep. Put the soil in a pile at the edge of the trench.

2. Loosen the soil in the bottom of the trench.

3. Next fill the trench halfway with compost or another organic soil amendment.

4. Dig a second trench adjacent to the first and place the soil on top of the amendment you placed in the first trench. Mix the soil and amendments together with the spade.

5. Fill the last trench with the soil you removed from the first.

CONTAINER MIXES

Because good drainage is much more important in containers than in the ground, garden soil is usually not good for growing plants in containers. A good container mix drains quickly, holds water, and is free of insects, disease organisms, and weed seeds.

Ready-made bagged container mixes are available in nurseries and garden centers. Because the quality of these mixes varies, usually the only way to judge a mix is to try it out. If your plants thrive in it, if you don't have to water too often, and if no problems develop in a few months, it is a good mix.

Ingredients of container mixes

Peat moss is a peat from northern sphagnum moss bogs. It has hollow fibers that are just the right microscopic size to hold water for use by plants. Peat moss remains stable in a container mix for several years. It is acidic and seems to have some properties that help prevent plant diseases. It is also quite expensive. The coarser grinds are better for container mixes because they drain faster.

Peat moss is very difficult to wet once it dries out, so it is usually sold slightly damp. Keep it in a sealed container until you're ready to use it. If it does dry out, add water to the container, stir it as best you can, and let it sit for a few days. To wet large amounts, spread it on the ground, sprinkle it with water, and roll it with a lawn roller. Don't squeeze wet peat moss; squeezing flattens the hollow fibers and reduces its ability to hold water.

Leaf mold used to be more widely available and less expensive than it is now. It is frequently specified as an ingredient in many older recipes for container mixes. Leaf mold is an excellent container mix ingredient, but it varies in quality. It holds water and nutrients almost as well as peat moss.

Blend the ingredients in container mixes by assembling them in flat layers on a clean surface. Then "turn" the pile by moving it, one shovelful at a time, to one side. Scatter each shovelful over a large area. Three turns will usually mix the ingredients thoroughly.

Ground wood is used in many forms. The most commonly used materials are sawdust, to which some nitrogen and iron fertilizer have been added, and ground bark. Wood dust, such as that from sanders, is too fine to be used. Most wood products are slightly acidic. They are not as satisfactory as peat moss in a container mix, but they are much less expensive.

Sand is added to give some body and weight to a mix. Large amounts of coarse sand increase drainage, but the main use of sand is to make a mix heavier. (If a mix is too light, pots may blow over in the wind.) Medium or coarse sand is better than fine sand in container mixes. The sand should be at least as coarse as table salt and should not be dusty. Beach sand usually contains too much salt for use in a planting mix, and the salt is difficult to leach out.

Perlite is an exploded pumice product. The particles of pumice are heated until they pop like popcorn. It is white and very light-weight, allows good drainage, but does not retain much water or nutrients. Perlite is stable and will last for many years in a mix.

Vermiculite is a type of mica that has been heated and exploded like perlite; the particles are composed of layers of mica that trap and hold water and nutrients. It is fragile and breaks up into powder in a few months to a year. It is available in two grades: coarser particles, which are sold as building insulation, and the finer horticultural grade. The former is better for most container mixes.

Other ingredients can be used if they are available. The materials listed above are available everywhere in the country; but local manufacturers might add ground nut shells, rice straw, ground corncobs, or other agricultural by-products.

Minerals and nutrients are often added in small quantities. Lime may be added to correct acidity,

Use a sheet of plastic or cloth to blend small amounts. Layer the ingredients on the sheet and mix by lifting one corner at a time.

especially if there is much peat moss in the mix. The most useful nutrient to add when the mix is being made is phosphate, which will last for a year or more in the mix. Most of the other nutrients help the newly transplanted plant to get off to a good start, but they are quickly leached out by watering and must be replaced with added fertilizer. Some commercial mixes have fertilizer added and others are sold without fertilizers.

Some recipes for soilless container mixes

All the recipes given here are for about 1 cubic yard of potting mix. The quantities add up to more than 27 cubic feet (1 cubic yard) because the particles fit into one another; the mix takes up less space than its separate ingredients. For making smaller amounts, substitute half-gallons for cubic feet and ounces for pounds in either of the recipes.

These mixes are made of readily available sterile ingredients. You can experiment with locally available materials that may be less expensive. It's a good idea to experiment with small batches at a time and to grow plants in the mix for several months before drawing a conclusion about it.

Heavy mix. This is a basic potting mix based on sand, sawdust, and peat moss. It is lighter than garden soil but heavy enough to keep most containers from blowing over in a breeze. It is also relatively inexpensive. This mix can be made lighter by substituting perlite for any part of the sand.

  11 cubic feet of peat moss
  11 cubic feet of sand
  11 cubic feet of sawdust
   5 pounds of 5–10–10 fertilizer
   5 pounds of ground limestone

Light mix. Based on peat, perlite, and vermiculite, this lightweight mix is good for large containers that must be moved. It does not contain any sand.

  21 cubic feet of peat moss
   6 cubic feet of vermiculite
   6 cubic feet of perlite
   5 pounds of 5–10–10 fertilizer
   8 pounds of ground limestone

Special mixes. For *acid-loving plants*, such as azaleas, rhododendrons, and camellias, you can use either of the mixes above; but leave out the limestone and add 1 pound of iron sulfate. Azaleas are often grown commercially in straight peat moss or a combination of peat moss and ground bark.

For *plants that need quick drainage*, such as cactus, increase the proportion of sand or perlite in one of the above mixes to 75 percent of the mix.

For *shade-loving plants*, such as begonias, piggyback plants, and gardenias, substitute ground bark or leaf mold for the sawdust in the heavy mix; reduce the limestone to 2 pounds; and add 1 pound of iron sulfate.

For *starting seeds*, use unmixed horticultural-grade vermiculite. Don't fertilize until the first true leaves open.

For *rooting cuttings*, mix 5 parts of perlite to 1 part of peat moss. Don't add nutrients until you transplant the seedlings to a potting mix.

Potting mix from garden soil

Soilless potting mixes use sterile ingredients and have both better drainage and better water-retaining properties than a soil-based mix. However, if you want to use garden soil in a potting mix, this combination works well:

  1 part garden soil
  1 part sand
  1 part peat moss or leaf mold

How to mix large amounts

Work on a large, smooth surface, such as a concrete driveway or patio. Layer the ingredients, making a flat-topped mound only a foot or two high. If the ingredients are too dry, put a sprinkler on the pile as you shovel on the ingredients. Using a square-nosed shovel, begin at one corner and spread each shovelful over an adjacent flat surface. What you're doing is making horizontal layers, taking vertical slices, and spreading them in horizontal layers again. Three turns should be enough to blend the ingredients thoroughly. Or you can simply turn the pile until it looks homogeneous and then turn it once more. (You can also use a cement mixer for combining ingredients, if you have access to one.) Store the mix in heavy-duty plastic bags or garbage cans until ready to use.

How to mix small amounts

Layer the ingredients on a sheet of plastic film. Lift one corner at a time to roll the mix across the sheet. Continue blending until it looks homogeneous; then mix for about 1 more minute.

MAKING COMPOST

A properly made compost pile gets hot enough (about 160°F) to pasteurize the compost, killing weed seeds, insect eggs, and most of the disease-causing organisms.

Composting requirements

To ensure that your pile will heat up properly, and to speed up the process, your compost pile needs the following:

■ Nitrogenous materials (manure, green plant matter, nitrogen fertilizers).

■ Carbohydrate materials (yellow plant matter such as dead leaves, sawdust, or straw).

■ Moisture.

■ Oxygen.

■ Enough mass to keep the heat from escaping. A pile about 3 feet square and 3 feet high is minimum.

Composting

Gather a cubic yard of material. Collect garden refuse, dried leaves, lawn clippings, and kitchen refuse such as fruit and vegetable materials, coffee grounds, and eggshells. Store it in 5-gallon plastic containers or in a bin until you're ready to assemble the pile. Screen the storage bin or cover the material with sawdust to reduce fly problems.

Cut the materials as finely as possible. Use a machete or a shredder. Small particles will provide a greater maximum surface area to be exposed to moisture, air, and soil bacteria in the composting process.

Build the compost pile. The compost system won't work unless there is a balance between nitrogen and carbon. Dried material is high in carbon, and green material and manure are high in nitrogen. Dried materials alone, such as all dead leaves, will not heat up because there is not enough nitrogen. If the pile doesn't have enough green material, add a few handfuls of a nitrogen-rich fertilizer to keep the balance.

Above: *This bin has removable front boards to make turning easy. Turn compost from one bin to the next.*

Right: *A simple bin can be made from a cylinder of wire fencing.*

If the materials are dry, sprinkle them as you build; but don't saturate. Some dry materials will help offset the moisture contained in wet green materials. If the pile becomes too wet, an anaerobic (without oxygen) reaction will take place, producing a sulfurous odor. Lawn clippings alone tend to mat in the compost pile, so mix some dead leaves or chopped-up shrub trimmings with them.

Vegetative kitchen wastes are considered to be green matter and are an excellent source of nitrogen. But do not add meat scraps, bones, or fat. These materials take too long to decompose, and they may attract flies and rodents. Animal manure, on the other hand, is a useful addition to the compost pile. If you don't have manure to add to the pile, sprinkle some garden soil or aged compost on each layer to provide the microorganisms necessary for the composting.

Check the temperature. Put an iron pipe or a crowbar in the pile to serve as a thermometer. Pull out the pipe to check the temperature at the center of the heap. If the compost pile is made properly, it will begin to heat up in a couple of days. After a week, the pipe will be too hot to hold.

The pile will begin to cool down after a few weeks. Turn the pile as soon as you notice the temperature dropping. The pile has cooled down because it is no longer getting enough oxygen. Turning it allows air to reach all parts of the pile and will cause it to heat up again. Turning also mixes the

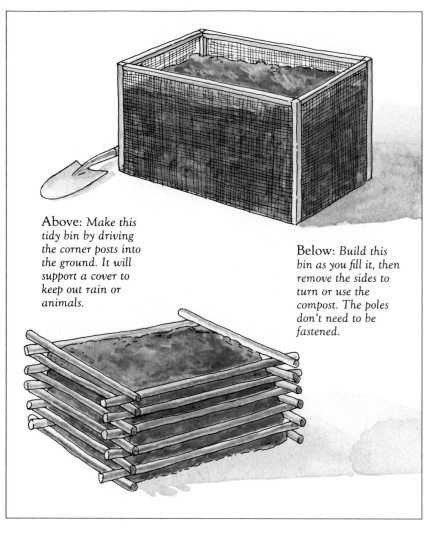

Above: *Make this tidy bin by driving the corner posts into the ground. It will support a cover to keep out rain or animals.*

Below: *Build this bin as you fill it, then remove the sides to turn or use the compost. The poles don't need to be fastened.*

ingredients and gives you a chance to place the outer layers in the center of the new pile so they can heat up too. The pile will probably need to be watered as you turn it.

Use the compost after it cools. If you want to sift out smaller particles for use in containers or a potting mix, make a frame of 2×2s and staple hardware cloth or 1-inch-mesh chicken wire to the frame. Larger pieces left after you sift the compost can be put in the next compost pile.

If you plan to store the compost before using, you can add earthworms to improve its quality after it has cooled. The worms will further digest the material and add their castings to the mix.

Compost in two weeks

You can make compost quickly by grinding or chopping the ingredients into pieces as small as possible and turning the pile every day. Use a grinder or shredder to prepare materials.

Composting problems

Here are some common composting problems and their solutions.

The pile doesn't heat up

■ The pile may be too small. Rebuild it and make it larger.

■ Check to see if it is too dry. Rebuild it; turn and water it thoroughly as you rebuild. Because it's difficult to get water uniformly through the compost by simply top watering, it is especially important to water the compost when you add dry materials.

■ If the pile has too much carbonaceous (dried) material and too little nitrogen, turn it and add some high-nitrogen fertilizer or some leafy green organic matter.

The compost smells bad

■ If it smells like ammonia, it has too much green (nitrogenous) matter. Layer in some straw, leaves, or sawdust.

■ If it smells like rotten eggs, it is too wet. Turn it and add some dry material.

The compost attracts pests

■ If the compost attracts insects, rodents, or dogs, there may be some meat or manure from a meat-eating animal in the pile. Remove the material or bury it deep within the pile. If the pile attracts insects, take measures to warm it up. Insects cannot tolerate the heat of a working compost pile, and after the pile cools down the compost is too decomposed to be of interest to them.

Composting structures

Many different kinds of structures can be used for holding the compost. They can be as simple as large plastic garbage bags or as elaborate as multiunit systems.

■ Form a length of welded-wire fencing into a cylinder 4 feet high.

■ Make an enclosure of hardware cloth or chicken wire stapled to four rectangular frames made from 2×2s.

■ Staple hardware cloth or chicken wire to 2×4s embedded in the ground as posts around the pile.

■ Build a rectangular enclosure with horizontally stacked fence posts, railroad ties, 3-inch poles, or 2×4s. This "log cabin" approach allows you to add and remove rails to keep the enclosure at the height of the pile, so you don't have to build or move the pile over a barrier. After the pile is built, you can remove the rails and the pile will hold its shape.

■ Use large plastic garbage cans with holes drilled in the side for aeration. Some manufacturers mount metal drums on rollers to make it easy for gardeners to turn materials by rolling the drum.

MULCHING

Traditionally, mulches have been organic materials such as straw, bark chunks, and wood chips; but now, newspaper, clear and black plastic, and other products are used with increasing frequency. The most important considerations in choosing a material are that it do the job effectively, be inexpensive and close at hand, and look attractive. The choices range from crushed granite rock to pieces of old carpet.

Main mulching materials

When choosing mulch materials, keep these questions in mind: How long will the mulch last? Will it break down to add organic material to the soil? Will it blow away in high wind? Will it float away or wash away in heavy rain? Is it free of weed seeds and herbicides?

Keep organic mulches pulled back from tree and shrub trunks. If the mulch is in contact with the trunk, it keeps the bark wet and can cause rot. Also, mulch makes an ideal environment for meadow mice to chew on the bark while protected in their burrows.

Bark chunks, such as fir bark, make an attractive, long-lasting mulch, suitable especially for gardens where appearance is important. The chunks are available in various sizes.

Wood chips are tree trimmings that have been put through a chipper. They are often available free from tree trimming companies, which would otherwise have to dump them. The chipped material is not as uniform or as attractive as bark chunks, but the chips make satisfactory mulch. The chips are often mixed with green leaves and twigs. This green matter decomposes and disappears during the first year. The depth of the mulch will decrease by as much as 50 percent during this time.

Pine needles are an attractive mulch and can often be gathered for free. They are acidic, fairly long

Ornamental mulches, *such as fir bark, should be kept away from the trunk.*

Vegetable garden mulches, *such as straw, decompose and improve the soil.*

lasting, and provide good ventilation for surface roots, making them ideal for azaleas, camellias, and rhododendrons. Pine needles can also be used to keep strawberry fruits off wet ground.

Ground corncobs, available in some areas, make an excellent mulch. They break down eventually to become a valued soil amendment for the garden.

Straw is a traditional mulch in rural areas. Straw breaks down quickly and can later be tilled in to improve soil structure. Try to secure a straw relatively free of grain and weed seeds.

Lawn clippings and raked leaves are mulches that work well together. Lawn clippings alone become matted if they are applied more than 2 inches thick, so mix in some dried leaves to reduce matting. If applied too thickly, green lawn clippings can build up heat as they compost and may damage plants. One way to apply lawn clippings is to spread them in a thin layer at each mowing. They will dry by the time you spread another layer.

Thin leaves, such as maple leaves, will also mat if used alone.

Either shred them or mix them with clippings, needles, or coarser leaves.

Crushed rock, gravel, and sand make attractive ornamental mulches. They do not have the soil-building properties of organic mulches, but they discourage weeds, control soil temperature, and help stop erosion. They don't reduce in volume over time, as the organic mulches do. Rock mulches are highly valued for their cosmetic properties; they are used primarily on pathways, landscaping areas, and at the tops of planting containers. Volcanic rock is a favorite soil topping in landscape containers.

How much mulch will you need?

In order to stop weed seeds from sprouting, the mulch needs to completely darken the surface of the soil. A fine mulch, such as grass clippings or sawdust, will be dark when only 2 inches deep, but 4 to 6 inches is best for bulkier mulches, such as bark chunks or wood chips.

Calculate how much you need with a pocket calculator, using one of the following formulas:

Black plastic mulches *do not decompose, but they do an exceptional job of preventing weed growth and conserving water in the soil. Use them in the vegetable garden or the cutting garden where appearance is not important. Or cover them with a thin layer of more attractive (but more expensive) mulch, such as ornamental rock, for use in the front yard.*

Cubic feet of mulch = area to be covered (in square feet) × depth of mulch (in inches) ÷ 12

Cubic yards of mulch = area to be covered (in square feet) × depth of mulch (in inches) ÷ 324

For example, if your garden is 20 by 20 feet (400 square feet) and you want to apply a 3-inch mulch, you can calculate the amount like this:

400 × 3 ÷ 12 = 100 cubic feet
or
400 × 3 ÷ 324 = 3.7 cubic yards

How far will a cubic yard of mulch go? If you spread it 2 inches deep, it will cover 162 square feet; 4 inches, 81 square feet; and 6 inches, 54 square feet.

When to apply mulches

Because mulches keep the ground from warming in the spring, apply them after the soil has warmed up. They are most useful during the hottest part of the summer. If the primary use of the mulch is to prevent weeds from growing, apply it before weed seeds germinate, in early spring.

Apply winter mulches when the first frost threatens tender plants or the first windy rains of autumn threaten soil erosion. Winter mulches also prevent the ground from alternately freezing and thawing, which causes small plants to *heave*, or lift from the ground. Once frozen, plants should stay frozen until spring.

Plastic mulches

In recent years black plastic has been used effectively as a mulch in home gardens and in commercial agriculture. It reduces watering needs and stops the growth of weeds. Rolls of plastic are generally available at nurseries.

Black plastic prevents sunlight penetration and has only a slight warming effect on the soil. Weed seeds that sprout in the warm, moist environment will die because they are deprived of light. Black plastic is often used in landscaping as a temporary barrier under a shallow ornamental mulch of rock or bark. The plastic prevents weed growth, and the ornamental material hides it. However,

the plastic will deteriorate in a few years. At that time, make the ornamental mulch deeper to prevent weed growth.

To keep plastic from blowing away, mound soil or rocks along the edges. Plastics can be an effective mulch for raised beds, where the wooden edge of the bed can be used as an anchor.

Water sprinkled from overhead enters only at the slits or holes in the plastic, where the plants are located. For more effective watering, you may want to install a buried soaker hose or drip system under the mulch.

Clear plastic warms the soil by trapping the sun's heat, much as a greenhouse does. It can be used to warm the soil in early spring, but remove it before you plant. During the summer, soil temperatures under a clear plastic mulch in direct sunlight can climb as high as 110°F. This temperature, over a period of a few weeks, has much the same effect as soil fumigation. It will kill weed seeds, disease organisms, and nematodes in the top inches of soil. To use clear plastic to sterilize soil, wait until the hottest part of the summer. Till the soil thoroughly, then water it well, just as if you were preparing to plant it. Then cover it with clear plastic for about 6 weeks.

RAISED BEDS AND CONTAINERS

Both raised beds and containers provide growing space if you want to have only a few plants, if you don't have soil space for a garden, or if your soil is unsuitable for planting.

Raised beds

Raised beds have several advantages over flat beds. The bed is narrow enough that you can work in it without walking in it, so the soil is never compacted. Raised beds drain better than flat beds, and they warm up faster in the spring. You can put a raised bed on any type of problem soil—even an unused driveway—fill it with potting mix or good topsoil, and have a successful garden.

If your raised beds are permanent, the paths between them are permanent too. They can be made of stones, gravel, or boards, for clean feet and ease of working. Make the paths about 16 inches wide, or the width of a garden rake. If you use a 2-wheeled garden cart, make the paths wide enough to accommodate it.

Beds can have no sides at all if they are raised only 4 to 8 inches. If you want to raise them higher, or for the most sophisticated type of gardening, build permanent sides. Make the sides of boards, railroad ties, stone, concrete blocks, and wood poles or posts driven close together.

To increase drainage, raise the beds at least 6 inches. For the most ease in working in the beds, make them 12 to 16 inches high and surround them with a railing you can sit on. The beds should be narrow enough so that you can reach the center without walking in the bed. Beds can be any length that you're willing to walk around to get to the other side.

Redwood and cedar boards are commonly used because they are so durable. Brush on a copper-based fungicide to extend the life of the boards as they weather in the elements. Don't use creosote or pentachlorophenol preservatives, which are toxic to plants.

The simplest sides are made of boards. For long-lasting beds, use 2-inch-thick redwood or cedar, held in place with 1×4 or 2×4 stakes. If the bed is 12 to 16 inches high, a cap makes a comfortable seat.

Use galvanized nails or aluminum roofing nails throughout garden construction because they won't rust. For the most durable construction, use galvanized bolts and galvanized angle irons to hold the boards together.

If gophers or moles are a problem, spread 1-inch-mesh galvanized chicken wire or ½-inch-mesh hardware cloth over the bottom before building the sides.

Custom uses of raised beds

Raised beds have many advantages for the home gardener, but some simple additions can make them even more useful. For instance, you can make covers to turn them into temporary greenhouses for starting seedlings, or bolt vertical racks or trellises to the bottom boards for seasonal needs, such as growing peas and beans. Netting, screens, or lath across the beds can reduce damage by birds and other pests and can protect against sun, wind, and rain.

Containers

Planting containers are made of many different materials. The most important factors are size and drainage. If you have to water a plant more often than once a day, the container is too small. The container must have drain holes. It is very difficult to raise healthy plants in undrained containers. Cover the holes with copper screen to prevent soil loss and to protect against the entry of slugs and sowbugs.

Pottery, if unglazed, allows water and air to pass through the container walls. This makes the soil in the pot dry out more quickly but helps prevent root rot in plants that are susceptible to it. This continual evaporation leaves concentrated soluble salts on the sides of clay pots. These pots should be soaked before reuse to dissolve these salts. Glazed pottery is not porous. Ceramic pottery does not deteriorate with time, but it breaks easily. Soak new pots before using so they won't draw water out of the container soil when you plant.

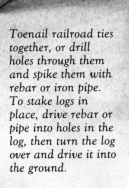

Toenail railroad ties together, or drill holes through them and spike them with rebar or iron pipe. To stake logs in place, drive rebar or pipe into holes in the log, then turn the log over and drive it into the ground.

This simple container is made by cutting a hole in the side of a bag of potting mix. Cut drainage slits around the edge of the bag.

Wash and disinfect old clay pots before reuse. Disinfect by soaking the pot in a solution of 1 cup of bleach to 1 gallon of water.

Colored plastic containers are sold at nurseries. More utilitarian 5-gallon plastic buckets, which make excellent containers, are commonly found as industrial discards. For drainage, drill a few ½-inch holes in the bottom. Cover the holes with fine-mesh copper screen to allow water passage but prevent soil loss. Plastic containers are light, inexpensive, don't build up salt accumulation on their sides, and can be cleaned easily. Plastic becomes brittle after a couple of years in the sun.

Double potting

Double potting—placing a container that drains within a non-draining decorative container—is a good way to bring a garden plant into the house for a couple of weeks while it is blooming. Put enough gravel or charcoal (which absorbs odors) on the bottom of the decorative container to bring the inner container to its rim. Fill the space between them with sphagnum moss or other loose material, and mulch the surface with something attractive. Water the inner pot lightly. The water level in the outer pot must not reach the bottom of the inner pot.

This method of double potting is a good way to bring an ornamental inside for a short time. The charcoal layer holds the pot above the drain water.

Pillow gardening

A type of container gardening that has gained in popularity in recent years is *pillow gardening*. Pillows are temporary containers made from polyethylene film. They will last for only one gardening season, but they are the most inexpensive way to add to your container garden. Place pillows on the deck or patio or along the edge of a driveway. Fill them with colorful annual flowers, or use them to extend your vegetable gardening space.

Cut 4-mil polyethylene into bands 3 or 4 feet wide and about a foot longer. Place the film where you would like the containers to remain. Lift the edges and staple or tape the corners into a box shape about 1 foot high. Fill the pillow with a lightweight potting mix (see page 22), and spread the mix out to fill the corners. The mix should be from 6 to 8 inches deep. Fold the edges over a couple of inches, then lay them across the potting mix and staple or tape the corners again, to strengthen them and make them more attractive. Cut slits for drainage every 6 inches where the pillow touches the ground. Treat the pillow like an ordinary container.

The easiest way to make a pillow is to use a 2-cubic-foot bag of potting soil from the nursery. Cut a rectangle out of one side, make a few slits for drainage at ground level, and plant in it.

PROPAGATING PLANTS

Propagating plants is the process of making many new plants from a few old ones. An ability to propagate plants not only saves you money, it also gives you the freedom to borrow any plants you like, from your own plants, those of your friends, or even wild plants.

Starting new plants is an exciting time in gardening. Watching your spring seeds germinate or your first cuttings form roots is especially rewarding. And with plants bought at a nursery, you can even propagate an instant garden.

Plants can be propagated in two ways: sexually, from seeds; and asexually, from some vegetative propagation method, such as dividing perennial chrysanthemums, rooting African violet cuttings, or grafting an apple tree. The technique used usually depends on the kind of plant. For example, all grains, most vegetables, and many flowers are started from seed. But most fruit and nut trees and many ornamental shrubs, such as camellias, are propagated vegetatively, partly because they tend not to grow true (similar in form to their parents) when started from seed. Timing is another other reason for vegetative propagation. For instance, cactus and other succulents are generally propagated vegetatively because their seeds may take several years to grow into full-size plants.

Each seed is the unique genetic product of its parent plants, and it can vary slightly or dramatically from them. Seeds sold commercially have a predictable form when grown. They are usually grown from seed themselves in large, isolated plots where the parent plants are known. But seeds saved from your garden plants may revert unpredictably to a parent if they are hybrids and may not develop into the form you expect. Tomatoes, for example, are either open-pollinated or hybrids. Seeds from open-pollinated plants can be saved and planted and will generally grow true, but seeds from hybrids will revert to near or distant ancestral forms. Seed growers have developed techniques of "line breeding" that ensure a plant will breed true, as a standard. But the seed grower, desiring a plant with special qualities, sometimes deliberately crosses two lines, to produce a hybrid, which definitely *won't* breed true.

Because plants have all their essential genetic information in each cell, vegetative propagation produces genetically identical plants that will vary only as a result of environmental factors. Plants can even produce an entire plant from one part. In some plants, stem cuttings can form roots, root cuttings will send up new shoots, or leaf cuttings will generate both new roots and new shoots. In others, stems and roots can be grafted to form a new plant. These are just a few of the ways that plants can be propagated vegetatively.

Germinating a seed

A seed consists of an embryo, an initial food supply for the embryo, and a protective coating. A seed can germinate if it is *viable* (capable of germinating) and if no internal or external mechanism, such as a required period of dormancy or a specialized seed coat that needs burning, inhibits germination.

Seeds will germinate when exterior circumstances are favorable. Generally, two conditions must coincide: (1) moisture must penetrate the seed coat while (2) the seed is subjected to the right temperature, which usually means adequate warmth. (However, some seeds require cold temperatures to germinate.) Sufficient oxygen must also be present, and for some seeds, such as strawberries and begonias, light is a prerequisite.

Moisture penetrating the seed coat is the first step in germination. Water also triggers chemical reactions that allow the embryo to use stored food in the seed to produce the new plant's first roots and stems. Thus, your ground or potting soil must be kept damp for germination to occur. The ideal amount of dampness will vary, with celery seeds requiring wet soil and spinach germinating well in moderately damp soil. Soggy soil may deprive the seed of essential

Propagating your own plants is the least expensive way to fill your garden with beautiful and unusual flowers.

oxygen and cause it to rot, especially if the soil temperature is lower than optimum for the seed to germinate.

The growing area must remain evenly moist during germination. A single drying out can kill the plant. Drying out is especially a problem with tiny seeds. Maintaining a moist environment is one of the chief reasons for germinating seeds in greenhouses or minigreenhouse coverings for seed trays.

When growing plants from seeds, you'll either plant the seeds directly in the soil outdoors or start them in a protected indoor environment.

Starting seeds outdoors allows the seeds to grow unchecked, once they germinate, without suffering any delay of growth resulting from the shock of being transplanted from indoors to outdoors. The disadvantage, of course, is that seeds don't always germinate easily in the rugged conditions outdoors, where they are subject to chance variations of temperature and moisture, as well as pests and disease. In nature, only a small percentage of seeds will actually germinate.

Starting seeds indoors allows you more precise control over the variables that affect germination. You can maintain an ideal soil temperature (about 70°F), and you can keep the potting soil properly moist. By covering the emerging seedlings with a plastic bag or glass cover you can keep the humidity at an optimum level, reducing the wet-dry-wet-dry interludes that thwart germination.

If you start seeds indoors, you can have plants ready for transplanting when warm spring weather permits. Your own or nursery transplants can help you get a head start in spring. Plants can be set out when they are large enough to survive a few nibbles from caterpillars—or even hefty tugs from birds—that like tender seedlings.

There are special pleasures in propagating plants from seeds, whether you start the seeds outdoors or indoors. For instance, you can spend long winter hours with

By combining seeds with nursery plants, you can have instant color in your garden as well as the variety and economy of planting from seeds.

seed catalogs, dreaming of future gardens. The variety of seeds available for each species of plant, from either catalogs or local nurseries, is much greater than the range of nursery plants for sale. And dollar for dollar, seeds are quite a value. Each seed packet contains a few to hundreds of potential plants, if you have the skills to germinate them.

Nursery plants

Nursery plants have several attractions. Skilled nursery operators, with a lifetime of seed-germinating and vegetative propagation skill, can usually do a better job getting plants started than a beginning gardener. And local nurseries have plants available when it's appropriate to plant them in your area.

Nursery plants come in a variety of containers and conditions. Bedding plants and vegetables are usually sold in flats or small cell packs.

Medium-size shrubs or trees, such as juniper ground covers, come in plastic or metal cans. Large trees and evergreen shrubs come with soil wrapped around their roots in burlap. These are called "balled and burlapped" (B and B) plants. During the winter dormant season, roses, fruit trees, grapevines, berry plants, and deciduous ornamental trees are some of the plants that may be sold "bare-root," meaning the plant is sold while it is dormant with no soil around its roots.

One of the advantages of buying plants in containers is that you can see the developed plant before you buy it, something that can't be said of seeds. This may be important if you're looking for an ornamental plant with a certain kind of flower or leaf color. The range of varieties sold in local nurseries will generally be the types known to succeed in your area.

Evergreen shrubs and trees are often sold balled-and-burlapped.

Purchased plants, especially for larger landscaping efforts, can produce an instant garden that would take years to develop from seeds or small vegetative cuttings. This is especially true for trees.

Propagating vegetatively

Because it begins with an adult plant, vegetative propagation avoids the time lost in the juvenile period of the plant's life. Vegetative propagation can often produce large numbers of new plants quickly and economically. For example, cuttings from a single mature oregano plant could probably supply your entire neighborhood.

There are four main techniques for vegetative propagation: division, rooting cuttings, layering, and grafting or budding.

Division is one of the easiest methods of vegetative propagation. Plants that have multiple basal stems can usually be divided. Simply dig up and divide the entire plant into two or more parts, ensuring that in each division you have some root, stem, and foliage. The stem is the vital part. Many ground covers, such as ivy, and herbs, such as chives, are propagated in this manner. Among houseplants, ferns can be divided easily.

Nurseries use a can cutter to slit the sides of cans for you. Be careful of the sharp edges where the can has been cut.

Bulbs and bulblike plants can also be divided in various ways. Dahlias and begonias have tuberous roots that can be cut apart and replanted if each cutting includes a bud. Potatoes, which are true tubers, can be cut in pieces, and each piece that has an eye can be planted. Other plants whose modified stems have become fleshy organs, such as tulip and daffodil bulbs, can be reproduced from parts of the bulb or can be separated out as they produce small bulbs.

Rooting cuttings is a widely used form of vegetative propagation, especially for ornamental shrubs. Cuttings may come from the stem, the leaf, or the root.

Layering is another method of vegetative plant propagation. Layering is the formation of roots along a stem while the stem is still attached to the parent plant. After roots form, the stem is detached.

Some plants layer naturally, such as blackberries, whose cane tips enter the soil and form roots.

In layering, new roots form when the downward flow of organic material from the leaves is interrupted, sometimes because the plant stem has been purposely nicked or girdled and placed in a dark, moist area (usually covered with soil). Darkness is a key factor in stimulating the formation of roots.

Grafting and budding are forms of asexual propagation that unite two plants to function as one plant. The two parts are called the scion (stem cutting) and the stock or understock (root system). For the graft to succeed, the moist cambium layers between bark and wood must fuse to form a path for the flow of water and nutrients.

Budding is a form of grafting in which a small piece of bark with a bud, rather than a whole stem, is used as the scion. Budding makes economical use of valuable plant materials, such as a new rose variety, and doesn't disfigure the plant if the bud doesn't "take." Roses and fruit trees are often budded.

STARTING SEEDS OUTDOORS

Your preparations for starting seeds outdoors will begin well before you put a hoe to the soil. As with many endeavors in life, the first key to successfully propagating plants is thoughtful planning.

Plan before you plant

Start by determining the right number of plants for your needs, the amount of space the mature plants will need, and the times at which the particular varieties you've chosen should be planted.

Seed catalogs and packets will provide useful information. First, make sure the season is right for planting the varieties you've chosen. Soil temperature is an important factor in seed germination: seeds of warm-weather plants, for instance, will rot before they germinate if the soil is too cold and wet.

Next, check the time required by your varieties to germinate and mature. You may want to plan a series of weekly plantings to prolong your harvest. Timing will also help determine the layout of your garden. Consider, for example, marking rows of seeds that take a long time to germinate, such as carrots, with fast-maturing varieties, such as radishes. The radishes can be harvested just as the carrots are beginning to leaf out. You can also use the space between late-maturing plants, such as tomatoes, for interplanting a crop that matures early, such as spinach. The early crop can be harvested before the later plants are large enough to shade the area.

Even in regions with a short growing season, it's often possible to grow two vegetable crops during the summer. Plant a cool-season crop as early as possible—even in the fall if your winters aren't too severe. As the spring crop reaches maturity, have a summer crop ready to plant in the space. Begin the summer crop indoors or in a hotbed or cold frame (see page 132) early enough that the plants are about 4 inches high when the spring crop is harvested.

Broadcasting *seeds results in dense, solid stands.*

Rows *can be made with the corner of a board.*

Plant height is another important factor to consider when mapping out your garden. Place tall plants (sunflowers, corn, pole beans) on the north side of your plot (not the south), so they won't shade other plants that need full sun. Some plants do, however, benefit from shade in the hot summer. Lettuce, for example, is less likely to bolt (go to seed) if it has some shade.

Preparing your garden

Before planting seeds outdoors, prepare the soil and add fertilizer (for general information on soil preparation, see Chapter 1; for fertilization, see page 79). If necessary, water the day before planting for adequate soil moisture. Rake the seedbed smooth. While you are waiting to plant, store your seeds in a cool, dark, dry place to preserve their viability. (See the box for life expectancies of representative varieties of seeds.)

Hills *are small groups of seeds. Make holes as deep as the first joint on your finger.*

Block *plantings are often used in raised beds to save space.*

Next, make furrows or dig holes for the seeds. The planting methods you will use depend on the kinds of plants you have chosen. Whether you are planting in rows, in hills, or on center, prepare the furrows and holes to the right depth for each kind of seed. Seed packets tell how deep to plant the seeds.

When planting in rows, align the rows north-south for maximum exposure to the sun. Use a board or string stretched between stakes to mark the rows. Make deep furrows with a hoe or the back of a rake.

Hills are used for vining plants such as tomatoes and squash. ("Hill" refers not to a mound but to a cluster of plants spreading in a circle from a central point.) Plant a dozen seeds per hill and thin to the most vigorous three or four plants as they mature. Use your finger or a stick to make holes for the seeds.

Block planting is an efficient way to manage space in small gardens. Determine the size of the

To sow small seeds, *put a piece of tissue paper in a shallow furrow. Mist the tissue to keep it from blowing away. The seeds are easy to see on the tissue.*

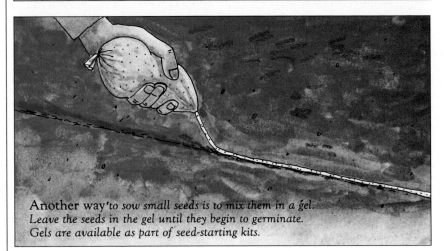

Another way *to sow small seeds is to mix them in a gel. Leave the seeds in the gel until they begin to germinate. Gels are available as part of seed-starting kits.*

mature plants, and then plant the seeds so that the leaves of the plants will just touch when they are mature.

Broadcasting seeds requires only a loose soil surface. This method simulates the way seeds are dispersed in nature. Lawns are often seeded by broadcasting.

Sowing the seeds

Place the seeds in the soil and cover them, unless the seed packet specifies planting on top of the ground. Some seeds need light to stimulate germination, but most prefer darkness and need to be covered. Press the covering soil down if it is dry or sandy, and leave it loose if it is wet or heavy.

Sow the seeds twice as thickly as you want the plants to grow, since some seeds won't germinate. Later, thin seedlings to the appropriate distance. Commercial seed tapes have the seeds already spaced at the right planting distance on the plastic tapes.

Large seeds are easy to place, since they can easily be shaken from the packet one at a time. Plant large seeds at twice their diameter.

Smaller seeds are often difficult to disperse evenly. To more easily plant small seeds, try one of these methods.

■ Take a pinch of the seeds between your thumb and forefinger. Rub your fingers together and let the seeds fall over the planting area.

■ Put a piece of tissue paper in a shallow furrow. Mist the entire area thoroughly to keep the tissue from blowing away and to moisten the tissue so that it will disintegrate. Shake the seeds onto the tissue, so you can see them, and distribute them evenly.

■ Mix the seeds thoroughly with an equal amount of flour, cornmeal, or sand and distribute evenly in the planting area.

■ Place the seeds in a commercial gel (sold in some nurseries and in seed catalogs) and mix until the seeds are evenly distributed. Leave the seeds in the gel until they begin to germinate. Then squeeze the gel from a tube over the growing area.

After dispersing the seeds, cover them with approximately ⅛ inch of fine soil. Cover large seeds to 4 times their diameter. If the soil is heavy, cover the seeds with sand, ground fir bark, compost, or peat moss.

After seeding

Because seeds need moisture for germination, don't let your garden get too dry. Keep the soil moist with frequent misting, but be careful not to wash out the seeds or developing seedlings.

In hot, dry weather, a light mulch of peat moss, ground fir bark, or compost over the seeds can help keep the seedbed moist. Shade the seed area with a board, a piece of burlap, or some straw if sunlight is intense and drying, but remove these dark covers as soon as the seeds begin to germinate. Look under the cover twice a day. If the seedlings develop in the dark, they will grow long and weak and be ruined. It also helps to plant a little more deeply than usual in dry weather.

Thin excess seedlings that would compete for light and soil moisture. If you thin by pulling out seedlings, be careful not to disturb the roots of those that remain. You can also thin by snipping the stems with scissors. Protect the remaining seedlings from insects and animals (see Chapter 9).

TIPS FOR STARTING SEEDS OUTDOORS

■ Plan your garden. Decide in advance what you want to grow and when to plant.

■ Plant in the right season for each variety.

■ Be sure the soil is moist, but not soggy, and loose.

■ Cover seeds to the right depth.

■ Keep soil moist until the seeds germinate.

STARTING SEEDS INDOORS

Starting plants indoors is a good way to get a jump on spring. Many vegetables and flowers can be started in a sunny window 4 to 6 weeks before they could normally be set out in the garden.

Materials and equipment

Containers for starting seeds can be reusable (plastic and clay pots, wood flats, aluminum trays) or suitable for only a single planting (peat pots and pellets); they can be newly purchased or recycled from other uses. Almost any kind of container can be used, as long as it has drain holes and will hold at least 3 tablespoons of soil. Paper and styrofoam cups, milk cartons, and yogurt and cottage cheese containers are some possibilities. Egg cartons are a little too small. Commercially available seed-starting kits, which come complete with soil and seeds, can be helpful for the beginning gardener.

If your containers have been previously used for growing plants, sterilize them before reuse. Clean them thoroughly with hot water and soap, soak for 10 minutes in a solution of 1 part household bleach to 9 parts water, rinse well, and let them dry.

Propagating units, either purchased or homemade, are used to maintain high humidity and warmth around the germinating seeds. A propagating unit can be as simple as a plastic bag over a pot or a piece of glass over a tray. More elaborate commercially available units are like miniature greenhouses, with plastic or glass covers and thermostatically controlled heating elements that will maintain a constant temperature of approximately 70°F.

Light is essential for growing sturdy seedlings. If your growing area does not have bright natural light (most outdoor plants need full sun for half a day), you may want to use fluorescent bulbs with a timer to provide more light to the developing seedlings.

Cover the seeding tray with a pane of glass or a piece of plastic film. Vent the glass or film enough that condensation doesn't form on the underside.

Water the seeding tray whenever the surface of the medium begins to dry out. Keep it moist but not soggy.

Sowing the seeds

First, prepare your seed-starting mixture. Horticultural vermiculite, unmixed, is useful for planting small seeds. Larger seeds can be planted in potting mix. Place the mixture in your containers to within ½ inch of the top and soak it thoroughly. Let it drain before planting your seeds.

Next, plant the seeds. There are two ways to sow, depending on the size of the seeds. Sow small seeds in horticultural vermiculite; then pluck out the seedlings as soon as you can handle them and transfer them to individual containers or flats. Plant large seeds in a potting mix in individual containers or flats. In both methods, make a shallow furrow with a ruler and sow the seeds. Then sprinkle milled sphagnum moss lightly over the seeds in the furrow. If the seeds are large, such as peas or beans, plant them to a depth twice their thickness.

If you are using peat pellets as containers, soak the pellets until they swell with moisture. Insert two seeds in the top of each pellet. Later, snip out the weaker seedling if both germinate.

Since most seeds germinate best in the dark, place newspaper or a piece of black plastic over the seeds until they sprout. If the directions on the seed packet say the seeds should not be covered, press the seeds gently onto the soil and place the container in bright but indirect light. Fluorescent lights can help if your seed-raising environment has poor light or if the seasonal light is low. Use a 40-watt bulb placed 6 inches from the seedbed for 24 hours a day.

After planting

Label the seed containers, using a pencil or waterproof-ink pen on a wood or plastic marker to indicate the name of the plants and the date of planting.

Transplant the seedlings by lifting them gently from below as you lift on their leaves. Plant them about 2 inches apart in flats, or in individual pots. Use pencil, India ink, or permanent markers to label the pots or flats. Ballpoint pen ink washes off when you water.

Keep the seeds warm and moist by covering them with plastic, glass, or moist paper towels. Moisture is especially crucial for small seeds, which can dry out easily. Remove the coverings after the seeds germinate.

Maintain a temperature of 70° to 75°F for the germinating seeds, unless package directions specify a higher or lower temperature. If your indoor temperature is lower than the desired range, use heater cables or a heating mat, both sold at nurseries, to encourage root growth. Sites in the home that raise the temperature just a few degrees, such as the top of a refrigerator or a television set, can sometimes be quite satisfactory.

When seedlings germinate, remove their dark covering and place them in bright light. Seedlings of sun-loving plants need full sunlight for at least 4 hours a day. Use scissors to thin seedlings that germinate too thickly.

As the seedlings develop, cool temperatures (65° to 70°F) and bright light are best for good growth. Too much warmth and low light will produce leggy plants. If direct sunlight is not available, cool temperatures can retard legginess and produce sturdy seedlings.

Water the seedlings every few days to keep the soil moist but not saturated. Use a small watering can with a fine sprinkling head, taking care not to wash out the seedlings as you water. Fiber wicks or fiber water mats can be used to draw water into the containers by capillary action. See page 76 for more information on watering plants in containers.

If your seeds were sowed in a starting tray, move the seedlings to 2-inch pots after the first set of true leaves appears. (The first set of true leaves appears after the first leaflike structures, called *cotyledons*, which nourish the stem tip and the foliage leaves that follow.) To move the seedlings, pluck them out of the soil, handling them gingerly. All parts of a young seedling can be damaged by handling, but the leaves are least likely to be damaged; so lift out seedlings by their leaves rather than by their stems or roots. Support the roots, along with some soil, with a fork or spoon in your other hand.

Begin feeding the young seedlings after the first true leaves have opened fully, a few days after germination. Feed weekly with a half-strength solution of a complete fertilizer high in phosphorus.

If your propagation environment has ever had loss of seedlings to damping-off fungus, apply a fungicide at the same time you fertilize. Clean containers, sterilized soil, and clean tools will reduce the prospects of fungus disease. If you're using a hose, be careful that it doesn't touch the ground, introducing contamination. Clean all containers carefully before reusing them for the next generation of seedlings. Disinfect tools by wiping them with rubbing alcohol.

Harden off seedlings when they are 2 to 4 inches high. Place them outside for gradually lengthening intervals over a week period. Start with an hour in the afternoon and work up to a full 24-hour cycle. Cold frames (see page 134) help in this acclimatizing of seedlings to the less-protected outdoor environment. Eventually the mature seedlings will be ready for transplanting (see page 38).

TIPS FOR STARTING SEEDS INDOORS

■ **Keep the planting mix moist.**

■ **Germinate seeds in a warm environment.**

■ **Grow seedlings in a cool, bright place.**

■ **Feed seedlings lightly with low-nitrogen, high-phosphorus fertilizer.**

TRANSPLANTING AND REPOTTING

Whether you are setting out small plants from the nursery or moving a large tree, a few simple techniques and precautions will help make your transplanting a success.

Transplanting small plants

Before transplanting small plants, water them well to be sure the roots are moist. Prepare the transplant area (for instructions, see page 20) and soak it thoroughly; then wait for it to drain so the soil won't be soggy. With a trowel, dig a hole in the ground slightly larger than the root ball of the plant.

To remove a plant from a pot without damaging its roots, turn the pot upside down, tap the rim on a hard surface, and catch the soil ball in your hand. For plants in plastic cell packs, push up on the bottom of the pack to loosen the seedlings. If plants are in a flat without individual partitions, gently separate the seedlings by hand; don't try to cut apart the intermingled roots.

Without delaying, place the plant in the hole and firm the soil around it. Hot sun and wind can dry the delicate roots in a very short time. Place the plant in the hole so the surface of the root ball is on the same level as the surface of the soil. If you're transplanting tomato plants, however, cover with soil to just below the first leaf at the bottom of the stem.

Newly transplanted seedlings need extra water and protection for the first several days. Water them daily if the weather is dry, but don't let the soil get soggy. Protect them from sun, wind, slugs, and snails by putting a pot or other covering over them for a couple of days.

Transplanting medium-size nursery plants

Moisten the plant's root ball thoroughly before transplanting.

Dig a hole roughly as deep as the root ball and twice as wide. Make the sides of the hole rough so the roots can more easily penetrate into the native soil. A small mound of soil in the bottom center of the hole will aid drainage.

If your plant is in a straight-sided metal container, you will usually have to cut the can to remove the plant. It's best to wait until you are ready to plant before cutting the container, since a cut container doesn't hold water very well. Have the can cut at the nursery if you intend to plant immediately; otherwise, cut it at home with tin snips.

A plant in a tapered metal or plastic container can usually be removed by turning the container upside down, tapping it on a hard surface, and knocking the root ball into your hand.

Peat or pulp containers can be planted whole. But remove or slash the container bottom and walls to allow roots to grow into the surrounding soil. Cut off the top lip of a peat pot to keep the water from being wicked out of the plant's root ball.

Examine the roots of any plants that appear rootbound. If the roots make a solid mass around the inside of the container, trim off the outer 2 inches of the root ball. Otherwise, make four vertical slashes an inch or so deep down the sides of the root ball and cut a cross on the bottom. Cutting the sides and bottom of the root ball will prune the roots. New growth will begin at the cuts. These new roots can more readily grow into the surrounding soil than the undisturbed roots would have. Before planting, stir some fertilizer into the soil at the bottom of the hole. Recent research on transplanting container plants shows that extensive amendment of the native soil is not as important as

Plant leggy tomatoes with the stem buried but with the roots near the soil surface, where they can get enough air.

Above: *To remove a plant from its pot, turn it upside down and tap the rim on a hard surface.*

Right: *Tear the rim from peat pots before planting, since any exposed rim will wick water from the root ball.*

Cut the outside of the root ball, about ½ inch deep, to encourage the new roots to grow into the native soil.

Transplant larger plants by digging a ditch around the plant, then undercutting from one side.

After planting, build a basin around the plant and fill it with water to settle the soil around the roots.

TRANSPLANTING TIPS

■ **Don't let the roots dry out. Work in the shade or on overcast days.**

■ **Shade new transplants for a few days. Remove the shade gradually.**

■ **Water the transplant frequently until it is established. This may take a week for small plants or several weeks for larger ones.**

■ **Plant most plants as high or a little higher than they were before.**

once thought. Since the plant must ultimately survive in the native soil, the transition from amended potting soil to the native soil should be as gradual as possible for the exploring roots.

Place the plant in the hole slightly above the soil line, to encourage drainage. (For severe drainage problems, see page 18.) Then build a ridge of soil in a circle around the plant, creating a basin. Fill the basin with water to soak the plant.

Put mulch around the plant (see page 26), but don't let the mulch touch the trunk. Provide support for the plant if necessary (see page 120).

Repotting plants in the same container

Moisten the root ball; then remove the plant from the container.

For small plants, trim off 1 inch from the sides of the root ball and 1½ inches from the bottom. Trim as much as 5 inches off the sides of larger container plants.

Replace the screen or pot shard over the drain hole in the bottom of the container and add about an inch of potting soil, or more for larger plants. Leave the soil loose; watering will settle it.

Replace the plant; then backfill with potting soil and fertilizer, tamping down the soil along the sides. Tamp just enough to fill in any voids but not enough to compact the soil. (Dowels are handy for tamping soil.)

Water the plant thoroughly and add soil if necessary. If the plant needs to be pruned, do so immediately after repotting.

Moving a shrub or tree

Ideally, shrubs or trees already growing in the ground should be moved only when they are dormant, or before active growth starts. Before you move the shrub or tree, soak the soil around the roots so it won't fall away from the roots as you move the plant.

Prepare the destination hole, making it as deep and twice as wide as the size of the root ball.

For small shrubs, cut all around the shrub with a spade, taking as large a root ball as possible. Gently lift the root ball from the ground with the spade and carry the shrub to its new site. Try to avoid breaking the root ball. For planting, follow the instructions given above for transplanting medium-size nursery plants.

Prepare larger trees and shrubs for moving by pruning their roots at least a month (or even a year) in advance. This pruning will reduce shock at the time of transplanting. With a spade, cut a circle around the plant to the spade's depth. The circle will mark where you will cut the root ball later. Make it as large as you will be able to handle. Continue to water the plant well to develop new rootlets within the root ball.

Make the destination hole as deep as and slightly wider than the root ball to be moved.

When you are ready to transplant, make a ditch around the plant just outside the circle you made for root pruning earlier. Dig deeply to get as large a root ball as possible; then cut through underneath. A mattock and spade will be useful in digging the hole.

Hold the soil to the roots with chicken wire, burlap, or a piece of canvas or heavy plastic. Work this supporting material underneath the plant as you dig around and under the root ball; then wire or tie it together around the trunk of the plant.

Slide the root ball out on a piece of sturdy cardboard or canvas. Transport the tree or shrub to its new location by sliding it on the cardboard or canvas or by wheeling it on a wheelbarrow or wagon.

Plant the tree or shrub according to the instructions for balled-and-burlapped plants (see page 42).

YOUR FROST DATES AND CLIMATE ZONE

Timing is all-important in planting. Ask your neighbors, the local nursery staff, or your farm advisor which plants grow best in your area and when to plant or transplant. These pages offer a guide to planting times and hardiness zones, but they give only a rough approximation. If your home is on a hillside facing south or near a large body of water, your location may be 10° warmer than the average in your region. And a garden on a north-facing hill can be 10° to 20° cooler than the rest of the region.

Plants too tender for your climate will require protection in severe winter weather. Many plants, such as bulbs and fruit trees, are sold with instructions such as "hardy to 10°F." These plants need to be dug up and brought indoors or carefully protected with a mulch if your winter temperature drops lower than that.

The dates of the final spring frost and the first autumn frost are also crucial when you plan your garden. Though each year will have some variation, the dates listed here will give you a general idea of what to expect for your region.

Some plants, notably fruit trees, require a winter chill at a specified low temperature for a certain period of time. The temperature and duration will be indicated by the orchardist. When buying trees or shrubs locally, you can usually assume that the nursery is selling plants known to flourish in your climate. But when buying mail-order trees or shrubs, ask if your winter will be cold enough, but not too cold, for a given variety.

Frost dates

Find the city nearest you on this list. The numbers are the average dates of the last frost in the spring and the first frost in the fall.

City	Last frost	First frost	City	Last frost	First frost
Albany, NY	4-27	10-13	Caribou, ME	5-19	9-21
Albuquerque, NM	4-13	10-28	Centralia, WA	4-27	10-17
Altoona, PA	5-6	10-4	Charleston, SC	2-19	12-10
Asheville, NC	4-12	10-24	Charleston, WV	4-18	10-28
Atlanta, GA	3-21	11-18	Charlottesville, VA	4-11	11-6
Atlantic City, NJ	3-31	11-11	Cheyenne, WY	5-14	10-2
Augusta, GA	3-14	11-1	Chicago, IL	4-19	10-28
Bakersfield, CA	2-21	11-25	Cincinnati, OH	4-15	10-25
Baltimore, MD	3-28	11-19	Cleveland, OH	4-21	11-2
Bangor, ME	5-1	10-4	Columbia, SC	3-14	11-21
Bend, OR	6-8	9-7	Columbus, OH	4-17	10-30
Berlin, NH	5-29	9-15	Concord, NH	5-11	9-30
Binghamton, NY	5-4	10-6	Corpus Christi, TX	1-26	12-27
Birmingham, AL	3-19	11-14	Dallas, TX	3-18	11-17
Bismarck, ND	5-11	9-24	Denver, CO	4-26	10-14
Boise, ID	4-23	10-17	Des Moines, IA	4-24	10-16
Boston, MA	4-5	11-8	Detroit, MI	4-21	10-20
Bridgeport, CT	4-26	10-16	Duluth, MN	5-22	9-24
Buffalo, NY	4-30	10-25	El Paso, TX	3-26	11-14
Burlington, VT	5-8	10-3			
Canton, NY	5-9	9-26			

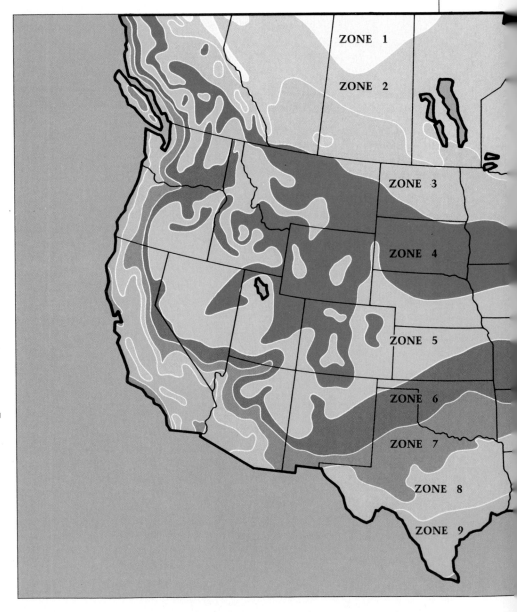

City	Last frost	First frost
Eugene, OR	4-13	11-4
Eureka, CA	3-10	11-18
Evansville, IN	4-2	11-4
Fort Smith, AR	3-21	11-10
Fort Wayne, IN	4-24	10-20
Fresno, CA	3-14	11-19
Grand Rapids, MI	4-23	10-30
Great Falls, MT	5-9	9-25
Green Bay, WI	5-6	10-13
Greenville, ME	5-27	9-20
Harrisburg, PA	4-9	10-30
Hartford, CT	4-22	10-19
Houston, TX	3-14	11-21
Huron, SD	5-4	9-30
Indianapolis, IN	4-17	10-27
Jacksonville, FL	2-16	12-16
Kansas City, MO	4-6	10-30
Knoxville, TN	3-31	11-6
La Crosse, WI	5-1	10-8
Las Vegas, NV	3-16	11-10
Lexington, KY	4-13	10-28
Little Rock, AR	3-17	11-13
Los Angeles, CA	1-3	12-28
Louisville, KY	4-1	11-7
Lubbock, TX	4-1	11-9
Marquette, MI	5-13	10-19
Marysville, CA	2-21	11-21
Memphis, TN	3-20	11-12
Miami, FL	-	-
Milwaukee, WI	4-20	10-25
Minneapolis/ St. Paul, MN	4-30	10-13
Mobile, AL	2-17	12-12
Montgomery, AL	2-27	12-3
Nashville, TN	3-28	11-7
New Haven, CT	4-15	10-27
New Orleans, LA	2-20	12-9
New York City, NY	4-7	11-12
Newark, NJ	4-3	11-8
Norfolk, VA	3-19	11-16
North Platte, NE	4-30	10-7
Ogden, UT	5-6	10-8
Oklahoma City, OK	3-28	11-7
Omaha, NE	4-14	10-20
Palm Springs, CA	1-18	12-18
Parkersburg, WV	4-16	10-21
Pasadena, CA	2-3	12-13
Peoria, IL	4-22	10-20
Philadelphia, PA	3-30	11-17
Phoenix, AZ	2-5	12-6
Pittsburgh, PA	4-20	10-23
Pittsfield, MA	5-12	9-27
Pocatello, ID	4-28	10-6
Portland, ME	4-29	10-15
Portland, OR	3-6	11-24
Providence, RI	4-13	10-27
Pueblo, CO	4-23	10-14
Raleigh, NC	3-24	11-16
Rapid City, SD	5-7	10-4
Red Bluff, CA	3-6	12-5
Reno, NV	5-8	10-10
Richmond, VA	3-29	11-2
Riverside, CA	3-6	11-26
Roanoke, VA	4-14	10-26
Sacramento, CA	2-6	12-10
St. Johnsbury, VT	5-22	9-23
St. Louis, MO	4-9	11-1
Salt Lake City, UT	4-13	10-22
San Diego, CA	-	-
San Francisco, CA	1-7	12-29
San Jose, CA	2-10	1-6
Santa Barbara, CA	1-22	12-19
Santa Fe, NM	4-24	10-19
Santa Rosa, CA	4-10	11-3
Savannah, GA	2-27	11-29
Scranton, PA	4-24	10-14
Seattle, WA	3-14	11-24
Shreveport, LA	3-8	11-15
Sioux City, IA	4-27	10-13
Sioux Falls, SD	5-5	10-3
Springfield, IL	4-20	10-23
Springfield, MO	4-12	10-30
Syracuse, NY	4-30	10-15
Tampa, FL	1-10	12-26
Texarkana, AR	3-21	11-9
Topeka, KS	4-9	10-26
Trenton, NJ	4-4	11-8
Tulsa, OK	3-25	11-1
Tucson, AZ	3-19	11-19
Washington, DC	3-29	11-9
Watertown, NY	5-7	10-4
Wichita, KS	4-5	11-1
Williamsport, PA	5-3	10-13
Wilmington, DE	4-18	10-26
Wilmington, NC	3-8	11-24
Winchester, VA	4-17	10-27
Worcester, MA	5-7	10-2
Yakima, WA	4-15	10-22

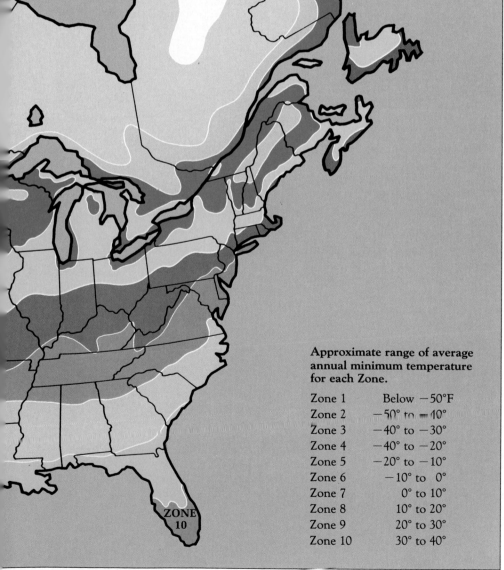

Approximate range of average annual minimum temperature for each Zone.

Zone 1	Below −50°F
Zone 2	−50° to −40°
Zone 3	−40° to −30°
Zone 4	−40° to −20°
Zone 5	−20° to −10°
Zone 6	−10° to 0°
Zone 7	0° to 10°
Zone 8	10° to 20°
Zone 9	20° to 30°
Zone 10	30° to 40°

ZONE 10

BALLED AND BURLAPPED PLANTS

Balled and burlapped (B and B) plants are trees and shrubs that are raised in a field and prepared for sale by extracting them from the soil and wrapping the root ball in burlap, tied with twine. In mild climates, plants sold B and B are usually evergreens (rhododendrons, azaleas, conifers) and large deciduous trees that don't tolerate bare-root transplanting. In severe winter climates, many different types of plants are sold B and B. Because plants raised in fields are much less susceptible to winter freezing than those grown in containers, many plants must be sold B and B.

In areas where winter freezing is not such a problem, only a few plants are commonly sold B and B. Those most frequently marketed in this form include rhododendrons and conifers sold as living Christmas trees.

The dormant season, autumn and early winter, is the usual time for planting B and Bs because there is less risk of transplant shock. However, because of the protection provided by the soil around the root ball, B and B plants can also be transplanted during the growing season.

Selecting a B and B plant

The plant should look healthy, with a good green color and no dead branches. There should be no signs of recent heavy pruning. Shake the trunk slightly. A trunk that is unduly wobbly may indicate that the soil is dry and loose around the root ball.

If you are buying a dormant plant that has no foliage, try to imagine how it will look with leaves. Be sure the branches are evenly spaced and that their overall shape is symmetrical.

After you make your selection and take the B and B home, keep the burlap on until you are ready to plant. Sprinkle the root ball and the foliage to keep them moist. Store the plant in a shady location, with a plastic sheet or moist organic materials such as sawdust, leaves, or straw around the burlapped root ball.

Transporting the plant

When transporting a B and B, be careful not to break the root ball. Cracking the soil in the root ball can sever small roots. Don't carry the plant by its trunk, and always set it down carefully.

Here are some ideas to help protect your back when you have to move heavy plants.

■ If the plant is small, you and another person may be able to carry it using a canvas sling or just your arms.

■ If the plant is large, slide it on cardboard, canvas, or a sheet of heavy plastic film. Use a car jack and a board to raise the plant; then slide the cardboard or canvas underneath. You can also use a wheelbarrow or small wagon.

■ For extremely large plants, hire a professional tree mover with a crane or power scoop.

Planting a B and B plant

Follow these steps when you plant a B and B tree or shrub.
1. Dig a hole roughly twice as wide and the same depth as the root ball.
2. Add fertilizer to the soil going into the hole (see page 82), mixing the soil to achieve a gradual transition from the soil type around the root ball to the native soil. Otherwise, the roots may remain in the amended soil. Roughen the sides of the hole to encourage root penetration into the native soil.
3. If drainage is a problem (for example, with clay soil), make a mound of soil in the bottom of the hole. It is better to plant too high than too low.
4. Determine how the tree or shrub will be oriented. If it is not perfectly symmetrical but has a dominant side branch, orient the plant so the branch will grow in the direction you wish.

Selecting a B and B plant. Examine the plant carefully. The leaves or needles should be a good green color, without spots or signs of insects. Unless the plant is a sheared Christmas tree, there should be no sign of recent pruning. The root ball should be solid and moist, and the plant should not rock or feel loose when wriggled.

The planting hole should be no deeper than the root ball. Many plants die from crown rot caused by the plant sinking so that some of the trunk is below grade. Set the root ball on undisturbed soil; then build a ridge around the hole to make a basin for watering.

5. Slide the plant into position. You can leave natural burlap on the root ball after planting because it will disintegrate. Cut off or bury any visible burlap between the stem and the soil line to prevent it from drawing moisture out of the soil. Some "burlap" is actually a synthetic plastic and must be removed at planting because it will not disintegrate. Inquire at the nursery about which kind of burlap is on the plants you buy.
6. Insert stakes to prevent the plant from leaning or falling in the wind. Use two stakes large enough for the plant's first few years of growth. (For information about staking trees, see page 120.)

If you plant too low *or want to turn the plant slightly after the hole is filled in, fill the hole with water so that the backfill soil becomes muddy and soupy. Then put a shovel under the plant and wriggle it as you lift.*

Staking. *After the plant is in the hole, but before you backfill it, drive a stake 18 inches into the bottom of the hole. The side of the stake should be solidly pressed against the root ball.*

7. Fill the space around the root ball with the soil you took from the hole.

8. Make a raised circle of soil around the planting hole to form a watering basin. The basin should be twice as wide as the root ball and a few inches high. Fill the basin with enough water to soak through the root ball.

After planting, water frequently for the first few weeks if the weather is warm and dry. The plant is very susceptible to drying out until its roots have grown into the native soil. For the first few months, water the plant consistently to encourage root growth, and never let the root ball dry out—but don't overwater. Feel the soil in the root ball (not the backfill soil). Water by filling the basin whenever the root ball soil is only slightly moist. If you live in a region that has a rainy season, break a hole in the side of the basin during this period so it doesn't trap too much water.

The roots should grow into the native soil in a few months. Within a year, the plant should be well rooted. If it still looks in the soil after a year, something is wrong. Dig the plant up and examine the root ball. If the roots are still tightly packed into the original root ball, it might be best to discard the plant and make a fresh start.

TIPS FOR PLANTING

■ Buy a healthy plant that is solidly rooted.

■ Keep the root ball moist and cool until planting.

■ Plant at the same depth as in the nursery or slightly higher.

■ Keep the root ball moist until it's established.

BARE-ROOT PLANTS

In the dormant season you'll find a wide variety of bare-root plants at nurseries. Plants that drop their leaves in the winter, such as fruit trees and roses, are completely dormant when out of leaf and can be dug up and transported without any soil around their roots.

Advantages of bare-root planting

Bare-root plants are cheaper than the same kind of plants sold in containers late in spring because they are easier to handle, lighter to ship, and require less attention in the nursery. There is also a larger selection to choose from.

Selecting and handling a bare-root plant

In the nursery, the plant may be kept in temporary storage in moist sawdust or sand, or the roots may be covered with a plastic bag. Even if the plant is prepackaged, try to examine the roots to be sure they are moist and plump, not shriveled and dry. The branches should be evenly spaced so that the plant will develop symmetrically.

When you arrive home with your plant, check the roots carefully. With sharp, clean pruning shears, remove any that are broken or damaged. Soak the roots for a couple of hours in a pail of water; then plant without delay, if possible. If you can't plant at once because the soil is too wet, plant as soon as the soil can be worked. Meanwhile, store the bare-root plant in a shady location with its roots and some stem in a moist medium, such as sawdust, or in a trench of loose soil. (This is called *heeling in.*)

Keep the plant cool. Bare-root plants don't survive long if they warm to the point that they break out of dormancy and begin growing. If that occurs, and if the roots begin to grow, plant as soon as possible. If the ground still isn't ready, put the plant in a container of soil and let it grow for a few months. Then transplant it to the ground in the summer.

Planting a bare-root fruit tree

Before planting, clip off any broken or damaged roots.

Make a hole wide and deep enough for the roots to fit without bending. Soak the hole well and put some native soil in the bottom. If the roots are radiating in a circle, make a cone-shaped mound and spread out the roots on this mound. Make the mound large enough so that the plant will be at the same depth at which it was grown in the nursery. A change of color on the bark just above the roots should show where the soil line was. If you can't find the original soil line, plant so that the top root is 1 inch below the surface. Plant slightly high to allow for some settling. This is especially important in heavy clay soil with poor drainage.

Some fruit trees have a thickened central taproot with a few smaller radiating roots. The cone-shaped mound would not be practical for such trees. But they too should be planted to their previous soil line.

If the plant is grafted, as many fruit trees are, the bud union (which should be clearly visible) must be at least 2 inches above the soil line. The bud union must remain dry and must not be allowed to send roots down into the soil. When planting, lay a board or rake handle over the hole and hold the bud union in place against it as you fill the hole with soil.

Don't fertilize the tree when you plant it. Dormant plants don't use fertilizer, and much of it will leach away and be wasted before the tree needs it. Instead, fertilize when the first leaves appear on the tree in the spring.

When the plant is in place, sprinkle soil into the hole, working it between the roots with your fingers. Then build a basin, 4 to 6 inches high and twice as wide as the tree's drip line, around the filled-in hole and fill it with water. While the soil is still soupy, wiggle the plant slightly to help eliminate air pockets.

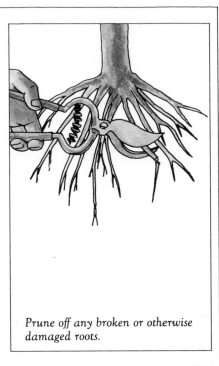

Prune off any broken or otherwise damaged roots.

Use a board to set the tree at the right level.

Bare-root plants usually don't need staking unless the location is especially windy.

Prune the tree after planting (see page 102). You probably won't need to water again until the tree leafs out. When it does, water into the basin. Break the basin if heavy rains overly saturate the soil.

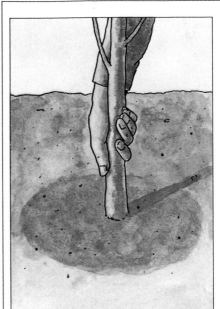

If the tree is too deep, lift it while the backfill soil is soupy.

If you can't plant a bare-root tree immediately, dig a shallow hole and "plant" it temporarily. Keep the roots moist at all times.

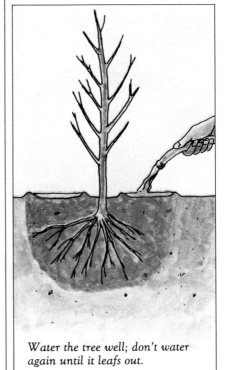

Water the tree well; don't water again until it leafs out.

Spread the roots of roses, asparagus, strawberries, and other plants without taproots.

Planting a bare-root rose

Rose plants are graded No. 1, 1½, or 2, depending on the number of canes (the branches) and their length. The highest grade is No. 1.

The technique for planting a bare-root rose is essentially the same as that for a fruit tree. Again, clip off any dried or broken roots, at the same time trimming all the roots back by about one-sixth. Dig a hole to fit the rose roots and make a cone of soil in the center. Spread the roots over the mound of soil.

In cold climates, place the bud union 1 to 2 inches below ground level to keep it from freezing in winter. Alternatively, you can put the bud union at the soil line, bringing soil up to just below the bottom branch, if you protect the bud union with a mulch during freezing weather. In mild climates, place the bud union 2 inches above ground level. More canes will develop from an exposed bud union than from one below ground.

Keep loose soil or moist organic matter around the canes until the rose breaks dormancy. The soil will protect against drying winds and keep the canes moist.

After planting, examine the branches of the rose plant. Although roses are top-pruned when they arrive at the nursery, trim the branches further if necessary to make sure that the top bud on each branch points in the direction you wish it to grow. Also eliminate all crossing stems so that the center of the plant is open. (For pruning instructions, see page 100.)

PLANTS COMMONLY SOLD IN BARE-ROOT FORM

- Fruit trees
- Deciduous ornamental trees and shrubs
- Grapes and berries
- Strawberries
- Asparagus and other perennials

PREPARING FOR A LAWN

Properly preparing the soil for a lawn is as crucial to the ultimate success of the lawn as the choice of grass type and the later care you give it. Regardless of the technique used to establish the lawn, the soil preparation is the same, except that the grade level should be ¾ inch lower for a sod lawn to allow for the thickness of the sod pieces.

Follow these steps when preparing for a lawn:

Investigate the soil if you anticipate problems with it. If the soil now grows healthy plants—even weeds—it will probably also grow a lawn. Testing can determine whether the pH is within suitable range or if the soil is too salty. Although you'll be able to perform some soil tests yourself, others can be carried out with more precision by a lab. Land-grant universities in many states provide these soil tests free or for a nominal charge. There may also be a commercial lab in your area. For information on soil testing, see page 14.

Clean the soil. Remove any plants that are growing there. If the area is now a lawn, remove the sod with a sod cutter. If there is a healthy growth of weeds or brush, kill these plants first with Kleenup, a herbicide that kills the roots and then breaks down in the soil. Remove the weeds after they are dead. Dig out any roots that will interfere with a tiller.

Remove any debris, such as construction wood, old tree roots, and rocks. Wood debris will cause mushrooms to grow in the lawn and may increase termite activity, with potential risk to the house. Rocks and concrete chunks will damage a tiller used in soil preparation and later will interfere with grass growth and water movement in the soil.

Rough-grade the area. Grade before adding any soil amendments or fertilizers. Create a slight slope away from the house, so rainwater will drain away from the founda-

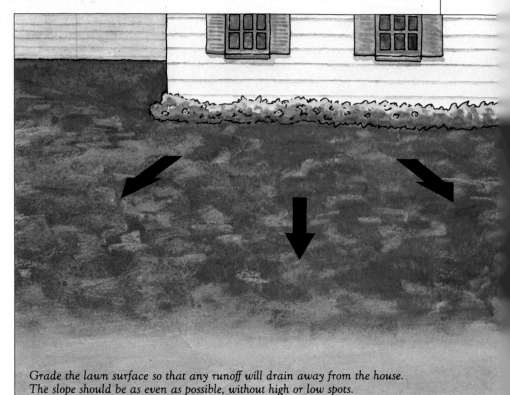

Grade the lawn surface so that any runoff will drain away from the house. The slope should be as even as possible, without high or low spots.

tion. Measure the grade with a mason's level and a string. If you live in an area of heavy rainfall, try to grade to at least a 1 to 2 percent slope (a drop of 1 to 2 feet per 100 feet). When grading around trees, minimize changes in the soil line around the tree base and avoid exposing tree roots. For drastic grade changes, remove and then replace the top 6 inches of native soil after shifting around the underlying subsoils.

Kill weed seeds. Sowing seeds or installing sod without controlling weeds can be self-defeating. This step is important, especially if many weeds have gone to seed where the lawn is to be. (If most of the weed seeds have sprouted already and have been killed, you can skip this step.)

For a month before putting in the lawn, water the site daily. As weeds emerge, kill them with a herbicide or with shallow tilling. Don't till too deeply, because you will only bring more seeds to the surface to germinate.

Spread soil amendments 2 to 4 inches deep.

Till the soil thoroughly. Make two passes at right angles to each other.

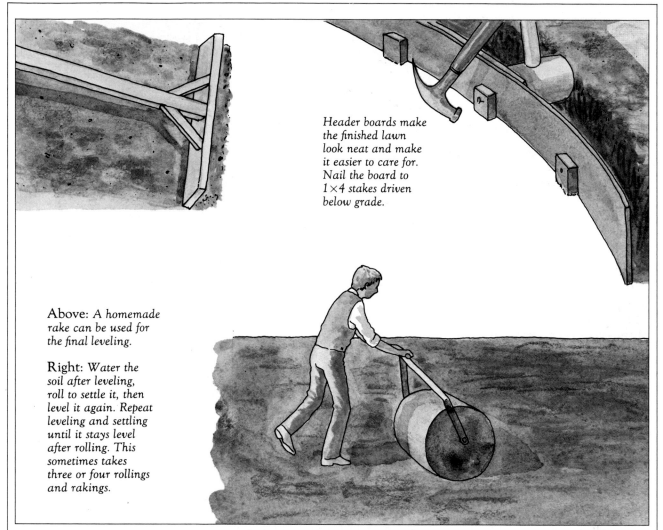

Header boards make the finished lawn look neat and make it easier to care for. Nail the board to 1×4 stakes driven below grade.

Above: *A homemade rake can be used for the final leveling.*

Right: *Water the soil after leveling, roll to settle it, then level it again. Repeat leveling and settling until it stays level after rolling. This sometimes takes three or four rollings and rakings.*

Vapam, a fumigant available to the homeowner, sterilizes the soil by killing everything in it, including weed seeds. Allow 6 weeks for the gas to escape from the soil before planting. Follow label instructions carefully.

Add soil amendments or topsoil, and lime if your soil test showed you needed it; then cultivate thoroughly with a tiller. Make several passes at right angles (for instructions on using a tiller, see page 20). For a lawn, the top 6 inches of soil should have good soil texture, which can be achieved by working 2 inches of organic soil amendment into the top 6 inches. For a list of suitable soil amendments and more on how much bulk is needed for various coverages, see page 16.

Install an underground irrigation system, if desired (see page 68).

Finish final grading at the site and fill in any excavated areas. Take time to rake and smooth the area thoroughly. A homemade board scraper or a landscaping rake can help in leveling. Later it will be difficult to correct high spots, which will tend to be scalped in mowing, or low spots, where excess water will gather. Use a string stretched between distant points to confirm your visual judgment that the grade is even.

Place header boards or mowing strips around landscape areas to minimize future maintenance and to prevent invasive grasses from extending beyond lawn areas.

Spread high-phosphorus starter fertilizer. A complete fertilizer should be applied after the seed. (For methods of applying fertilizer, see page 84.)

Lightly roll the site with a roller half-filled with water. After rolling, rake the ground level again, water to settle it, and roll it again. If the roller causes spots to settle, repeat the cycle several times if necessary until the ground stays level after rolling. Then proceed to put in the lawn (see page 48).

PLANTING AND PROPAGATING BULBS

Bulbs and bulblike plants (including corms, tubers, tuberous roots, and rhizomes) have specialized modified parts that store food. They are perennials whose fleshy storage organs survive underground after their foliage dies back each year. The bulbs are stimulated to produce new foliage and flowers when triggered by a seasonal change from wet to dry or cold to warm.

Some bulbs should not be left in the ground during their dormant period. In the fall, after the foliage has yellowed or been killed by a frost, dig up the bulbs and dry them for a few days in a shady spot. Then brush off the dirt and store them at 35° to 45°F in a shallow pan of dry sand, peat moss, or perlite until the next proper planting time.

Some bulbs can be *naturalized*, or left in the soil for perennial flowering without further attention. But only certain bulbs naturalize well. These include daffodils, crocus, allium, brodiaea, galanthus, and scilla.

During the period after the flower has died, the leaves are making next year's bulb. Since bulb size determines the size of the flowers produced by a plant, allow the leaves to remain on your plants until they turn yellow.

These plants are propagated in two basic ways. Tuberous roots, stem tubers, and rhizomes are cut apart, or *divided*. Bulbs and corms have detachable parts that can be *separated*.

Dividing tuberous roots

Dahlias, begonias, and other tuberous roots store food in swollen specialized roots for next year's shoots. Dahlias have annual, elongated, swollen roots that disintegrate as the plant grows and blooms. New roots form at the end of the growing season. Begonias have perennial discus-shaped tubers that grow larger in diameter each year.

1. Dig up the dahlia or begonia in the autumn and clean off the soil.
2. Dust with captan (a fungicide).
3. Store the plant in a newspaper wrap or other dry medium at 40° to 50°F until the buds begin to swell as spring approaches.
4. Cut into pieces, making sure each division has one bud. When dividing them, make sure the elongated root parts are cut so that each division has a bud piece of the stem (crown). For begonias, cut the discus-shaped root into as many pieces as there are buds.
5. Dust the cuts with captan and let them callus in a warm, dry place for 2 days.
6. Plant the divisions in a pot or outdoors, if the temperature is already warming.

Dividing potatoes and other tubers

The "eyes" of potatoes and other tubers are buds.
1. In early spring cut the potato into sections, making sure that each section has an eye.
2. Dust each section with captan and set it in a warm, dry place to callus over for a day. This section is called the potato *seed*.
3. Plant the potato seed in your garden, either shallowly or about 1 foot deep. If you plant shallowly, continue to mulch the emerging green stem; the potatoes will grow under the mulch, which makes picking easy. Light must not reach the developing tubers or they will turn green and spoil.

Dividing rhizomes

Rhizomes are modified stems that grow just below surface level or on the surface, forming roots and buds at nodes. Divide them while they are not in active growth. For bearded iris, the best time is right after they finish blooming.
1. Lift the clump and wash off clinging soil.
2. Cut off the old flower stalk and shorten the leaf blade back to 3 inches. Cut off sections that show new shoots. Make sure each section has a bud and roots.

Hyacinth. *Score by making cuts in the bottom. Keep it in sand in a humid place until small bulbs form on the scores. Then plant the entire bulb upside down.*

Potato. *Use certified potatoes for seed. Cut each potato into several pieces, being sure that each piece has one or two eyes.*

3. Dust the sections with captan and allow to callus in a shaded place for 2 days before planting.
4. Replant the rhizome on a ridge of soil with its roots trailing down the side.
5. Press down the soil, and water the rhizome. Fertilize when it shows signs of growth.

Separating corms

Corms are fleshy central underground stems to which leaves are attached. Small separate corms, called *cormels*, develop on the underside of the parent corm. They can be removed by separating and then planted. (A single gladiolus may develop up to 50 cormels.)

Follow these steps to separate cormels:
1. Dig up the corm in the autumn or when the plant is dormant.
2. Separate out the cormels and store them in vermiculite in a

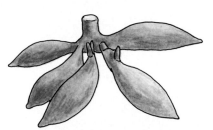

Dahlia. *Store the root until spring. When the buds turn pink and begin to swell, separate into several roots, each with a bud.*

Gladiolus. *Tiny cormels form around the edge of the large corm. Plant these outside in the garden in the spring.*

Tuberous begonia. *In the spring, when the buds begin to swell and turn pink, cut into several sections, each with a bud. Plant these inside in leaf mold until the tops are 4 inches high.*

Tulip. *Small bulbs often form at the base of the new, large bulb. Separate these small bulbs and replant them. They will take a year or two to flower.*

Iris. *Divide the rhizome so that each piece has a shoot. Discard old sections without shoots.*

Lily. *Break off outer scales. You can remove the outer two layers of scales without harming a large bulb.*

paper bag in the refrigerator. Add a few drops of water if the corms begin to shrivel during the winter. 3. Plant the cormels outdoors at a depth twice their size. Cormels usually take 2 years to reach flowering size.

Propagating true bulbs

True bulbs are tiny, fully formed plants surrounded by fleshy scales. The old bulb exhausts its food supply while flowering. Then the leaves manufacture the food that forms the new bulb.

Bulbs are of two types. The *tunicate* bulbs (daffodil and tulip) develop fleshy leaves and will seldom dry out. *Scaly* bulbs (fritillarias, lilies) have dry, scaly leaves and readily dry out.

Separation is the primary method of propagating true bulbs. Dig up the bulbs after the foliage has turned completely yellow. Separate and replant them at a depth about twice their size.

Bulb scaling is a method of propagation that can be used with some lilies. Remove individual bulb scales in October or November, dust them with captan and a rooting hormone, and place them in a bag of damp vermiculite. Keep them at room temperature until roots begin to grow (about 2 months); then chill them in a refrigerator for another 2 months to break dormancy.

Scoring and scooping, two alternative propagation techniques, can be used for hyacinths and daffodils. *Score* a bulb by making two

cuts at right angles in the basal plate of the bulb; then dust it with captan and place it upside down in moist sand in a warm, dark, humid place. *Scoop* by cutting off the base of the bulb with a knife or sharpened spoon, dust the base with captan, and store it upside down in an environment as described for scoring. With either procedure, bulblets will develop on the cuts in about 2 months. The bulb can then be planted, upside down. At the end of the growing season, separate the bulblets.

Scoring creates fewer but larger bulblets than scooping. These scored bulblets will reach flowering size in about 2 years. Scooping produces numerous bulblets that need about 3 or 4 years of growth before they reach flowering size.

DIVIDING PLANTS

The *crown* of a plant is the place where the roots and shoots meet. Many perennials, and some woody plants, grow new shoots directly from the crown rather than from a trunk. These new shoots often form their own root systems and become individual plants, although they usually remain attached to the parent plant. After several years of this growth, the center of the plant may become crowded and die, leaving a ring of new plants around the dying core.

These plants can reliably be propagated by *division*, a method in which the new plant, with stem, root, and leaf or bud, is separated from the parent plant. Plants with fibrous crowns, runner plants, and offset plants can all be divided.

Dividing plants with fibrous crowns

The crowns of day lilies, chrysanthemums, and many other herbaceous perennials are composed of multiple stems, usually in a rosette pattern. Increasing numbers of these stems usually result in exhausted, woody interiors and an excess of outer shoots that crowd each other. A portion of stem and roots, either a single unit or a clump, can be broken off and replanted. Division will both rejuvenate your older plants and increase your supply.

Divide in spring before growth begins or in fall after growth has stopped. If, like day lilies, the plant blooms in spring and summer and then produces vegetative growth, divide them in the fall. If, like chrysanthemums, the plant blooms in late summer and fall, divide in fall or early spring. Divide potted plants when they crowd their pots.

Follow these steps to divide plants with fibrous crowns:
1. Dig up the clump to be divided.
2. Shake off the soil and cut back the tops of the stems to reduce water demand on the roots.
3. Pull apart the plants. This can be done by hand if the clump is small. Two spading forks, back to back, can be used to break apart

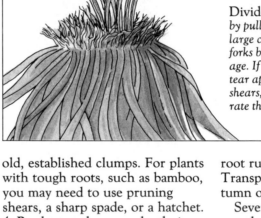

Divide multistemmed plants *by pulling the stems apart. On large clumps, a pair of spading forks back to back provide leverage. If the stems are too tough to tear apart, use a knife, pruning shears, or even a hatchet to separate them.*

old, established clumps. For plants with tough roots, such as bamboo, you may need to use pruning shears, a sharp spade, or a hatchet.
4. Replant at the same depth, in prepared soil, and water well.
5. Fertilize when there are signs of new growth.

Dividing strawberries and other runners

A *runner* is a horizontal stem that arises from a crown bud and grows laterally. A new plant forms at the end of the stem, and eventually the connection to the parent plant disintegrates. Strawberry runners form in the warm midsummer period, when days are 12 to 14 hours long. As they develop, check your plants and thin out the new runners if they become too numerous.

To divide strawberries and other runners, guide developing runners to the places where you want them to root. Hold each stem to the soil with a large wire staple. (Or fill containers with potting mix and root runners right in the pots. Transplant the new plants in autumn or early spring.)

Several methods of renewing strawberry beds are commonly used. Since strawberries bear most heavily in their second year, most of the methods aim at replacing the plants every third year. One way to do this is to maintain strawberries in a 3-row system. Each spring, dig out the 3-year-old plants and renew the row by tilling in organic matter. In midsummer, as runners begin to form on the 2-year-old plants, guide the first ones to form to the empty row and root them there, about 12 inches apart.

A more casual way to renew a strawberry bed is to maintain it as a single matted bed, at least 4 feet wide, allowing runners to root wherever they will. Each winter, till one-third of the bed to remove the oldest plants. Train runners to root in the empty space.

Plants that form runners *can be divided by rooting the plantlets that form at the ends of the runners. The plantlets can be rooted in the ground, then transplanted, or they can be rooted directly in a pot. Encourage rooting by holding them tight to the soil and keeping the ground moist.*

Plants that form offshoots *can be propagated by removing the offshoot and replanting it. Offshoots of soft plants, such as echeverias, can be broken off with your fingers. Use a knife for woody plants.*

Dividing offset plants

Offsets are plantlets that develop from the roots or crown of the parent plant. They can be separated and rooted. If they are left in place, the original plant will become a clump.

To divide offsets, remove them by cutting close to the central stem with a sharp knife. If an offset is already well rooted, treat it as a rooted cutting and repot it. If it has not rooted, handle it as a stem cutting for rooting (see page 54). Replant divided offsets in pots with rooting medium. Some African violets form offsets. Break them off by pressing a finger between the offset and the parent plant. Removing offsets from violets not only gives you new plants, it makes the parent plant more attractive.

PLANTS PROPAGATED BY DIVISION

Fibrous crowns	Hosta	Offsets
Agapanthus	Kaffir lily	Some African violets
Alyssum	Lily-of-the-valley	Agave
Astilbe	Ornamental grasses	Aloe
Some bamboos	Pinks	Bromeliad
Begonia	Shasta daisy	Cactus
Bellflower	Violets	Chinese evergreen
Bleeding-heart		Echeveria
Candytuft	Runners (stolons)	Hen and chicks
Chives	Ajuga	Jade plant
Chrysanthemum	Some bamboos	Sedum
Coralbells	Cinquefoil	Yucca
Day lily	Geum	
English daisy	Piggyback plant	
Ferns	Saxifrage	
Gazania	Strawberry	

ROOTING CUTTINGS

Cuttings are incomplete pieces of plants from which the missing parts can be grown. Unlike a division, a cutting lacks one or two of the three main plant parts: roots, stems, or shoots.

General procedures

Root cuttings in a mixture of 5 parts perlite to 1 part peat moss. The peat moss adds structural strength to the perlite so the cuttings don't fall over. Besides supporting the cuttings, the rooting medium keeps them moist while permitting air to penetrate to the base of the cuttings. Cuttings must have moisture if they are to survive and develop roots. To make sure they don't dry out, cover them with a pane of glass or a piece of plastic film, vented just enough so that condensation doesn't form inside the covering.

Place the cuttings in bright light, but not direct sunlight. Light is necessary for leafy cuttings to produce the plant hormones that cause roots to grow. Artificial light can be used.

Maintain temperatures as close as possible to 70°F for the air in the rooting area and 85°F for the rooting medium. The warmer temperature stimulates root growth, and the cooler air slows metabolism in the leaves. Bottom heat, if needed, can be applied with heater cables.

In many plants, root formation can be increased by dipping stem and leaf cuttings in rooting hormones, or *auxins*, which are commercially available in powder and liquid forms. Consult the package for directions.

To help prevent plant disease and insect infestations, keep your rooting bench, containers, tools, growing medium, and the cuttings themselves as clean as possible. Check carefully all incoming cuttings for insects such as aphids, mites, larval whiteflies, and mealybugs. Remove the insects and dust or drench with a fungicide if necessary.

Most cuttings will root in about 6 weeks, although cuttings from

For a few cuttings, cover a pot with a plastic bag held in place with a rubber band.

Cover a flat of cuttings with a pane of glass, vented slightly. Or put plastic kitchen wrap over it.

Mark the bottom end of hardwood cuttings with a slanted cut.

Softwood cuttings have several leaves left on.

rapidly growing shoot tips might root in as few as 3 weeks. Hardwood cuttings may take as long as a year. Tug gently at the cutting every couple of weeks to see if roots have begun to form. Transplant the cuttings when the roots begin to branch, or when the root ball is dense and about 2 inches in diameter. Over a period of 2 weeks, expose them slowly to dry air and full sun.

Rooting hardwood stem cuttings

Take the cuttings early in the dormant season. In mild-winter regions, start to root in the fall; in regions where the ground freezes, store cuttings through the winter for spring planting. The storage time allows the base end to callus over, which helps rooting in some species.

1. Cut an 8-inch, midbranch, pencil-thick section from the previous season's growth. The cutting should have three leaf buds, with the base cut just below a bud. Distinguish the top from the base by cutting the top straight across and the bottom at a slant.

2. When storing cuttings, place them on their sides or upside down in a bucket of moist sand or wood shavings, with several inches of sand over them. Keep the cuttings at a temperature of approximately 32° to 40°F.

Rex begonias *are rooted by first cutting the veins of the leaves to be used. Place the cut leaves on top of the rooting medium, pinning them down where the veins have been cut.*

Sansevieria *leaves should be cut into 3-inch sections. Insert them into the rooting medium to three-quarters of their length. Roots and stems will emerge from the base of the cutting.*

Streptocarpus *leaves are split down the center of the midrib. Place them in the medium just deeply enough to cover the midrib. New plants will form at each cut vein.*

African violets *are placed in the medium using the leaf stalk to hold the leaf upright. The base of the leaf should be covered.*

3. When you are ready to plant, dip the base (the slanted end) of the cutting in a rooting hormone.

4. To plant cuttings, make a hole with a pencil in your rooting medium and insert the slanted end of the cutting 3 inches deep.

5. Roots will form under the soil level. Transplant when the roots begin to branch.

Camellias and holly are among the plants propagated as *semihardwood* cuttings. In summer, make the stem cuttings with three or four leaves, just as the new leaves have matured and the stem is stiff but not yet woody. Cut the base just below a node, dip the base in hormone, and plant at once in your rooting medium. Keep the cutting moist. Rooting may take several months.

Rooting softwood stem cuttings

To root softwood stem cuttings, use the following procedures:

1. Make the cuttings in spring or summer.

2. Choose for the cutting 8 inches of pliable yet mature new growth that will bend without snapping.

The stem should have leaves attached.

3. Cut just below a leaf node. Remove the leaves from the lower third of the cutting. If the leaves are large, cut off half of each remaining leaf to reduce transpiration. Try to leave about 2 square inches of leaf.

4. Dip the base in rooting hormone and tap off the excess.

5. Make a hole with a pencil in your rooting medium and insert the cutting to a 3-inch depth.

6. Root in a moist and brightly lit spot, but without direct sunlight.

7. Transplant as desired when roots have formed.

Rooting herbaceous stem cuttings

In addition to hardwoods and softwoods, various herbaceous plants can be propagated by rooting cuttings. Among them are chrysanthemums, geraniums, and marguerite daisies.

Follow these procedures to root herbaceous stem cuttings:

1. Cut off the top 5 inches of a stem, with the leaves attached. If the leaves are large, trim back half of each leaf to reduce transpiration. Keep about 2 square inches of leaf.

2. For plants that exude a sticky sap, such as geraniums, let the stem base callus over for a few hours to reduce the possibility of decay.

3. If you wish, dip the base of the cutting in rooting hormone. Although helpful, this practice is less essential than with hard- and softwood cuttings.

4. Make a hole with a pencil in your rooting medium and insert the cutting to half the length of the stem.

5. As with other cuttings, maintain high humidity, warmth, and adequate light.

Rooting leaf cuttings

Choose recently mature leaves for cutting. New plants form under the rooting medium wherever a leaf vein was cut. Several methods are used, depending on the shape of the leaf.

LAYERING

Layering is a way to get new roots to grow on the stem of a plant while the plant remains rooted and nourished. Its main advantage is that the plant's source of water and nutrients is not disturbed during propagation.

Successful layering requires four main conditions. As with other propagation techniques, maintain (1) adequate moisture, (2) good aeration, and (3) moderate temperatures in the rooting area. In addition, (4) eliminate light from the area to be rooted.

Tip layering. *Bury the tip of the cane in late summer.*

The following spring, move the new plant to its permanent location.

Tip layering

In this method, you bury the tip of a branch.
1. In late summer select a stem bearing the tip of the current season's growth and bend it down to the ground.
2. Dig a small hole with a trowel, insert the tip to a 4-inch depth, cover with dirt to hold the tip firm, and water the area. Roots will form and a new shoot will begin to grow in a few weeks. The newly rooted tip can be dug up in late fall or early spring.

Layering. *Select a flexible branch from last year's wood. Make a cut a few inches from the end. Dig a shallow trench and peg or staple the cut to the bottom of it, with the tip of the branch exposed.*

Simple layering

This is a good way to fill in space in a hedge. It is also the simplest way to propagate most shrubs.
1. In early spring or late fall select a dormant year-old branch.
2. Make a cut three-quarters of the way through the stem a few inches from the end. To keep the cut open, insert a matchstick, a pebble, or a grain of wheat. As the wheat germinates, it releases hormones that help promote rooting.
3. Dig a shallow trench and bend the branch to the trench. Bend the branch at the cut so the tip is vertical and tie it to a stake. A wooden peg, a piece of bent wire, or a stone can keep the base of the bend in place.
4. Cover the base of the bent stem with soil or rooting medium, but leave the tip exposed. Remove all leaves that would be buried.
5. Roots will form on the buried

bend. Keep the root area moist.
6. Cut the rooted branch from the parent plant in the following autumn or spring and place it in the desired location.

Layering saplings

Whole shrubs and trees, one year old, can be bent over and laid in a trench in early spring. As stems begin upward growth and develop leaves, gradually cover the parent plant with soil. In autumn or early the following spring, remove the soil from the trench, remove the new stem sections with roots, the parent plant, and replant.

Air layering

Air layering is a useful method for rerooting leggy houseplants. Follow these steps:

1. In spring select a stem of the previous season's growth. In summer choose a stem of the current season's growth that has already hardened but is not yet woody. Leaf growth above the point of air layering will stimulate root formation. If you are rerooting a leggy houseplant, choose the spot where you would like the new soil level to be.
2. Slit the stem at an upward angle and insert a matchstick, a pebble, or a grain of wheat to hold the cut open.
3. Apply a rooting hormone to the cut area.
4. To maintain high humidity and darkness around the cut area, wrap a handful of damp sphagnum moss

Serpentine layering. *This variation on simple layering produces several new plants from a single flexible stem.*

Stooling. *A sprouting stump produces the new plants.*

Air layering. *Make the cut where you want the roots of the new plant to form.*

Tie the bottom of a piece of plastic and stuff with damp sphagnum moss. Then tie the top.

PLANTS THAT CAN BE PROPAGATED BY LAYERING

Tip Layering
Blackberry
Loganbery
Raspberry

Simple layering
Barbarry
Clematis
Dieffenbachia
Horse chestnut
Lilac
Magnolia
Thododendron
Viburnum
Wisteria

Air layering
Azalea
Dieffenbachia
Magnolia
Philodendron
Rubber plant

Stooling
Clonal apple stock
Lilac

Natural suckering
Poplar
Cherry
Lilac

around the cut, encase with black polyethylene plastic or aluminum foil, and tie both ends securely with rubber bands or tape.

5. Check the wrapping weekly and moisten the moss as needed.

6. Rooting will occur in 2 to 3 months. Cut the top off just below the new roots and plant. Prune the top if the foliage area is especially large compared with the roots.

Stooling and natural suckering

Stooling is a propagation method in which the parent plant is cut back to a height of an inch above the ground during the dormant season. In spring, as new shoots develop in the crown area, mound soil or sawdust over the plant, around the stems. Roots will form along the stems. The following autumn, remove the soil from around the crown, cut off the rooted stems as close to the parent plant as possible, and transplant them where desired. The parent plant can be left to produce more shoots for the following seasons.

Natural suckering occurs in some plants without a gardener's interference. These plants send out suckers that root and can be removed and replanted. Suckers are usually removed toward the end of the growing season or in early spring.

GRAFTING AND BUDDING

Grafting joins together a stem cutting, or *scion*, from one plant with the root system (*stock*) of another plant to form a third variety. In budding, the scion is a small piece of bark with a bud rather than a whole stem.

General procedures

The key to success with grafting or budding is to bring the *cambium*—the thin layer of slippery tissue just under the bark—of the stock and scion into contact and keep them alive until they grow together, usually a couple of weeks.

Collect scions just before bud break in early spring, or if winter cold is severe, in the autumn before the wood freezes. Each scion should have two or three leaf buds. Take them from the middle of the stem. Store scions in moist sawdust or moist peat moss in a plastic bag in the refrigerator until the stock is ready for grafting.

Budding can take place whenever the stock is in vigorous growth in spring. During spring growth, the bark will *slip* (lift) easily. The bark usually won't slip after growth slows in summer.

The *bottom* of the scion must fuse to the *top* of the stock. Keep track of which end of the scion is up by marking the top with a straight cut and the bottom with a slanted cut. The scion will die if it is inserted upside down into the stock.

Join grafts quickly and then protect them from air so that exposed cambium is not killed by drying out. Tie grafts together with rubber grafting bands, nursery tape, plastic electrician's tape, or wide rubber bands. The tie material must hold the parts firmly together yet be able to stretch, disintegrate, or be cut as the stem thickens.

To prevent drying, apply grafting wax or asphalt emulsion sealing compound to the graft. Also dab some on the cut end of the scion to keep it from drying out. Asphalt emulsions, consisting of asphalt and water, are simplest for a home

gardener to use. It is not necessary to wax the bud grafts; just wrap them tightly.

Whip grafting

Whip grafts are used in early spring on plants with stems up to ¾ inch in diameter. They have a high rate of success because there is much cambium-layer contact between the two parts. Stock and scion should be the same diameter for best results.
1. Choose a stock with 2 inches of wood below a bud. Cut it off flush just beneath the bud. Then cut it as shown in the illustration.
2. Choose a scion about the same diameter as the stock. Cut it the same way as you did the stock.
3. Slip scion and stock together, with the cut surfaces, or *tongues*, interlocking and the cambium matching. If the stock and scion are not the same diameter, match cambium layers on one side.
4. Tie the graft with a rubber band and wax it.

Cleft grafting

Cleft grafts are often used for *topworking* trees—for changing from one variety to another.
1. Select two pencil-thick scions about 4 inches long. Cut the base of each into a long, tapering wedge. Make one edge of the wedge thicker than the other.
2. Saw off the stock branch at a right angle. With a butcher knife, make a vertical split 2 to 3 inches into the stub of the stock.
3. Hold the split stock open with a screwdriver and insert the scions at each end, lining up the cambium on the thick edge with the cambium of the stock. Remove the screwdriver and the scions will be held snugly.
4. Apply wax, making sure you cover the entire stub of the stock. (Ties are not needed because the pressure holds the scions snugly.) In a few days, inspect the graft and rewax any open areas.
5. If both grafts take, trim off the weaker one in the following year. Stake and train the scion that summer. It will grow quickly.

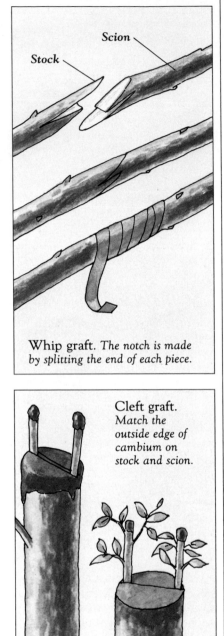

Whip graft. *The notch is made by splitting the end of each piece.*

Cleft graft. *Match the outside edge of cambium on stock and scion.*

Bark grafting

This method is used to graft new tops to large trees. Fruit trees with stock measuring 4 inches or wider are often bark-grafted.
1. Have 3 pencil-thick scions, each 5 inches long, ready for each stock.
2. Prepare the stock when the tree is in active growth in the spring—the time the bark is pliable and likely to slip. Cut off the branch you wish to replace, leaving a stub 1 to 12 inches in diameter.
3. Cut one side of each scion with a wide, 2-inch-long slice. Make a shorter slice on the other side.

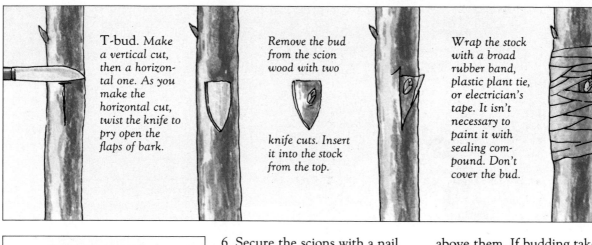

T-bud. *Make a vertical cut, then a horizontal one. As you make the horizontal cut, twist the knife to pry open the flaps of bark.*

Remove the bud from the scion wood with two knife cuts. Insert it into the stock from the top.

Wrap the stock with a broad rubber band, plastic plant tie, or electrician's tape. It isn't necessary to paint it with sealing compound. Don't cover the bud.

Bark graft. *Cut the bark loose and insert the scion between it and the wood.*

4. Make a 2-inch-long vertical cut in the bark at the top of the stub of the stock. Lift back the bark on each side of the cut.
5. Insert the scion between the wood and the bark with the long-slice side of the scion facing inward. Be sure the cambium of the stock and the cambium of the scion are in contact.

TIPS FOR GRAFTING AND BUDDING

■ The cambium on scion and stock must be in firm contact.

■ Keep the graft from drying out until a callus has formed. Check the seal every week and patch it if it has cracked.

■ Make a few more grafts than you want and prune off the excess. There are always a few that don't take.

6. Secure the scions with a nail through the bark, then wax the graft.
7. After a year, trim to leave only the strongest scion.

T-budding

Use a T-bud graft on thin-barked fruit trees, roses, and ornamental shrubs whose stock stems are ¼ to 1 inch in diameter.
1. Make an inch-long vertical cut through the bark to the wood of the stock. Then make a horizontal cut through the bark at the top of the vertical cut. Twist the knife to open the two flaps.
2. Cut behind the bud, from ½ inch below to 1 inch above the bud. About ¾ inch above the bud, cut horizontally so the bud *shield* can be removed.
3. Insert the bud shield into the stock, pushing it down under the two bark flaps. The slippery cut side of the shield will touch the slippery surface of the wood under the flaps.
4. Wrap the union tight with a rubber band or electrician's tape, leaving just the bud exposed. The bud should unite with the new stock in 2 to 3 weeks. When the bud has taken, remove the tape.
5. Rub off any competing buds that develop on the stock near the desired bud.
6. The following spring, after budding, encourage grafted buds to grow by cutting off the stock just

above them. If budding takes place in early spring, the stock can be cut about 8 weeks later in the same season, after you're certain the bud has taken.

POTENTIAL GRAFTS

What can be grafted to what? Generally, almost all grafts within a species, and many between different species in a genus, are successful, but almost no grafts between different genera are successful. Here are some combinations of stock and scions that make successful grafts.

Almond: almond, peach, nectarine

Apple: apple (but don't combine vigorous and slow-growing varieties)

Apricot: apricot, plum

Sour cherry: sweet or sour cherry

Orange: sweet or sour orange, grapefruit, lemon

Peach: peach, almond, apricot

Pear: pear, quince

Plum, European: European plum, almond, nectarine, Japanese plum

Plum, Japanese: Japanese plum, apricot, nectarine

Camellia: any camellia

Rhododendron: any rhododendron

WATERING

Although all gardeners water, watering is probably the least understood of the gardener's arts. Improper watering accounts for more plant failures than any other cause.

Proper watering is one of the most important—and most difficult— gardening techniques to learn. Plants cannot live without water. Water is essential to almost all the processes that go on in the plant's system. It makes up a large part of the plant's structure. An actively growing plant may be 85 to 90 percent water. Most plants are sensitive about how much water they need; few will thrive in both very dry and very wet conditions. On the other hand, a great many plants will grow well within a range of moisture conditions. Learning how to water requires an understanding of both the moisture needs of different kinds of plants and how water behaves in the soil.

Water use by the plant

Water is the life-sustaining liquid needed both for the physical movement of materials through the plant and for the chemical processes that make all the plant's food. Plants use water as the medium for transporting dissolved minerals from the soil to the leaves. This upward flow of water and minerals occurs in microscopic tubes, called the *xylem*. The xylem tubes extend from the roots, through the stem, and into the

An automatic sprinkler system is the best way to water thickly planted areas like this hillside.

leaf. Water then passes through the leaf material, where part of it evaporates (a process called *transpiration*) through microscopic openings on the undersides of leaves, called *stomates* (or *stomata*). In the process of transpiration, the evaporating water cools the plants, just as a wet towel cools by evaporation.

Three factors can reduce the flow of water up the xylem to the leaves. The soil may be too dry, the root system may not be functioning properly, or the xylem may be plugged or cut for some reason. If the xylem flow is slowly reduced over a period of time, the leaves begin to show nutrient deficiencies, usually by turning pale green and yellow. If the xylem flow is suddenly reduced, and the transpiration rate is high, perhaps because of hot weather or wind, the leaf wilts, then scorches or sunburns as it overheats.

Once in the leaf, water is used in the process of photosynthesis. *Photosynthesis* is the chemical reaction that locks up the sun's energy in the form of simple compounds that form the basis for all of plant and animal life. Photosynthesis can only occur when the stomates are open. If a plant is stressed due to lack of water, it will close its stomates, which stops photosynthesis and plant growth.

The plant does not transpire all of the water in its system. Some of it flows back from the leaves carry-

ing sugars and other chemicals to the flowers, fruits, growing tips, and roots. This second transport system in a plant is called the *phloem*. The phloem nourishes the other plant parts. If you peel back the bark of a tree, the phloem is visible as the white part of the bark. The flow of water in the phloem is by diffusion and is much slower than water movement in the xylem.

Plant requirements for water

The plant's size and its ability to conserve water affect its need for water. Plants native to desert or windy locations develop ingenious mechanisms to conserve water. Such plants often have small, thick leaves with waxy coverings.

Three broad plant groups can be identified as an aid in determining when to water. The first group of plants can't tolerate drought. They thrive in soil that should be kept moist. These plants should be watered when the soil is damp but not muddy. When you touch damp soil, it feels cool and wets your finger but does not muddy it.

The second group may be described as average plants. Soil in their root zone should be just barely moist before watering. When you touch it, the soil feels cool and moist but doesn't dampen your fingers. Moist soils are crumbly at this point but not dusty.

The third group can't tolerate wet soil. Water these plants when the soil is dry and no longer cool to the touch. But don't let the soil stay dry too long; although these plants tolerate drought, they grow better when watered regularly. Among plants in this group are many cacti and succulents.

Water movement in the soil

Water moves through the soil because of the forces of gravity (pulling downward) and capillary action (the force with which water molecules cling to each other and to soil particles). Gravity is relatively easy to understand, but capillary action is less familiar to us. You can observe capillary action by rolling up a paper towel and inserting the bottom of it in a glass of water. Water will climb through the towel because of the capillary action of water molecules clinging to towel fibers and to each other.

When water enters the soil it moves downward in the pore spaces between the soil particles. As water fills the pores, the soil becomes saturated and the water moves deeper, replacing the air in pores. The rate at which this *wetting front* moves depends on the soil texture: it moves faster in sand, with its large pore spaces, and slower in clay, which has small pore spaces. Eventually the force of gravity pulling downward is balanced by the capillary action of the water molecules clinging to soil particles, and the water stops draining downward.

At this point, the soil is like a sponge that has been soaked in a basin of water, then lifted and held above the basin until it stops draining. Gravity has pulled out all the water it can, but water is still held in the sponge by capillary forces.

If you squeeze the sponge, water runs out freely. As you continue to squeeze, it becomes more and more difficult to get water to flow from the sponge, until finally no more water will flow no matter how hard you try.

As the soil dries through evaporation from its surface and removal of water by plant roots, like the sponge, it eventually will release no more water. This occurs when

Top: Drip irrigation can be the salvation of gardeners too busy to water regularly. Drip emitters put moisture just where plants need it.

Bottom: Watering tape, such as this, is part of a drip irrigation system. The water seeps slowly from the tape to this young cabbage.

the soil is so dry that plant roots cannot overcome the very strong capillary forces that keep the last remaining layers of water clinging to the soil particle surfaces.

Soil should be watered before it gets this dry. Plants will show water stress before this point, with foliage wilting or discoloring. Plants should be watered when they have used about half the water available to them, before they undergo water stress.

Water and soil type

Knowledge of your own soil will help you water properly. Sandy soils have large pores and dry out quickly; they need to be watered more frequently. Clay soils have small pores and dry out slowly. It is easy to overwater clay soil, keeping the pores full of water so that air is excluded. The ideal soil (the "good garden loam" described in gardening books) has a mixture of large and small pores. The small pores hold water, and the large pores allow air to enter right after watering.

If your soil isn't ideal, the best way to improve it is to add organic amendments. Organic amendments provide a mixture of large and small soil pores that increases the soil's water-holding capacity, yet allow for good drainage and aeration. Organic matter in the soil acts as a sponge, holding water in sandy soils, and allowing air to penetrate clay soils.

The art of applying water must also take into consideration the speed at which soil can absorb water. To prevent runoff and erosion, apply water at the rate at which the soil can absorb it. Hand sprinkling and some sprinkler systems can apply water at a rate that causes puddling and runoff. A gardener may then assume, incorrectly, that the soil is wet through the depth of the root zone of plants. In fact, the soil may be wet only an inch or so deep. Apply the water more slowly, so that it has time to penetrate the soil. Or water in cycles, by sprinkling until the water begins to puddle, turning the water off for a half hour or so, then watering again.

As plants get larger in the container, they use water faster. These flats of ivy need daily watering.

Water and weather

The speed with which the plant's leaves transpire water is of crucial interest to the gardener. A plant must be able to balance its water uptake with its water transpiration for growth to occur. Several factors must be in balance. Watering is a difficult gardening art to master because so many variables are involved. Several of these variables are related to the weather.

Humidity, temperature, wind, and the length of the day all affect the rate at which plants use water. In hot, dry, windy weather, plants need large amounts of water to keep their leaves cool. Even in winter, the combination of low humidity caused by cold and high winds can dry and scorch the leaves of plants.

Day length is an important factor because plants transpire water only during daylight. June is the month with the greatest water demand because it has the longest days, even when it isn't the hottest month of the season.

Watering plants in containers is more critical than watering plants in the ground because the soil volume from which roots can pull water is small. Moreover, the container's large surface area will be affected much more readily by temperature, wind, and humidity than will the ground soil, whose vast volume buffers rapid change in the external environment.

WATERING BASICS

The soil in the root zone of your plants acts as a reservoir for water. Depending on its texture, it holds a certain amount of water from one period of rainfall or irrigation to the next.

When it rains, or when you water, the water fills the pores between soil particles. The soil at this stage is *saturated*—it is holding all the water it can. When the rain stops, gravity pulls the water from the larger soil pores and air from the surface replaces it. But capillary action keeps the smaller pores filled with water. After a few hours, gravity has moved the water downward in the soil as far as it can. Now all the water is held in capillary-sized pores and all the larger pores are full of air. The soil's reservoir is holding all the water it can.

Water *transpiring* (evaporating) from the leaves draws water into the roots much as sucking on a drinking straw draws water into the bottom of the straw. As plants extract water from the soil, the soil's reservoir is depleted. The effect is like wringing out a sponge: the first squeeze of a wet sponge wrings out a great deal of water with little effort, but as the sponge grows drier, it takes more and more effort to extract water, until finally you can't wring any more out at all. Water flows less and less easily into the plant as the soil's reservoir is exhausted.

Soils of different texture retain different amounts of water. If you add an equal amount of water to sand, loam, and clay soils, the sand will need the most depth to contain it, and the clay the least depth.

As water is added to soil, the first inch of soil must become very wet before the water can move to the second inch. Short waterings wet the top inch but don't even dampen the soil below it.

When to water

The right time to water your plants is when the root-zone water supply is about half empty. The plants are not suffering for lack of water, but the soil has dried enough to let some air into it. At this point the soil an inch or so below the surface feels cool to the touch, but it will not wet or muddy your finger.

Test the soil by digging a shallow hole with a trowel, or simply by scratching the surface soil away with your finger. To test more deeply into the soil, use a soil sampling tube (see page 14) or dig a hole with a shovel. Usually you won't need to check the soil very deeply, however. Even large trees use the water in the surface layers of soil first; so testing the soil just under the surface shows if the reservoir is depleted.

How much to water

Each time you water, fill up your soil's reservoir and add a small amount more. This slight overfilling ensures that salts from irrigation water or fertilizer are leached below the root zone and don't accumulate to the point that they damage plant roots.

To know whether you have watered enough, dig a hole a few hours after watering and check the depth of the saturated zone. If the soil below the root zone of the plants is saturated, you have watered enough. As a rule of thumb, assume that the root-zone depth for lawns and annual flowers is 1 foot; for vegetables and perennial flowers, 2 feet; and for trees and shrubs, 4 feet. Fortunately, however, you don't need to dig a hole 4 feet deep to see if you have watered long enough. Time your water application, dig a hole to see how deeply the water penetrated, and use your results to calculate how long you'll need to water to reach the depth you want.

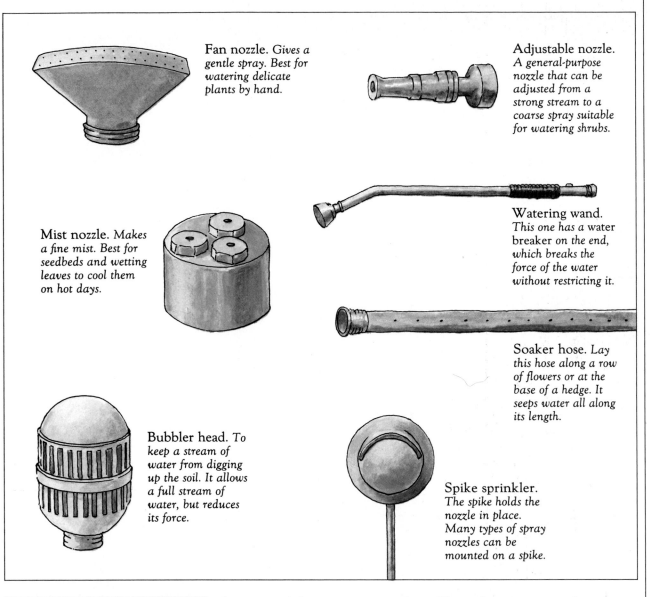

Fan nozzle. *Gives a gentle spray. Best for watering delicate plants by hand.*

Adjustable nozzle. *A general-purpose nozzle that can be adjusted from a strong stream to a coarse spray suitable for watering shrubs.*

Mist nozzle. *Makes a fine mist. Best for seedbeds and wetting leaves to cool them on hot days.*

Watering wand. *This one has a water breaker on the end, which breaks the force of the water without restricting it.*

Soaker hose. *Lay this hose along a row of flowers or at the base of a hedge. It seeps water all along its length.*

Bubbler head. *To keep a stream of water from digging up the soil. It allows a full stream of water, but reduces its force.*

Spike sprinkler. *The spike holds the nozzle in place. Many types of spray nozzles can be mounted on a spike.*

Testing your soil

A simple test can reveal your soil's ability to retain water and can help you determine whether to amend the soil to alter its water-retaining capacity.

Prepare these three soil samples: (1) your garden soil with the moisture content just right for watering, (2) the same soil mixed with an equal amount of peat moss, and (3) garden soil that has been dried in an oven for 2 hours at 200°F. Fill three pots with the soil and tamp it down slightly. Set each pot over the mouth of a glass jar.

Pour about a pint of water into each pot. Note how long it takes the water to begin to drip into the jars; these rates will show how fast your soil drains. When the water has stopped dripping, measure the amounts that have drained through the three samples. The amount of water retained in the first pot shows the capacity of your soil's reservoir. Compare the amounts left in the first and third pots: the difference between them indicates how much of each pint is still in the soil when it is time to water. Compare the amount of water left in the first and second pots to determine how much your soil's retention would be changed by amending it with peat moss.

Observe your plants

Besides examining your soil, check your plants for signs of distress to help you determine when to water.

Plants that are getting the right amount of water have healthy green leaves, full foliage, and normal growth rates. The leaves are turgid (not wilted). The following signs can indicate that a plant is receiving too little water:

■ In some plants, leaves turn from shiny to dull as a first signal of water stress. The color may also change from bright green to blue green or gray green.

■ New leaves and leaves that aren't stiff wilt. Stiff leaves, such as holly leaves and pine needles, don't wilt as they dry out, but new growth on these trees does.

■ Little or no growth occurs.

■ Flowers fade quickly and fall prematurely.

■ Older leaves turn brown and dry and fall off.

METHODS OF WATERING

The ideal of all watering systems is to replace the amount of water transpired by a plant through its leaves and evaporated by the soil surface. Several methods of watering are commonly used, each with its own strengths and limitations.

Hand watering, using either a watering can or a hose, is an accurate but time-consuming method. When watering by hand, be sure that you do more than just wet the soil surface. Apply the water slowly enough so that it seeps in rather than runs off. In the hot summer, watering by hand can become a full-time occupation (but a pleasant one).

Furrow irrigation saturates the furrows between plants. Furrows are most useful when plants are in rows, as in vegetable gardens. Water is let into each furrow from one end, usually with a garden hose, until the entire furrow is filled and water soaks into the soil. Because the leaves don't get wet, leaf diseases are avoided, which makes this an attractive method for plants that are particularly susceptible, such as squash or peas.

The pitch, or downhill slope, of furrows should be balanced with the rate at which the soil absorbs water so that all plants in each furrow receive the same amount of water. If the pitch is too steep, plants at the downhill end will be overwatered and those at the uphill end will be underwatered; if the pitch is too slight, water may never reach the plants at the downhill end. If adjusting the pitch of furrows is impractical, break them into short segments: the shorter the furrow, the less difference the pitch makes (but the more often the gardener has to move the hose).

Basin irrigation is suitable for many large vegetable plants and for single trees and shrubs. A ridge of soil is built around the plant, the resulting basin is filled with water, and the water seeps into the root

Basin irrigation *can be done with bubbler heads on a sprinkler system. Have one head in each basin.*

Drip irrigation *carries the water to each plant.*

Hand irrigation *can be accurate and gentle, but it is time-consuming.*

area. Water may be applied in the basin with a hand-held hose or with an automated bubbler system. The plant foliage remains dry, avoiding some diseases.

Flooding is often used in flat areas. Lawns, vegetables, and fruit trees are flooded within low dikes to ensure good saturation.

Soaker hoses ooze water out slowly, as a drip system does. Canvas soaker hoses must not be used on the surface or they will rot. Vinyl soaker hoses can be laid on the surface or buried. Soakers can be hooked up to automated systems.

Sprinklers are commonly used for lawns and ground covers and are useful for covering large areas evenly. They can be attached to a hose end or installed as part of a permanent, automated system, complete with timers. Several types of sprinkler heads are available that provide different watering patterns.

Sprinklers are an economical way to deliver water to a large, heavily planted area. They are the only practical way to water lawns or large areas of ground cover. Water delivery will be uneven on windy days, however.

Furrow irrigation *can be used only where the plants are in straight rows and appearance is not important.*

Sprinkler irrigation *is the only practical method where water must be applied evenly over a large area, such as a lawn.*

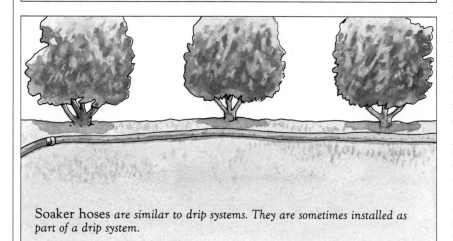

Soaker hoses *are similar to drip systems. They are sometimes installed as part of a drip system.*

The drawbacks of sprinklers make them particularly risky for vegetable and flower irrigation. They can be wasteful if used on a lightly planted area. Moreover, because sprinklers unavoidably wet leaves as well as roots, plants with susceptible foliage may suffer mildew and other diseases.

Sprinkler irrigation also has certain disadvantages for gardens in which deep mulch is used to control weeds. The mulch soaks up large amounts of water, which is evaporated again to the air without ever reaching the soil beneath. And in gardens that are not mulched, sprinkling can promote germination of weed seeds because it wets the entire surface of the soil (rather than wetting only a selected area, as furrow and drip irrigation do). Gardeners in areas where summer rain is frequent will fight most of these problems in any case and sprinkler irrigation may very well be the easiest way to water during a dry spell. For more information on sprinkler systems, see page 68.

Drip irrigation makes the most economical use of water and watering time. Drip emitters deliver from ½ to 5 gallons of water per hour; they are sometimes left on for as long as 16 hours a day. Once a drip system is installed—about a half-day job for a small garden—watering is completely automatic (if the system is automated with a clock) or is a matter of turning a faucet on and off every day or so. Drip irrigation is excellent for watering without causing runoff or loss of water through evaporation. It is a wise choice for slopes, where erosion would be a problem with other methods, and for complex plantings, which it can maintain easily and at low water cost.

Drip systems do a good job of keeping soil relatively moist, without swings of wet-dry cycles. The continuous supply of water washes salts deep into the subsoil, and since the leaves don't get wet, mildew is not a problem. Most important, plants grow better than they do with other systems. Weed growth is reduced, however, since water wets the surface only at the emitter. For more information about installing a drip system, see page 70.

Capillary watering makes use of water's capillary action—its ability to climb molecule by molecule up wicks or through porous soil, against gravity. Containers placed on fiber mats or in wet sand, or with wicks of fabric, nylon, and glass wool can be watered by means of capillary action. For more information, see page 76.

INSTALLING A SPRINKLER SYSTEM

A sprinkler system is a convenient, effective method for watering large lawn or garden areas. The system can be operated manually, or it can be automated with a timer and electric valves.

Planning your system

First, on a piece of graph paper, make a scale drawing of the area you want to water. If you are going to automate your system with a timer, select a location for it. Position the timer inside your house, garage, or carport, where you can get to it in rainy weather or in the dark. Select locations for the groups of sprinkler valves (called valve *manifolds*). Each manifold should be easily accessible and should not be in an area that will be covered by the sprinkler system. Usually the front and back yards are controlled by separate manifolds. Decide where to tap the house water supply. The easiest spot is usually at an outdoor faucet. On your map, draw a line showing where the pipe will be laid from the faucet to the valve manifold location.

Next determine the flow rate, in gallons per minute (gpm), that is available to run your sprinklers. Measure how many seconds it takes your outdoor water tap, turned wide open, to fill a 1-gallon container; then divide the number of seconds into 60 to determine your flow rate in gallons per minute. If a gallon bucket fills in 5 seconds, the flow rate is 60 ÷ 5, or 12 gallons per minute.

Using a sprinkler parts catalog, available from an irrigation supplier, check the specifications for different sprinkler heads, including the width of coverage and how many gallons per minute the head uses. Plan where to place sprinkler heads, spacing them so that the water from each head almost touches each adjacent head. It is better to have them too close than too far apart.

Now group the heads together into circuits, drawing circles around groups of heads. All the plants covered by a single circuit should have the same watering needs. Each sprinkler circuit is composed of several heads that are connected by pipe and operated by a single valve. All the heads in a circuit come on together. Only one circuit is on at a time. The combined flow rate (sometimes called *precipitation rate* in catalogs) of all the heads on each circuit should not use more than about 60 percent of the available flow rate.

On the plan, connect the heads with pipe, with all the pipe on each circuit ending at the valve. Since pipe is not very flexible, plan to lay it in straight lines, with 45° or 90° bends. For ease in ditching, run pipes in shared ditches whenever you can, and try to avoid going close to trees or under walks or driveways.

Make a shopping list of parts. Include sprinkler heads, anti-siphon valves, and enough PVC pipe and fittings to tie the system together. Use ¾-inch Schedule 40 pipe between the house plumbing and the valves and ¾-inch Class 200 pipe between the valves and heads. Schedule 40 pipe has threaded joints like those on iron pipe. Class 200 is glued together with smooth joints. Buy the right kind of tee to connect with your house water line and a *gate valve* to shut off water to the entire system. If you intend to automate your sprinkler system, buy electric (instead of manual) valves, a controller (the time clock), and enough wire to reach from the controller to the valves.

Installing the system

Follow these basic steps to install your sprinkler system:
1. Drive stakes into the ground where the heads will be. Draw lines on the ground with agricultural lime where the pipes will go.
2. Turn off the main water valve to your house and cut the water line where you intend to tie the sprinkler system into it. A riser to an outdoor faucet is usually the most convenient spot. If you live in an area where the ground freezes in

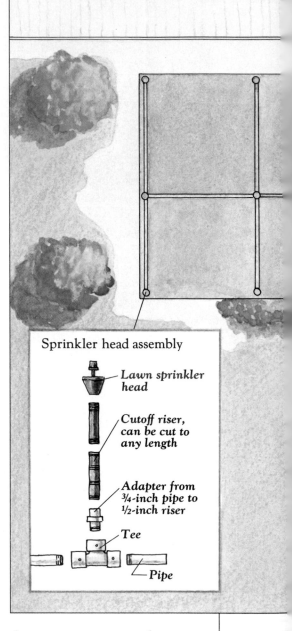

Sprinkler head assembly

Lawn sprinkler head

Cutoff riser, can be cut to any length

Adapter from ¾-inch pipe to ½-inch riser

Tee

Pipe

the winter, connect to the water line in your basement or near the water meter.
3. Make the attachment to your water line. The type of attachment will depend on the type of pipe you have. Turn off the main water line at the main shutoff valve or the water meter, cut into the line, install the tee, a short piece of pipe (a *nipple*), and a gate valve, which will function as a main shutoff valve for your sprinkler system. After you have attached the gate valve and shut it off, you can turn the household water back on. Dig the ditch (about 8 inches deep) to the valve manifold location and lay pipe in it.

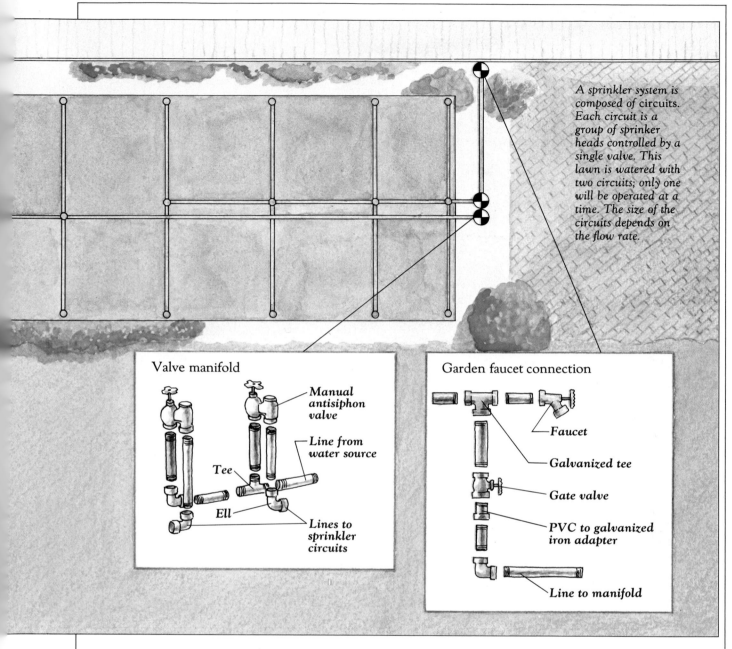

A sprinkler system is composed of circuits. Each circuit is a group of sprinker heads controlled by a single valve. This lawn is watered with two circuits; only one will be operated at a time. The size of the circuits depends on the flow rate.

Valve manifold

Manual antisiphon valve

Line from water source

Tee

Ell

Lines to sprinkler circuits

Garden faucet connection

Faucet

Galvanized tee

Gate valve

PVC to galvanized iron adapter

Line to manifold

4. Assemble the valve manifold (it's easiest to do this at a shop bench); then carry it to its location and put it in place. The manifold consists of the valves, the risers to position them above the ground (the instructions that come with the valves will tell you how high they must be, or ask your dealer), and the pipe going from each valve to its circuit.
5. Attach the manifold to its pipe, turn off the valves, and open the shutoff valve to test for leaks.
6. Dig trenches for the pipe, approximately 8 inches deep.
7. Put the sections of pipe together and install the heads.

Making PVC connections

1. Class 200 PVC pipe can be cut with a hacksaw. Make the cuts as square as possible; a miter box helps to keep them square.
2. Remove the burrs by scraping with a knife or with sandpaper. Avoid getting pieces of PVC in the pipes.
3. Spread PVC cement (which is really a solvent; the connections are welded together) on both surfaces to be attached.
4. Fit the parts together, seating the pipe all the way into the fitting.
5. Turn the pipe a quarter turn in the fitting to spread the solvent.

6. Wipe off the excess solvent.
7. Don't handle the joint for a couple of minutes as it sets up. Don't put pressure in the lines until the next day.
8. After the glue has hardened, run a test for leaks and to see that the sprinkler heads cover your lawn or garden adequately. Add or eliminate sprinkler heads as needed.
9. Fill in the trenches.
Keep a copy of your installation plan so you can locate underground parts easily.

INSTALLING A DRIP SYSTEM

Drip systems deliver water one drop at a time. Because of this slow rate of delivery, the system doesn't need to be as carefully balanced as a sprinkler system. Sections can be added to an existing system whenever needed.

Drip components

The key element in a drip system is the *emitter*. Each emitter allows only a drop of water at a time to escape, even though the water in the supply line may be under several pounds per square inch (psi) of pressure. Emitters are available in various styles that release from ½ to 5 gallons per hour (gph); a rate of 1 gph is most commonly used. Some emitters deliver the water as a fine mist or a light sprinkle. Others, used mainly for rows of vegetables or flowers, are soaker hoses and release water from the entire length of the hose.

The emitters are joined by *hose*, flexible pipe usually made of black polyethylene that is connected with *compression fittings* inserted into the hose. The emitters are usually inserted into holes punched in the hose.

A *pressure regulator* on the line may be necessary to reduce the ordinary household water pressure (about 50 psi) to the lower level used by most drip systems (about 15 psi). In simple drip systems, the pressure regulator is usually a washer with a small hole. Some systems operate at household pressure and don't need a pressure regulator.

A *filter*, a crucial ingredient for a drip system, prevents small particles of sediment from clogging the emitters. This is the single most common problem with drip irrigation. When heads become clogged, they must be checked and cleaned out. Filters should be checked periodically to remove sediment.

A *backflow prevention device* is essential if the system is connected to your household water. It prevents fertilizer or dirty water from backing up into your drinking water supply lines.

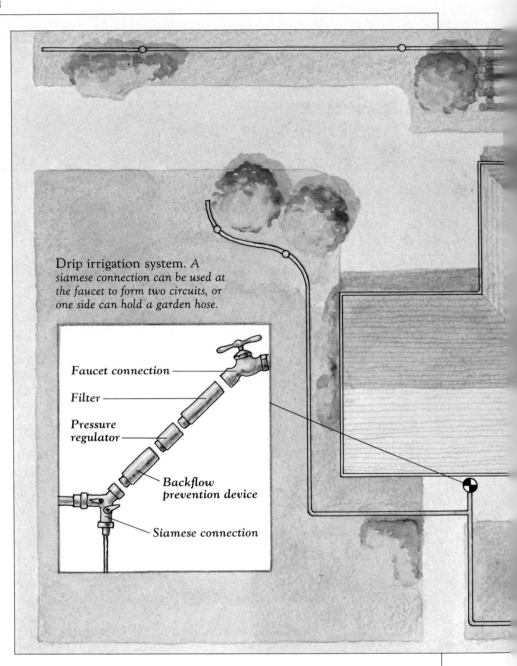

Drip irrigation system. *A siamese connection can be used at the faucet to form two circuits, or one side can hold a garden hose.*

Faucet connection
Filter
Pressure regulator
Backflow prevention device
Siamese connection

A *timer* (optional) is a clock that turns the system on and off.

A *fertilizer injector* is a useful optional element that makes it possible to add soluble fertilizer into the watering stream.

Installing the system

1. A simple drip system can be attached to a garden faucet. Attach the filter, backflow prevention device, and fertilizer injector (if you are using one) to the faucet. If you wish to use more than one circuit, install a *siamese connector*, which will allow you to direct water into

either or both circuits. You may wish, for example, to place container plants, which may need to be watered for only a few minutes each day, on a different circuit from shrubs, which may be watered for several hours every few days. Battery-operated timers are available that also attach directly to the faucet.

2. Lay out hose throughout the garden so that it passes by the plants you want to water. Use ½-inch hose for main lines and ⅜-inch hose for laterals, or wherever a lower flow of water is expected. Be careful when installing not to

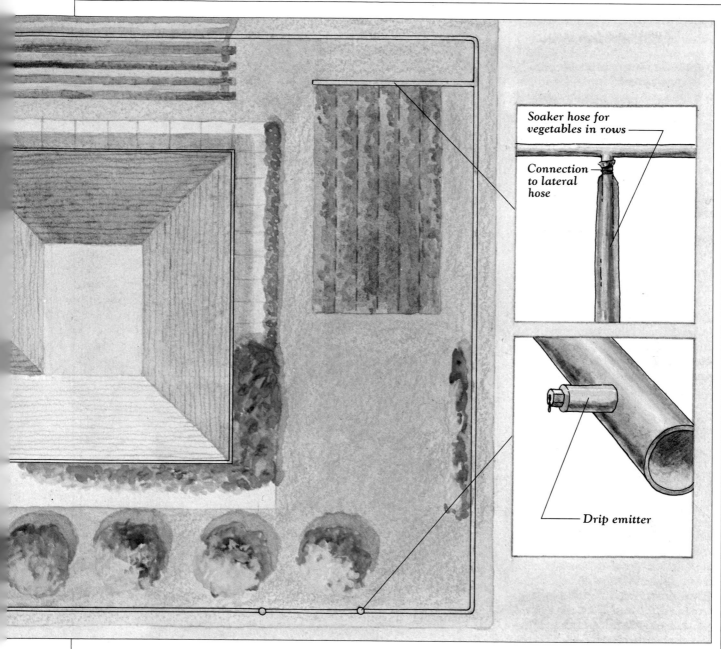

*Soaker hose for
vegetables in rows*

Connection
to lateral
hose

Drip emitter

get any dirt in the pipes. Leave the end of each hose open for now.
3. Install emitters at the base of each plant. Use more and larger emitters for larger plants. As a general rule, use 5 emitters for a fruit tree, 2 or 3 for a shrub, and 1 for a flower or vegetable.
4. Flush the system by turning it on and letting it run for a few minutes to wash any dirt from the lines. Then turn it off and cap or crimp the ends of the hoses.
5. Turn the system back on and check each emitter to make sure it is working.

6. Set the timer, if you are using one. Follow the manufacturer's directions. If you are watering an orchard, set the timer to water for several hours every day. Flowers and vegetables need about 30 minutes a day. Containers should be watered daily (if they contain large plants and are in the sun) until water begins to drip from their drain holes.

Maintaining the system

Watch the plants. If one plant wilts on a hot afternoon, put another emitter at its base, or change

to a larger emitter. If several plants wilt, leave the water on longer at each irrigation. Adjust the irrigation time to the season. Plants use the most water in June, a little less in May, July, and August, and less yet in other spring and fall months.

Clean the filter periodically, and each month check for clogged emitters.

Once a year, or more often if your water is dirty, open the ends of the lines and flush them out.

WATERING VEGETABLES AND FLOWERS

Whether you are growing vegetables or flowers, you'll want to choose a method of irrigation that ensures a consistent, even supply of water to the plants. Vegetable and flower gardens are most commonly watered with furrow irrigation, sprinklers, and drip systems. For more information about these systems, see pages 66, 68, and 70.

Strive for consistency

It is important that irrigation be consistent. Many problems with both vegetables and fruits—including root rot and blossom-end rot of many vegetables, cracking of cabbage heads, and bud drop of many flowers—are a result of inconsistent watering.

Changes in water supply can make a root system less effective. Plant roots will grow where the water is; if watered with a drip system, for example, they will grow mostly in the wet areas under each drip emitter. If you are using drip irrigation and switch to overhead sprinkling, the small, dense root systems your plants have developed will have difficulty finding enough water until the plants can produce larger, more diverse root systems.

Plant tissues also adapt to a certain level of available water. Plants that are watered frequently are succulent and soft and will be damaged by even a short period of drought. But if you live in an arid region and practice dry-land gardening, your plants will become accustomed to a smaller amount of water; their tissues will be tough and able to withstand longer dry periods.

Although it's convenient—and sometimes necessary—for plants to be able to withstand drought, in many cases drought-resistant tissue makes a plant less desirable. The best lettuce, cabbage, and celery is grown as quickly as possible with lots of water. This produces sweet, tender vegetables. Lettuce grown without a steady supply of water is

Impulse sprinklers *on a tall pipe can be placed in any part of the garden. They should be high enough to get water over the tops of tall crops.*

Soaker hoses *are ideally suited to row crops.*

Quick drip. *Punch holes in a coffee can for a simple drip system.*

tough and bitter. However, herbs and some winter squash improve in flavor when grown under dry conditions.

Watering vegetables

Provide enough water to wet the root zone. Shallow-rooted vegetables have their main roots in the top 2 feet of soil; moderately deep-rooted vegetables, in the top 4 feet of soil; and deep-rooted vegetables, in the top 6 feet of soil. Because even the deeper-rooted vegetables draw most of their water from the upper levels of their root zones, it is most important to wet the top foot of soil for all varieties.

Vegetables need a steady supply of water, especially when they are flowering or fruiting, when they are very sensitive to fluctuation in soil moisture. As a general rule, vegetables need 1½ to 2 inches of water per week. One inch of water will wet dry garden loam to a depth of approximately 1½ inches. Reduce this amount to account for seasonal rainfall or increase it to counteract extreme conditions of excessive heat, wind, or low humidity. Remember, too, that 1 foot of sandy soil holds only about ¾ inch of usable water but the same amount of clay soil holds 2 to 2½ inches. You won't need to irrigate clay soil as often.

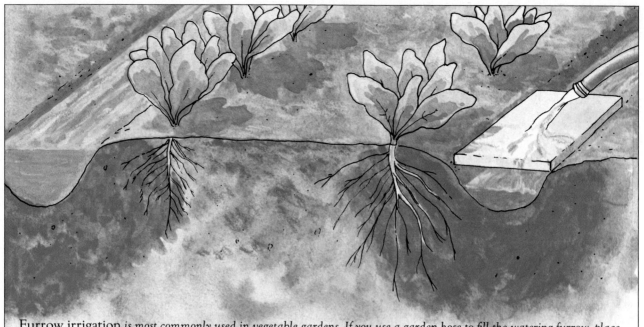

Furrow irrigation is most commonly used in vegetable gardens. If you use a garden hose to fill the watering furrow, place a board under the end of the hose to prevent erosion. Most of the roots will grow in the area that is usually wet, close to the furrow. Few weeds will grow in the center of the beds because the surface soil stays dry there.

Mulches are helpful in maintaining constant soil moisture. The leaves of developing plants also shade the soil and reduce evaporation. Plant vegetables so that the leaves of mature plants will form a canopy covering the entire ground.

Some vegetables need less water as they mature. Onions will keep better if they go dry in the last month. Melons and winter squash will have better flavor and will keep better if left somewhat dry during the last few weeks.

All the major watering methods can be used for vegetables. Morning is the best time to sprinkle because the leaves dry quickly, so diseases don't have time to take hold. Other methods of watering can be used at any time of day.

Vegetables respond particularly well to drip irrigation. A drip system under a black plastic mulch is a method of vegetable gardening that has long been used by commercial growers and is increasing in popularity with home gardeners. The mulch conserves water and eliminates weeding, and the drip system delivers water and soluble fertilizer to the plant roots. If the drip system is automated with a timer, this combination removes much of the maintenance work from vegetable gardening.

Watering flowers

All methods of irrigation are used to water flowers in different settings. But both sprinkler irrigation and rainfall can weight large flower heads so much that they break. Support flower heads with a stake (see page 122) to keep them from breaking.

Annuals, struggling to move rapidly through their life cycle to produce seeds, need a steady supply of water. Irregular watering can cause flowers to form and to drop from the plant prematurely.

Perennials usually have more established root systems and can be treated as small shrubs. Water deeper but less often than for annuals. If you are growing perennials in a climate that is too warm to force them into dormancy, you can sometimes make them go dormant by witholding water. If your climate is dry in the fall, just stop watering. If it rains occasionally, cover the soil over the plant roots with plastic sheeting.

Roses are often watered in basins with bubblers on automated systems. They are heavy users of water and grow best with a steady supply.

After **bulb** flowers have dropped and the bulb has rebuilt its supply of food for next year's production, withdraw water so the bulb will dry out and store well. Be cautious with overhead sprinkling, which might damage the single flower of some bulbs as it emerges. Choose another watering system at flowering time.

ROOT DEPTH OF VEGETABLES

Shallow
  Cabbage
  Cauliflower
  Celery
  Lettuce
  Onion
  Radish
  Sweet corn
  White potato

Moderately deep
  Carrot
  Cucumber
  Eggplant
  Pea
  Pepper
  Snap bean
  Summer squash

Deep
  Asparagus
  Cantaloupe
  Globe artichoke
  Pumpkin
  Tomato
  Watermelon

WATERING PLANTS IN CONTAINERS

Knowing when and how much to water container plants is essential to their success. Many factors affect the frequency and quantity of watering—kind of plant, size of container, potting mix, location, season, and many others.

Drip irrigation. *This method can be used only where there are no saucers under the containers. Use the smallest emitters available—usually ½ gallon per hour—with a light potting mix. Spray emitters are available that spread the water over the entire surface of the soil.*

When to water

Water container plants when the soil is just barely moist. When it's time to water, the soil just under the surface will feel cool to the touch but not wet or muddy. If you are having problems with root rot (whole plants dying suddenly), be sure to wash your hands between pots to avoid spreading the fungus.

As you become familiar with your containers, you will be able to tell by their weight whether they need water. Another way to tell when they need water is by the sound the pot makes when tapped with a knuckle. A hollow sound indicates that it's time to water.

How much to water

A container plant needs enough water to wet the bottom layer of soil. This will be apparent when water begins to drain from the container. The space between the rim of the container and the soil level should hold enough water to wet all the soil in the pot, and then some. If it is too small, you have to fill it more than once, making the watering job more time-consuming.

Water draining from the bottom of the container not only tells you that you have wet all the soil in the container, it also flushes out soluble salts. Fertilizer salts, and any salts that are dissolved in the irrigation water, will accumulate in the potting mix if it is not flushed regularly. Concentrations of these salts, even fertilizers, are toxic to plants; they cause the tips of leaves to die and turn black.

Always give the plant the same amount of water. You should vary only the frequency of watering, not the amount. If the container is in a saucer, empty the saucer after the pot has finished draining, usually about 10 minutes. If it is too big to lift, use a turkey baster to remove the water.

A common problem with containers is that the root ball shrinks somewhat if the soil becomes overly dry. Water will then run around the root ball, down the sides of the container, and out the drain hole without wetting the roots. You can poke holes in the root ball to get better drainage, or try adding a tablespoon of liquid detergent to a gallon of water to break the surface tension. Alternatively, you can totally immerse the container in a tub of water for an hour to rewet the root ball.

Watering houseplants

During the dormancy period, or when the plant is "resting," usually winter, watering must be reduced.

Houseplants generally need less warmth but more humidity than most gardeners realize. Thin and papery leaves need more humidity than thick, leathery ones. The low humidity in most houses can be a problem, especially in winter. You can increase the humidity around your houseplants by setting containers in a pan with pebbles or gravel and water.

Hand irrigation. *Watering wands make hand watering easier. The type of wand illustrated makes the watering of hanging containers a neater process.*

When the air has too little moisture, plants may develop brown and shriveled leaf tips, yellow and wilting leaf edges, shriveled and falling buds and flowers, or falling leaves. Too much humidity may cause gray mold on leaves or flowers. Patches of rot may appear on leaves and stems, especially of cactus and other succulents that are sensitive to too much water.

The high sodium levels of softened house water will cause a toxic buildup of salts in indoor plant soil. Water is softened for home use in some areas because of high

Wick irrigation. *The method shown is a good way to keep your plants watered while on vacation. Use nylon clothesline for the wick. Fray the ends.*

Sand tray irrigation. *This tray will water any container set in it. The tray must be perfectly level. Line it with a sheet of heavy polyethylene and fill with about 2 inches of sand. Cut a notch at the level of the sand to drain excess water. The tray illustrated is watered with a drip system, using double-walled tubing as an emitter.*

natural levels of calcium in the water, which interferes with sudsing of soaps and other cleansing agents. The softener replaces the calcium in the water with sodium. The accumulation of sodium in the soil is injurious to plants. Use an outside water tap or rainwater for your houseplants if you have softened house water. Plants damaged by sodium buildup should be immersed in and then flushed with salt-free water.

Methods of watering

Container plants can be watered in several ways:

Watering by hand. Use a watering can or a bubbler attachment at the end of the hose. A "wand" will save bending and reaching. Apply enough water so that some drains from the bottom of the container. Water should flow freely away from the container and not collect at its base. Be sure the drain hole is not clogged.

Drip watering. Drip systems, with either drip or mist emitters, are an effective way to water a great many containers. An automatic system can be helpful, especially for plants that require frequent watering. You will probably need to increase the amount of water dripped into the containers during hot, windy summer weather.

Wick watering. The capillary action of water rising in a fabric wick can be used to deliver water steadily and slowly to plants. For a homemade system, use a margarine tub with a top and a section of nylon clothesline as a wick. Fray the edges of the wick to get better water pickup. This is a good low-maintenance, long-term system for watering indoor plants when you go on vacation. Commercial wick watering devices are available in some nurseries.

Sand tray watering. Place containers in a tray of moist sand. Be sure there is contact between the soil in the container and the sand in the watering tray, since this method depends on capillary action. The tray of moist sand has another advantage in that it raises the humidity around the plants.

Immersion watering. Immersion can sometimes be helpful, especially for containers where the soil has dried back from the edges so that water runs around the root ball without wetting it. If the soil cakes on the top so that water cannot penetrate, immersion can be used to wet the entire root ball. Place the container in a tub and add water until it comes over the top of the container. Leave it in the water for about 15 minutes, or until all bubbles have escaped. Then remove the container and allow it to drain.

Immersion is excellent for water-loving plants such as ferns; for plants grown on slabs of fiber, such as staghorn fern; and for wire-basket containers lined with sphagnum moss. Allow them to drain thoroughly before returning to their growing space.

FEEDING

Applying fertilizers can be as simple as watering. The choice of fertilizer and when it is applied affects not only the health of a plant but also its growth pattern.

Plants make their own sugars from air and water, using the energy of sunlight. Plant "food" is sunlight. The fertilizers we apply to the soil are minerals that form some of the necessary raw materials for plant functions. Since the soil is composed of minerals, we are actually supplementing what is already there. Except in hydroponic gardening and, to some extent, container gardening, plants can grow and survive without added fertilizers. After all, wild plants have been doing it for eons.

But if we want our plants to look their best and reach their full potential of yield and growth, we must add fertilizer. We can do this in a multitude of ways. Fertilizers come as natural organic products, such as steer manure, as soluble salts, as liquids, as pellets, spikes, and briquettes. To know which fertilizers to choose, we must understand our plants, our soil, and our own preferred way of working.

Nutrients in the soil

Of the more than 100 chemical elements that have been isolated, 17 are known to be essential to plant growth. All 17 are essential, but they are needed in varying amounts. Three elements come to the plant from air or water (carbon, hydrogen, and oxygen). The

A drop spreader is the most precise way to apply fertilizers to a lawn.

rest are usually absorbed from soil by plant roots. They are divided into three groups: the three *primary nutrients* (nitrogen, phosphorus, and potassium), the three *secondary nutrients* (calcium, magnesium, and sulfur), and the eight *micronutrients* or *trace elements* (zinc, iron, manganese, copper, boron, molybdenum, cobalt, and chlorine).

Soil chemistry is complex and dynamic. Dozens of elements are present in soil in thousands of combinations. As the soil changes temperature, as water moves through it, as plants and animals live in it, these elements recombine endlessly, sometimes into forms that can be absorbed by plants, and sometimes into unavailable forms. With only a few exceptions, mineral nutrients are absorbed by plants as dissolved salts. If an element is in a form that is insoluble, it is not available to the plants.

Nitrogen

Nitrogen is the one plant nutrient that must be added for optimum plant growth anywhere in the world. It is needed in large quantities and is in chronic short supply. All plants and microorganisms compete for the available nitrogen because it is a constituent of protein, the basic substance of all living matter. In its most common mineral form, nitrate, nitrogen is

highly soluble and mobile, so it is easily washed from the soil by rain or irrigation. In nature, nitrogen is recycled endlessly through plant and animal tissues. Free nitrate is absorbed and built into living matter, which dies, decomposes, and becomes nitrate again.

Nitrogen is also the only plant nutrient that can be used to regulate the form that plant growth will take, rather than just keeping a plant healthy. Nitrogen stimulates shoot growth in plants. If a high level of nitrogen is present in the soil, the internal resources of plants are directed to make vigorous shoot growth. This means that other types of growth—such as flower, fruit, and root growth—slow down. If you are raising lettuce, this is highly desirable; lettuce that grows rapidly is succulent and sweet. But if you are raising tomatoes, the plant might go on making vigorous leafy growth well into the summer, only beginning to make blossoms and fruit as cool weather approaches.

Fertilizers without nitrogen or with only a little nitrogen are sold to promote flowering and fruiting. It isn't the presence of phosphorus and potassium that promotes flowering, it is the absence of nitrogen.

Nitrogen is leached from soil or absorbed by plants within weeks of application. It usually needs to be applied every month or so during the growing season.

Phosphorus

Phosphorus must be added to the soil in most parts of the country. But arid regions often have so much phosphorus in the soil that it causes salt problems. Phosphorus is highly reactive, bonding quickly with a wide variety of elements. In the soil, it is usually combined with oxygen to form phosphate. Phosphate combines with calcium and other minerals to form almost insoluble compounds. Because phosphorus compounds are usually insoluble, they are very stable in the soil. Unlike nitrogen fertilizers, phosphorus fertilizers can be applied in large quantities every few years; they do not leach from the soil.

Because of their low solubility, phosphates are present in the soil water in extremely low concentrations, only two or three parts per million. But their presence is constant; as soon as the dissolved phosphate is removed by plants, more dissolves to replace it. As a result, plants with large root systems, such as trees, are able to absorb enough for their needs. But plants with small root systems, especially seedlings, don't have enough root area to absorb such dilute chemicals. Mature trees seldom need added phosphorus, even in regions that have phosphorus-deficient soils. But seedlings almost always benefit from extra phosphorus. Without large amounts of phosphorus, top growth slows until the root system has grown large enough to absorb the needed amounts. Since absorption by roots slows in cold soils, phosphorus often needs to be added under those conditions too. Winter and early spring crops grow better with added phosporus.

Potassium

Potassium is the third primary nutrient. Like phosphorus, it must be added in most areas, but not usually in arid regions. It is highly soluble in water, but since it adheres tightly to clay particles in the soil, it is not easily leached. A single application will last for a growing season in good soil.

Top: Iron deficiency in azalea leaves. Symptoms of iron deficiency appear on the newest leaves; the veins usually remain green.

Bottom: Hose-end attachments can be used to apply liquid fertilizer. A concentrated fertilizer solution is placed in the jar.

This root feeder dissolves a pellet of fertilizer in the stream of hose water, then carries it to deep tree roots.

But chelates are expensive and must be added at regular intervals. A more permanent solution is to make the soil more acid, thus freeing the iron and manganese already present for plant use. This can be done by applying acidic materials, such as soil sulfur or iron sulfate. Soil acidity can be maintained by using fertilizers that have an acidifying effect on the soil. Ammonium sulfate is often used for this purpose. Also, several fertilizers are blended especially for plants that need acid soil. These fertilizers contain chelated iron as well as having an acid reaction on the soil.

Kinds of fertilizers

Aside from the nutrients they contain, there are other differences between fertilizers. The most important difference for the home gardener lies in the form in which they are applied.

The most familiar fertilizers are fertilizer salts, in the form of crystals or granules. These are scattered on the soil and watered in. The irrigation dissolves them and carries them into the soil.

Other fertilizers are liquids or soluble powders that are dissolved in water before application. These fertilizers are diluted with water and are applied by watering. They can be applied with a watering can or a hose attachment, or through an automatic watering system attached to a drip irrigation system.

Fertilizers can also be applied as solid chunks that are placed individually in the soil where the plant can reach them. They are always slow-release fertilizers and come in the form of briquettes, spikes, and coarse salts.

Nutrients can also be applied in the form of organic matter. Manure is the farmer's ancient source of plant nutrients; compost, dry leaves, and most other forms of organic matter will decay to release plant nutrients. Organic matter is bulky, but it improves soil structure as well as adding nutrients. Since most of the nutrients are insoluble until the protein that contains them decomposes, the effect lasts for a long time.

The secondary nutrients

Calcium, magnesium, and sulfur are called the secondary nutrients. They have this name not because their importance is secondary but because they are found in most soils and seldom need to be added as fertilizer.

Calcium and magnesium are the elements that are largely responsible for the acidity or alkalinity of soil. They are moderately soluble, so in regions of high rainfall they are washed from the soil and carried away. Soils in these regions are usually acid, and lime (calcium carbonate) is often added every year to make the soil less acid. In areas of low rainfall, and where the soil is derived from limestone, the soil is high in calcium and magnesium and is usually alkaline.

Sulfur is present in most commercial fertilizers, even though it is not listed on the label. As sulfate, it is highly acid and is often used to make alkaline soils acid.

The micronutrients

Micronutrients are essential for plant growth, but they are needed in very small quantities. They are usually added only when a deficiency is noted. They are seldom truly deficient in soil, but are sometimes unavailable to plants, especially in alkaline soils. Iron and manganese deficiencies are seen in the West almost as commonly as nitrogen deficiency. Alkaline soils cause these elements to form insoluble compounds. Adding iron or manganese alone seldom helps, since the added iron is immediately bound into an insoluble form in the soil.

These nutrients can be added as *chelates,* a word derived from the Greek word for claws. Chelates are organic ring-structure compounds that combine with and protect a nutrient, such as iron, making it difficult for the nutrient to react chemically with soil particles so that it remains available to plants.

FERTILIZERS

Fertilizers are chemical "packages" that supply plants with nutrients. Properly used, they can help produce healthy, vigorous plants. Here are a few general pointers on selecting and using fertilizers.

How to read a fertilizer label

Law requires that the minimum guaranteed contents of the product be printed on fertilizer labels. The information on the labels is standardized. The percentage by weight of three nutrients is always given in the same sequence: nitrogen, phosphorus (phosphate), and potassium (potash)—commonly abbreviated NPK (the chemical symbols for the nutrients). A fertilizer with the label 12–8–16, for example, has 12 percent nitrogen, 8 percent phosphate, and 16 percent potash by weight. Fertilizers with different numbers but the same NPK ratio are equivalent but have different concentrations. For example, 1 pound of 10–20–20 has the same amount of nutrients as 2 pounds of 5–10–10.

Fertilizers that contain all three primary nutrients are called "complete" fertilizers. If a fertilizer lacks any primary nutrient, a 0 appears in that place in the NPK sequence. Ammonium sulfate (21-0-0), for instance, has nitrogen but no phosphate or potash.

Nutrient balance

The most important factor in selecting fertilizers is the relative balance between nitrogen and the other two major nutrients. High-nitrogen fertilizers, those with a ratio of 2:1 or greater, stimulate foliage growth. This is desirable in lawns, leafy plants such as lettuce, and most young plants. But it can be detrimental in other cases. For instance, too much leafy growth in a tomato will delay its fruiting, and you may want your hedge to grow slowly so you don't have to prune it so often. As a basic rule, use high-nitrogen fertilizers when plants should be making more leafy growth.

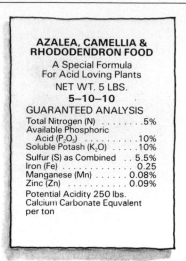

AZALEA, CAMELLIA & RHODODENDRON FOOD
A Special Formula
For Acid Loving Plants
NET WT. 5 LBS.
5–10–10
GUARANTEED ANALYSIS
Total Nitrogen (N) 5%
Available Phosphoric
　Acid (P_2O_5) 10%
Soluble Potash (K_2O) 10%
Sulfur (S) as Combined . . 5.5%
Iron (Fe) 0.25
Manganese (Mn) 0.08%
Zinc (Zn) 0.09%
Potential Acidity 250 lbs.
Calcium Carbonate Equvalent
per ton

Fertilizer labels *always show the percentages of nitrogen, phosphorus, and potassium.*

Nutrient persistence

Several forms of nitrogen may be found in fertilizers:

Nitrate is water-soluble and in a form that plants absorb easily, but it does not remain in the soil. Heavy rain or irrigation will leach it out in a couple of weeks.

Ammonium is also water-soluble, but many plants cannot absorb it. Ammonium attaches to soil particles and does not leach from the soil. However, bacteria in the soil slowly oxidize it into nitrate, which does leach.

Organic nitrogen, usually in the form of protein, is not soluble or available to plants. It is slowly broken down into ammonium by bacteria in the soil.

The proportion of these three forms of nitrogen in a fertilizer indicates how soon the nitrogen will be available to plants and how long it will last in the soil.

Phosphate forms compounds in the soil that are only slightly soluble and remain in the soil for long periods. A single heavy feeding of phosphate will remain in the soil for several years, or in a container mix for a year.

Nitrogen deficiency. *Leaves turn yellow, beginning with the oldest leaves.*

Potassium deficiency. *Oldest leaves turn yellow, then burn, at edges and between the veins.*

Potash leaches from the soil slowly, but not as slowly as phosphate. A single feeding with potash will last for a growing season, or for a couple of months in a container.

Acid reaction

When used over a period of time, fertilizers can make the soil more acid or more alkaline, depending on the kinds of ingredients used. Some fertilizers have strong acid reactions; they are used in areas with alkaline soil or to feed plants that prefer acid soils, such as azaleas, camellias, and rhododendrons. Others have weak acid reactions and are best used in naturally acid or neutral soils. The degree to which a fertilizer will make a soil more acid can be determined by checking the *calcium carbonate equivalent* listed on the product label. This number refers to the pounds of calcium carbonate (lime) required to neutralize the acid produced by a ton of the fertilizer. The higher the number,

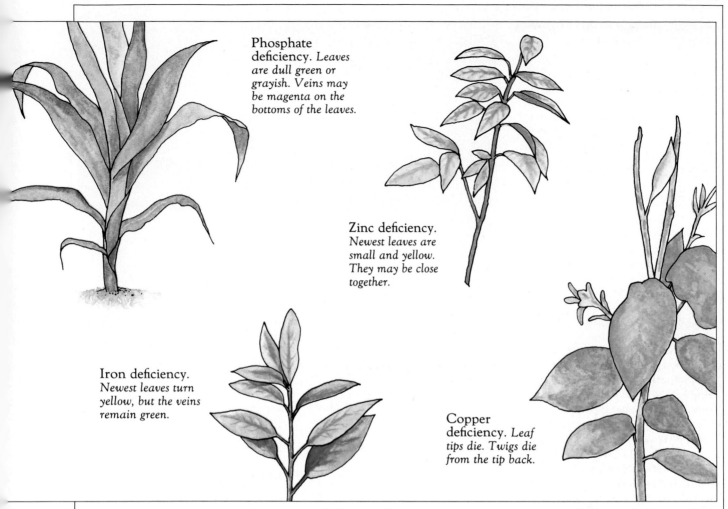

Phosphate deficiency. *Leaves are dull green or grayish. Veins may be magenta on the bottoms of the leaves.*

Zinc deficiency. *Newest leaves are small and yellow. They may be close together.*

Iron deficiency. *Newest leaves turn yellow, but the veins remain green.*

Copper deficiency. *Leaf tips die. Twigs die from the tip back.*

the more acid the fertilizer. For example, an equivalent of 200 pounds indicates that the fertilizer has a moderate acid reaction; an equivalent of 1200 pounds indicates a strong acid reaction.

Signs of nutrient deficiencies

Nutrient deficiencies will cause various problems for your plants. *Chlorosis,* or yellowing of the leaves, is usually due to a nutrient deficiency.

Some of the common signs of various nutrient deficiencies are described below:

Nitrogen. Older leaves turn yellow, die, and drop. Growth is slow. New leaves are smaller. Plant may have heavy bloom but light fruit set, with small, highly colored fruits that mature early.

Phosphate. Leaves are dull gray green to dark green and are set close together on shorter stems. Veins, petioles, and lower leaf surfaces may be reddish purple. Light bloom is followed by fewer and smaller fruit.

Potash. Older leaves are crinkled and curl upward. Pale yellow chlorosis followed by scorch begins on leaf edges and progresses inward between the veins. Shoots die back late in the season. Lateral buds grow in a zigzag pattern and produce short, brushy growth.

Calcium. Foliage is abnormally dark green. Terminal buds and root tips die. Buds and blossoms drop prematurely. Stems are weak.

Magnesium. Older leaves have a yellow V shape between the veins. Leaves curl upward along the margin.

Sulfur. Young leaves turn light green to yellow. Plants may be small and spindly, with retarded growth and late maturity.

Iron. The newest leaves turn yellow between the veins, leaving green "Christmas tree" appearance along the midrib. Older leaves remain green.

Manganese. Chlorosis of young leaves appears between veins; green color changes gradually from the veins outward. Tomatoes are dwarfed.

Copper. Growth is stunted. Terminal shoots in trees die back. Leaves have poor pigmentation. Leaf tips wilt and die.

Zinc. Leaves are yellow and small. (This deficiency is sometimes called "little leaf.") Leaves may be deformed and mottled. Shoots may have short internodes and small diameter; twigs may die back. Flowers have light fruit set; fruit is small, pointed, and highly colored.

APPLYING FERTILIZER

Most fertilizer packages have instructions that give the amount and frequency of application. You can either follow those directions or feed half as much as directed but twice as often.

Unless you have very poor soil or are feeding container plants, you add fertilizers simply to supplement the nutrients already present in the native soil. Potash and phosphate are present in most soils in the dry West, for instance, but they must be added in areas that get more than about 40 inches of rainfall a year. Nitrogen is always needed, since it doesn't remain in the soil for very long.

Dry chemical fertilizers are usually the most economical buy. Slow-release forms save the most time. Foliar feeding gives the quickest response and ensures that all the nutrients are absorbed. Liquids or soluble powders can be added to the irrigation water. Organic fertilizers add organic matter as well as nutrients. After adding any fertilizer to the soil, be sure to water thoroughly to dissolve and dilute the nutrients and to keep salts in the fertilizer from harming your plants.

There are several effective ways to apply fertilizers.

Broadcasting

This method is best for spreading large amounts of fertilizer over a large area. Lawns, trees, vegetable gardens, and flower beds can be fertilized this way. Both granular fertilizers and bulk organic materials can be spread by hand or with a spreader device, such as a lawn spreader or crank-type hand-held spreader.

Banding

Banding is often used for rows of vegetables or flowers, especially to get plants started. Place the fertilizer in a furrow 2 inches to the side of, and 2 inches deeper than, the seed furrow. Placement of the

Banding. *Place fertilizer between the seed and the water source so that the water will dissolve the fertilizer and carry it to the plant. If you are watering with a drip system, place the fertilizer at the emitter.*

band of fertilizer must be coordinated with the watering plan. For furrow irrigation, place the band in a furrow between the seed furrow and the irrigation furrow. With overhead sprinkling, place bands on both sides of the seed furrow.

Side dressing

Side dressing is the placement of fertilizer alongside a plant or row of plants, usually midway through the growing period. It is often used to supplement the fertilizer applied at the time of planting.

Watering with fertilizer solution

Some fertilizers, clearly marked on the package as completely water soluble, are ideal for applying as part of the watering process. You can use this method with drip irrigation and sprinkler systems and for houseplant watering.

Dissolve a small sample of the fertilizer to see if it leaves any residue that could plug up your system. If it does, you will have to strain the liquid or pour the dissolved portion into another container, leaving the residue behind.

Soil injection is a specialized method of applying fertilizer solution that is sometimes used with trees. A root irrigator is inserted into the root ball, and water pressure forces the fertilizer into the root area.

Slow-release *fertilizers should be placed in the root zone of each plant. A bulb planter makes holes for briquettes.*

Foliar feeding

Spraying plants with water containing fertilizer is known as foliar feeding. Fertilizer applied in this way is readily absorbed by the leaves and can cause a rapid change in the plant's condition. This method is often used to overcome deficiencies of micronutrients or to provide nutrients that would be unavailable to the plant through the soil, such as iron and zinc.

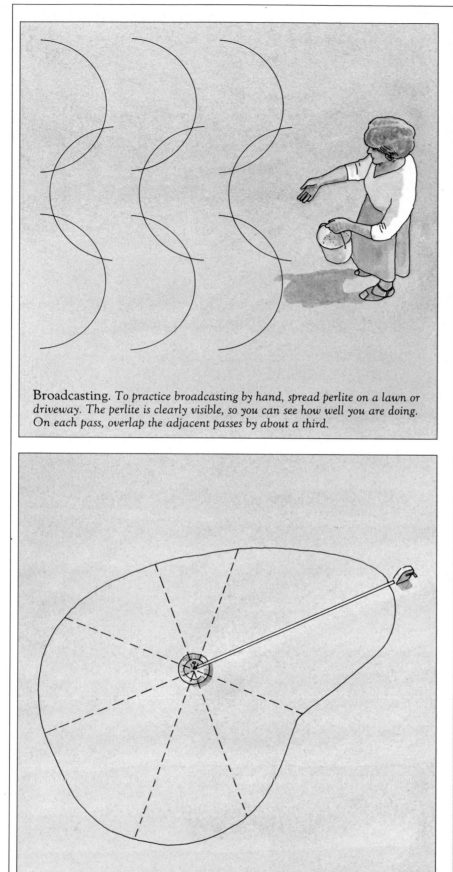

Broadcasting. *To practice broadcasting by hand, spread perlite on a lawn or driveway. The perlite is clearly visible, so you can see how well you are doing. On each pass, overlap the adjacent passes by about a third.*

Measure areas *of odd shapes by finding the average radius. Measure 8 radii, equally spaced, using a paper plate marked in eighths as a guide. Add all the measurements and divide by 8. For more accuracy, use 16 or even more radii. The more measurements you make, the more accurate the outcome.*

Using slow-release fertilizers

Slow-release fertilizers last for several months to a couple of years in the soil. They are more expensive than soluble types but are valuable where low maintenance is a goal. These fertilizers come as small pellets, chunks of mineral, briquettes, or spikes that are driven into the soil with a hammer.

ESTIMATING AMOUNTS

■ A pint of most chemical fertilizers weighs about a pound.

■ To find how much chemical fertilizer you need to provide a given weight of actual nutrient, divide the number of pounds of nutrient you need by the percentage of that element in the fertilizer. Say, for example, that you want to add 2 pounds of actual phosphate to your vegetable garden and that your bag of fertilizer contains 20 percent phosphate. Just divide the 2 pounds (the amount you want) by 20 percent (the percentage in the fertilizer):
$2 \div 0.20 = 10$
You will need to apply 10 pounds of the fertilizer to get the desired amount of phosphate.

■ There are two ways to estimate the number of square feet in a given area. First, for a rough approximation, you can multiply the estimated average width by the estimated average length. The result will usually be within 10 or 20 percent of the correct area, which is close enough for applying fertilizer.

A second, more accurate, way is to mark a paper plate into eight equal sections (as if you were cutting a pie) and use a large nail to stake it in the center of the area to be measured. Leave the head of the nail protruding slightly. Hook the end of a 50- or 100-foot tape rule over the nail. Using the lines on the paper plate as guides, measure from the nail to the edge of the area in 8 directions, then divide the total by 8 to find the average radius. Use this average radius to find the area of a circle:
radius × radius × 3.16 = area

FEEDING LAWNS

Feed new lawns with a fertilizer that is high in phosphorus and nitrogen to give the grass seedlings a good start. After the lawn is established, nitrogen is the main nutrient that grass needs. A pound of actual nitrogen per thousand square feet per application is a good rule of thumb for quantity. See page 84 for a method of calculating the amount of fertilizer you will need to get a given amount of the nutrient.

Nutrients that lawns need

Although nitrogen is the main nutrient that grass needs, others are also important. Phosphorus helps grass maintain a strong root system. It is needed in lesser amounts than nitrogen. Phosphorus also tends to remain in the soil rather than leach through.

Potassium contributes to hardiness and resistance to disease. This nutrient leaches from soils, though more slowly than nitrogen. A good management plan calls for applying 1 pound of actual potassium per 1000 square feet per year. Apply it just before periods of stress—hot summer weather for northern lawns, fall for southern lawns.

Cycles of application

Fertilizing lawns will increase their vigor and color. Spring feeding helps to get the lawn growing, outdistancing weeds and pests, before hot summer weather appears. An autumn feeding is helpful to keep cool-season grass thriving in mild regions and to get grass off to a quick start the following spring in cold regions. It also improves cold-hardiness and density. Fall feeding can shorten the dormant season of warm-season grasses and may maintain their color during the cool season.

The amount and timing of fertilization is important to lawns. Bermudagrass, a heavy feeder, can use 1 pound of actual nitrogen per 1000 square feet every month to 6 weeks during its growing season.

For warm-season grasses, apply nutrients every month or 6 weeks

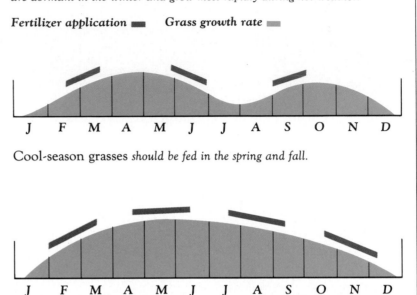

Cycles of lawn growth. *Cool-season grasses grow most rapidly in the spring and fall and are partially dormant during hot weather. A heavy fall feeding helps them repair damage done during the summer heat. Warm-season grasses are dormant in the winter and grow most rapidly during hot weather.*

Fertilizer application ▬   Grass growth rate ▬

J F M A M J J A S O N D

Cool-season grasses *should be fed in the spring and fall.*

J F M A M J J A S O N D

Warm-season grasses *should be fed throughout their growing season.*

during the growing season—April through September in many warm climates. Begin feeding as soon as growth starts in the spring, and continue feeding until growth stops in autumn.

For cool-season grasses, apply quick-release fertilizers three or four times throughout the growing season. Feed nitrogen in these proportions: one-fourth in early spring, one-fourth in late spring, and one-half in early fall. Feed potash in late spring.

Controlling diseases with fertilizer

All plants are more resistant to plant diseases when they are healthy and well fed, but lawns are particularly sensitive to fertilization practices. Unlike most other plants, grasses have the ability to store nitrates for future use. When fed large amounts of nitrogen fertilizer, grass plants grow as fast as they are able, but they also store extra nitrates in the spaces between their cells. These extra nitrates make the grass particularly attractive to fungi. The rapid rate of growth caused by high nitrogen

levels also causes the grass plants to become succulent and less resistant to plant diseases.

CATEGORIES OF LAWN GRASSES

Cool-season grasses are grown mainly in northern climates and at higher elevations in the West. These grasses thrive in cool weather and will tolerate frozen soil, but when stressed by hot weather, they may become dormant.

Bluegrass
Bentgrass
Fescue
Ryegrass

Warm-season grasses, grown primarily in the South, thrive in hot weather. They are stressed by cold weather, becoming dormant in temperatures below 50°F, and will die if the ground freezes.

Bahiagrass
Bermudagrass
Carpetgrass
Centipedegrass
St. Augustinegrass
Zoysia

Drop spreader. *Make 2 passes at each end of the lawn as a turning space. Close the hopper while turning.*

Broadcast spreader. *The pattern thrown by broadcast spreaders is heavier in the center. Overlap about a third on each pass to get even coverage.*

Iron chlorosis in lawns

If your lawn doesn't get greener and begin to grow after you've fed and watered it, it may be deficient in iron. The likelihood increases if you have an alkaline soil, since such soils tend to make iron un-available to plants. Iron chlorosis can be corrected in a lawn by using a fertilizer that contains an iron supplement.

TIPS FOR LAWN FERTILIZING

■ Nitrogen will not be available to grass if the soil is waterlogged or overly compacted. Reduce water-ing and aerate the soil whenever necessary.

■ For sandy soil, make frequent applications of small concentra-tions of nitrogen.

■ Beware of root competition be-tween lawns and shrubs or trees. Apply fertilizer to match the com-bined plant needs.

■ If you remove lawn clippings (a natural source of nitrogen), you'll need to add more fertilizer.

NITROGEN REQUIREMENTS

Grasses vary in their nitrogen re-quirements. Long-term fertilizer needs may even be a consider-ation in choosing a particular grass. The lists below are ar-ranged according to the nitrogen requirements of various grasses in areas with a long growing season. Nitrogen requirements will be lower for areas that have short warm seasons. The grasses listed start with those that have low nitrogen requirements (2 to 4 pounds per 1000 square feet per year, depending on conditions) and progress to ones with high nitrogen requirements (6 to 8 pounds per 1000 square feet).

Zoysia
Red fescue
Tall fescue
St. Augustinegrass
Common Bermudagrass
Highland bentgrass
Colonial bentgrass
Kentucky bluegrass
Perennial ryegrass
Dichondra
Hybrid Bermudagrass
Creeping bentgrass

FERTILIZING TREES

With trees, it's important that the fertilizer penetrate into the root zone. Although some trees may have roots dozens of feet deep, most of the nutrients and water a tree receives are absorbed in the top 2 feet of soil. Tree roots may explore hundreds of feet from the trunk, particularly if the tree is growing in dry or infertile soil. But most of the feeder roots are in a broad band approximately under the outer edge of the tree top (the *drip line*). In general, you should fertilize the tree from a point midway between trunk and drip line to a point 2 feet beyond the drip line.

Fertilization assists in rapid development and maintenance of attractive, healthy landscape plants. Young trees grow more rapidly following fertilization and will more quickly reach their mature size. Older ornamental trees need little fertilization if they have good leaf color and are growing reasonably well.

Leaves of fertilized trees are larger and greener than those of unfertilized trees. Fertilization makes trees more able to withstand insects and diseases. And fertilization may reverse the decline of trees that are not growing well.

However, overfertilization can provoke overly vigorous growth, increasing the tree's susceptibility to cold and to some diseases. When a tree grows very vigorously, much of the growth is vertical (rapidly growing vertical shoots are called *watersprouts*), which spoils the shape of the tree.

Once trees and shrubs are established and have grown to the desired size, restrained fertilizing can restrict further growth and reduce the need for pruning.

Amounts of nutrients for trees

For young trees getting established and for all fruit trees, a complete fertilizer is best. The fruit harvest

Fertilize trees in a lawn *by boring holes around the drip line of the tree. Proportion the right amount of fertilizer among the holes.*

and pruning of fruit trees remove substantial amounts of nutrients from the trees, which must be replaced through the soil to maintain tree health. Use about 6 pounds of 12-6-6 fertilizer, or its equivalent, for each mature fruit tree. For smaller trees, apply the fertilizer to an area starting a foot from the trunk and extending a foot beyond the tree canopy or drip line.

Mature ornamental trees and shrubs do not need complete fertilizers; nitrogen is usually the only element they require. The method for determining the appropriate amount of actual nitrogen to use when fertilizing mature ornamentals is shown in the chart. Apply the fertilizer evenly around the area under the tree's leaf canopy, extending from a point midway between trunk and drip line to about 2 feet past the drip line. Be careful not to get the fertilizer too close to the trunk.

When to feed trees

Fertilize deciduous trees in spring as soon as leaves first appear. Needle-leaf evergreen trees (conifers such as spruce, fir, pine,) should also be fed at this time, the beginning of the active growth period. Fertilize again in the fall, before mid-November in many climates, when cold weather will not permit new growth. Nutrients will then be stored in the roots for a vigorous bud break or growth spurt the following spring.

For fruit trees, fertilize early-bearing varieties by dividing the fertilizer into two applications; feed two-thirds in early spring and the rest in June. In areas where the soil freezes in the winter, make an application in late fall instead of spring. Fruit trees in containers benefit from monthly feedings during the growing period.

Citrus trees flourish when given three feedings: late winter, mid-summer, and late summer. Use a fertilizer with the full spectrum of micronutrients, especially zinc.

Trees in sandy soils benefit from more frequent applications.

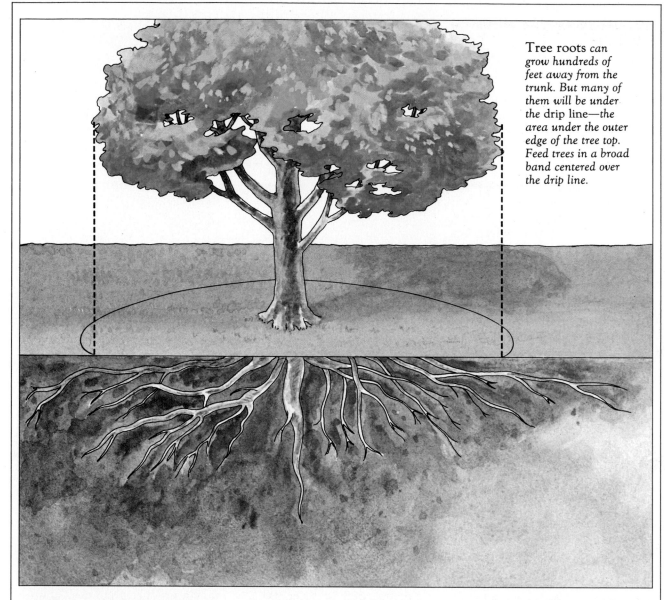

Tree roots can grow hundreds of feet away from the trunk. But many of them will be under the drip line—the area under the outer edge of the tree top. Feed trees in a broad band centered over the drip line.

Feeding trees in lawns

Because lawn grass is such a voracious feeder and grass roots make such a dense network in the upper foot of soil, trees growing in lawns are often underfed, even when the lawn receives more fertilizer than the rest of the garden. If you would like to increase the growth rate of a lawn tree, use one of these three methods:

■ For quicker greening, use a nitrate-based nitrogen source (rather than an ammonium or urea fertilizer). Spread it across the entire lawn, but use twice the recommended quantity in the feeding zone of the tree. Water the fertilizer in as usual, but then put a sprinkler under the tree and water even longer. Put on a total of 2 or 3 inches of water (as measured in a can). This heavy watering will carry the nitrogen below the reach of the grass roots.

■ Inject a liquid or soluble fertilizer below the level of the grass roots with a subirrigation tool (available in most garden centers).

■ With a soil auger (which can be rented), dig holes about 2 or 3 inches in diameter and 2 feet deep every couple of feet around the drip line. Pour dry fertilizer or slow-release pellets into the holes and fill with soil.

ESTIMATING NITROGEN NEEDS

Determine the amount of actual nitrogen according to the diameter of the tree trunk at a point 4 feet above the ground, as follows:

Trunk diameter (inches)	Actual nitrogen (pounds)
1	0.15–0.30
2	0.30–0.60
3	0.45–0.90
4	0.60–1.20
5	0.75–1.50
6	0.90–1.80
7	2.10–4.20
8	2.40–4.80
9	2.70–5.40
10	3.00–6.00

See page 84 for the method of calculating the amount of actual nitrogen in a fertilizer.

FEEDING VEGETABLES AND FLOWERS

Both vegetables and flowering plants benefit greatly from regular feeding. Here are some general guidelines for achieving the best results with fertilizers.

Vegetables

Vegetables grow quickly and need a steady, reliable supply of fertilizer for optimum growth. Most are heavy feeders. For the highest quality greens, apply large amounts of nitrogen, which promotes more leafy growth.

As a general rule, the faster a plant grows, the more fertilizer it should be given. If you are using a commercial vegetable mix, follow the instructions on the label. If you are using general-purpose or generic chemical fertilizers, follow the guidelines given in the chart.

If you use manure or compost as your fertilizer, spread it from ½ to 1 inch deep before tilling. If possible, work it into the ground a month or two before planting. Apply only half as much if you're using poultry manure.

Culinary herbs generally require less fertilizer than vegetables. Minimal fertilizing stresses the plant, forcing a concentration of oils that enhance the herbs' taste.

Here are some guidelines for feeding certain vegetables. For instructions on the various application methods, see page 84.

■ **Tomatoes and peppers.** Two or three applications are best. At planting, use 1½ pounds of 10–12–6 per 50 feet of row, mixed into the soil. After plants are growing well, side-dress with 1 pound per 50 feet of row every 3 to 4 weeks, splitting the application along each side of row.

■ **Corn.** Apply 2 pounds of 8–10–8 fertilizer per 100 feet of row in a band on both sides of and 2 inches away from the seed. When plants are 8 inches tall, side-dress with 3 pounds of 8–10–8 per 100-foot row of corn.

Siphon injectors *draw water from a liquid concentrate (in the bucket) and inject it into the irrigation water. This is a convenient way to fertilize outdoor container plants, or any other plants that are watered with a hose.*

■ **Onions.** These are heavy feeders. Apply 5 pounds of 8–10–8 per 100 square feet at planting time. Side-dress with 1 pound per 25 feet of row each month.

■ **Potatoes.** These heavy feeders need 2 pounds of 10–10–10 or 2½ pounds of 8–10–8 per 100 square feet of planted area.

Flowering plants

For most flowers, apply 2 pounds of 10–10–10 or its equivalent per 100 square feet. Work it into the soil at planting time or in the spring. Side-dress or broadcast another pound in midsummer. Here are special instructions for a few favorite flowers.

■ **Bulbs.** Fertilize bulbs at planting time with a long-lasting phosphorus source, such as a spoonful of bone meal per bulb or 3 pounds of 20 percent superphosphate per 100 square feet of planted area. When the bulbs emerge, feed with a complete fertilizer.

■ **Annuals.** Each year apply a total of 1 to 2 pounds of roughly 10–10–10 fertilizer per 100 square feet of flower bed. Work about a third of the fertilizer into the soil at the time of planting and then feed monthly throughout the growing season.

■ **Roses.** Roses are high-powered flower producers and need abundant and attentive feeding. Apply a complete fertilizer in early spring, just after pruning, before the leaves are fully open. Repeat every 3 to 4 weeks. Feeding should stop 6 weeks before the first anticipated autumn frost to prevent damage to new growth.

■ **Azaleas.** Azaleas, camellias, and rhododendrons should be fed lightly after bloom and monthly through August. Use a fertilizer formulated for acid-loving plants.

■ **Hydrangeas.** Hydrangeas grow best in acid soil. They are unusual in that acid soil turns the flowers blue and alkaline conditions turn them pink. For blue flowers, keep alkaline soils acid by adding aluminum sulfate.

Side dressing is used with growing plants. Spread the fertilizer over the root zone and water it in, or scratch it lightly into the soil with a rake. Heavy feeders, such as annual flowers and vegetables, are frequently side-dressed for a supplemental feeding during the growing season.

■ **Geraniums.** Use nitrogen sparingly for these flowers. Otherwise, they will produce copious leaves and few flowers.

Container plants

Container plants can be fed with granular fertilizers, slow-release capsules, or with liquefied nutrients. Because of the small amount of soil, plants in containers are more dependent on the gardener for feeding than are plants in the ground. Always dampen the soil before adding fertilizer, and be careful about concentrations. Too much fertilizer can damage or kill your plants.

Liquid feeding twice a month is preferred by many container gardeners. Follow directions on the package regarding strength and frequency of use, or feed at half strength but twice as often. Never feed more than recommended.

For outside container plants, which are often watered directly from a hose, attach a siphoning fertilizer injector to the end of the hose. Most siphon injectors dilute the fertilizer solution 1:15, so make the solution to be injected into the hose 15 times more concentrated than you wish to apply it. Since

1 cup contains 16 tablespoons, it is easy to translate tablespoon recommendations into cup amounts.

Ferns can be damaged by over-fertilizing. Use a low-analysis fertilizer diluted to half strength. Fish emulsion (5–1–1) is safe for ferns.

Since many container plants are indoor house plants, be aware of their seasonal growing cycles. In response to the low light of winter, many indoor plants may become dormant. Don't feed them during this period, but resume when they begin to grow again in the spring.

Foliage plants in containers will respond more readily to a high-nitrogen fertilizer (such as 12–6–6), since nitrogen stimulates leaf growth. Flowering plants will respond more to a low-nitrogen fertilizer (such as 5–10–5). Follow package directions carefully for the small amount (teaspoons) needed per gallon of water.

A newly potted plant in a rich potting soil will need feeding in 3 weeks to 2 months, depending partly on the amount of watering and its leaching effect on nutrients. Fertilizer generally leaches more quickly from perlite than from vermiculite.

NITROGEN EQUIVALENTS

The following fertilizers will all add about 0.2 pound of actual nitrogen. This amount of nitrogen is about the quantity that will be needed by 100 square feet of general planting, such as a typical flower bed.

Fertilizer	Pounds
5–10–10	4
6–20–10	3¼
8–24–8	2½
10–10–8	2
16–16–16	1¼

A pint of dry fertilizer weighs about a pound; a half-pint weighs about ½ pound. Dry coffee weighs about half as much as fertilizer, so a 1-pound coffee can holds about 2 pounds of fertilizer.

PRUNING

Pruning is the art of directing plant growth by cutting. Its success depends on understanding how the plant responds to pruning cuts.

Since the beginning of civilization, pruning has been a crucial art of husbandry. While Isaiah spoke of "beating spears into pruning hooks," the ancient Chinese were developing their own methods of pruning. Pruning is both a science and the accumulated wisdom of generations of gardeners. Much of this wisdom lies in understanding how a plant will respond to each pruning cut.

Why prune?

Pruning serves many purposes, both for the plant and for the gardener, but three main reasons for pruning stand out.

Pruning directs and stimulates plant growth. Pruning can control the size of a plant and can alter the direction of its growth. Pruning can affect the amount of sunlight that falls on the inner branches of a plant and on plants below. Often, an older, neglected shrub or tree can be provoked into rejuvenated growth through severe pruning. Pruning can enhance a plant's shape by removing misshapen branches.

Pruning improves plant health. Skillful pruning can do much to prevent future diseases by bringing

Regular and consistent pruning not only keeps plants healthy and vigorous, it also helps them to blend into a group, as in this perennial border.

sunlight and air circulation into the middle of the plant. With less plant material competing for water and nutrients, the remaining plant parts generally become stronger. Pruning can remove diseased or infested plant parts, isolating a problem. When a plant has been damaged, such as a tree with branches shorn off in a windstorm, proper pruning can cut a damaged limb flush with the trunk, eliminating the jagged stub that would allow rot to enter the tree. Anticipated wind or snow load damage can be reduced by pruning vulnerable branches.

Pruning increases flower, fruit, or leaf production. Pruning back part of the new wood on apple trees each winter forces plant energy into making bigger apples on spurs on the older branches. Thinning peaches will result in fewer but larger peaches. And reducing the number of strawberry runners will result in fewer but larger strawberries. Removing some of the buds in a cluster of camellia blossoms will force the plant energy into the remaining flowers, making them larger.

Pruning expresses the artistry and style of the gardener. The art of pruning makes plants an artistic medium for the gardener. Hedges, for example, can be sheared into a natural look or can have a more formal manicured look. Your plea-

sure and pride in your garden can be greatly enhanced as you shape it, over years, with pruning. As an exterior decorator, you can prune shrubs so their texture, color, and flowering will lend interest to the garden. Among the most dominant and lasting expressions of the gardener's art are trees, which develop their forms for a generation before reaching artistic maturity.

Plant responses to pruning

To understand why a plant responds as it does to pruning, it is important to understand some of the forces that shape plants. Some of these are internal, such as the competition between plant parts for nutrients, and the flow of plant hormones. Other forces are external, such as where light is available. The way a plant responds to pruning also depends on the time of year that the pruning is done.

Plants have two "circulatory" systems. (They are not truly circulatory because the sap does not travel in a circle.) One system carries water and dissolved mineral nutrients from the soil to the leaves and branches. The other system carries sugars and complex organic chemicals made in the leaves to all the other parts of the plant. The parts of the plant can be thought of as being in competition for both streams of nutrients.

Shearing hedges is a form of simple topiary in which a row of shrubs is pruned to an elongated square.

A properly pruned rose will respond in the spring with a burst of vigorous growth. Heavy pruning, such as this, elicits an especially vigorous response.

During the summer, deciduous plants store energy, in the form of granules of starch, in their roots. In the spring, they break down the starch into its component sugars, which dissolve and are carried up the stem to the opening buds. The more sugar a shoot receives, the faster and larger it grows. If half the buds on a fruit tree or a rosebush are pruned off during the winter, each remaining bud will have twice as much sugar and will grow twice as vigorously.

Another force that governs plant response to pruning is the flow of growth hormones, especially a hormone called *auxin*. Auxin is formed in comparatively large quantities in the growing points of all plants, and in lesser quantities in the leaves. In small quantities, auxin stimulates plant growth. But in large quantities, it represses growth. The growing point of every branch, as long as it is actively

growing, produces enough auxin to keep all the other buds on the branch (there is a bud at the base of every leaf on most plants) from growing. On an apple tree, for example, each bud that breaks in the spring will grow a single unbranched shoot during that growing season. The next spring, all the dormant buds along that shoot break into growth and begin growing at once. Each of them produces enough auxin to keep the buds on its shoot dormant. If you pinch off that growing tip, several buds near the end of the branch will be released from dormancy and begin growing. But once they are growing actively, no other buds will break dormancy. This principle is behind the use of pinching, heading, and shearing to make a plant thick and bushy.

Leaves use light for energy to form sugar from air and water. The more light a leaf receives, within limits, the more sugar it makes,

and the faster the shoot to which it is attached will grow. If a leaf is in such a dark location (such as the interior of a tree) that it can't make even the sugar it needs to support itself, it is sacrificed by the tree: its protein is withdrawn for use elsewhere, and it turns yellow and drops off. To a large extent, we regulate plant growth by allowing light to reach certain leaves. By thinning out the top of a tree, we allow leaves to grow not only within the tree but under it as well.

Also, a plant that is growing in a dark location grows in a more open pattern, with each leaf isolated so that none shade the others. A plant in a light location grows more densely, with the leaves packed more closely together.

Because the roots are packed with stored energy during the winter, pruning at that time causes the tree to respond with increased vigor in the spring as growth begins. But this vigorous response is dependent on the stored starches.

This espaliered apple tree has been trained to a four-wire cordon. It has borne fruit for two generations of gardeners. Espaliering not only makes fruit trees more interesting, attractive, and easy to care for, but also increases their productivity.

The less energy a plant has stored, the less vigorous is its response to pruning. A tree pruned in early summer, when its stored reserves have been exhausted in new growth, will not respond with a burst of energy, but it will be less vigorous than usual the following spring. The reason is that late summer is the time that trees replenish their starch supply. Removing leaves at this time diminishes their ability to make starches, so less is stored for the following spring's growth. If you want to reduce a tree's growth, or avoid a vigorous response to pruning, this is the time to do the heavy pruning.

Pruning for fun and art

Several specialized forms of pruning shape plants into forms far removed from that intended by nature. Some of these are done as highly sophisticated art forms. Others are done just for fun or as a means of artistic self-expression.

Bonsai is the art of dwarfing trees in containers that has been prac-

ticed in China and Japan for hundreds of years. There is no secret to creating bonsai trees; rather, there is a body of skills and specific techniques. Properly done, a bonsai is a miniature tree, or even a grove of trees, that gives the effect of great age. The trees are carefully grown and shaped over years or even generations to express an artistic gesture. The art of bonsai is too complex to begin to cover in this book, but many books devoted to it are readily available.

Espaliering is the art of training fruit or ornamental trees on a trellis. The art originated in Europe, where it was developed to gain the highest yield from fruit trees. The trees were kept small and carefully shaped so that each leaf received the maximum light and warmth. Today it is still used for commercial raising of fruit, but it is most commonly carried out by home gardeners, who find the allure of growing large crops on small, attractive trees irresistible.

Topiary uses living plant matter as a medium for sculpture. If bonsai attempts to imitate natural forms, topiary ignores nature. Small-leaved evergreens, usually yew or boxwood, are shaped into geometric forms or whatever shapes strike the artist's fancy. Topiary often has a humorous expression, shaping shrubs into fat dancing elephants or squat ducks.

Pleaching is accomplished by a combination of grafting and pruning. The branches of trees are bent across a path and grafted together to form an arcade. This has never been a widely popular craft and is seldom seen today.

Pollarding occurs when a tree is pruned back to the same place each year. The ends of the branches to which it is pruned grow into swollen masses of bud tissue, sprouting dozens of vigorous shoots each spring. Pollarded trees are dense and small. This is perhaps the most highly controlled way of pruning a tree. It is often done with sycamores.

PRUNING TOOLS

Good quality tools will make pruning easier. They are sturdier and hold a sharp edge longer than inexpensive tools. Here are several factors to consider when selecting pruning tools:

■ The quality of the steel in the cutting edge is important. High quality steel, either forged or stainless, will take and hold a cutting edge better than other types.

■ Choose tools of a weight that you are comfortable with.

■ Take the time to see how the tool feels in your hand. For example, pruning shears with a spring mechanism that reopens the shears after each cut should open to fit your hand. If it opens too far, your hand will tire quickly. With hedge shears, snap the shears open and shut a few times. Is there a rubber cushion to absorb the shock of the cut? If not, your arms will absorb the shock and soon tire.

Basic tools

Four basic tools will be adequate for most pruning chores:

Hand pruners, or hand pruning shears, have a hook and a blade. They easily cut branches up to ½ inch. There are two types: scissors and anvil. The anvil type presses the wood against an anvil. The bypass type cuts like a pair of scissors. When using hand shears of the scissors type, always lay the blade, not the hook, on the side toward the plant. If the hook is on the side toward the plant, the cut will leave a small stub that may let rot enter the plant.

Maintain your hand pruner by keeping it clean and dry. After each use, wipe the blade with an oily rag. Sharpen it by taking it apart and renewing the edge on a whetstone.

Lopping shears have long handles, giving you good leverage to cut branches as thick as 1¼ inches. This is the tool to use for branches over ½ inch in diameter. Loppers usually have a bypass blade design, similar to that of hand pruners.

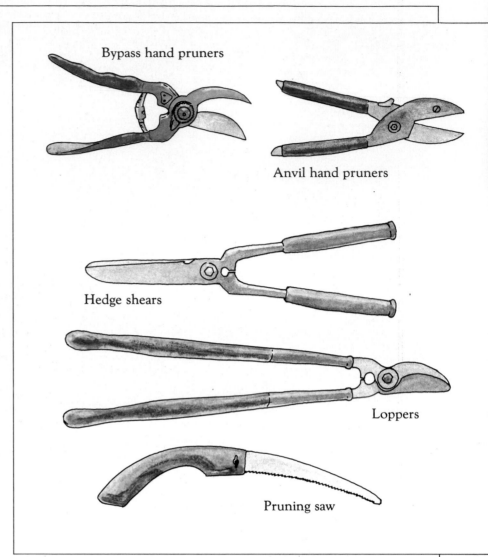

Bypass hand pruners

Anvil hand pruners

Hedge shears

Loppers

Pruning saw

Variations on basic design include some anvil-style models and some heavy-duty ratchet or gear designs that give you the force to cut branches up to 1¾ inches.

The length and strength of the handles will determine how much leverage you have for large cuts. Handles are usually made of wood or metal. Either can be strong if well made.

Loppers can reach high and deep into dense foliage. As with the hand pruning shears, put the blade on the side toward the plant when cutting.

Hedge shears can be used on hedges with wood up to ½ inch thick. The blades range from 6 to 12 inches long; longer blades cut more accurately on a level plane. Handles are made of wood or tubular steel. A notch in one blade helps to hold the vegetation while cutting larger stems, but hand

pruners or loppers will work better on thick stems. The main difficulty with hedge shears is that vegetation sometimes slips out while you are cutting. Models with serrated cutting edges or wavy blades have been devised in attempts to cope with this problem. This tool is useful for pruning not only hedges but ground covers, some shrubs, perennial flowering plants, and faded flower heads.

Maintain them by keeping the metal clean, dry, and lightly oiled to prevent rust. Sharpen the blade by unbolting it, placing it securely in a vise, and then drawing a whetstone along the blade at the original bevel angle.

Electric hedge trimmers can make quick work of extensive hedge shearing and do a neater job

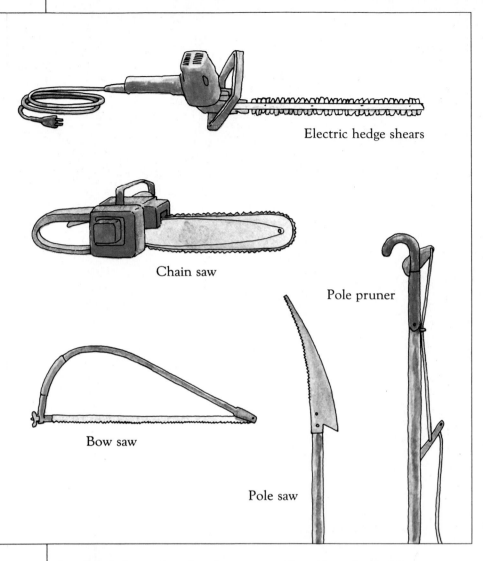

Electric hedge shears

Chain saw

Pole pruner

Bow saw

Pole saw

to remove any rust or rough spots on the surface of the saw. A smooth blade slips easily through a cut without dragging.

Other pruning tools

One variation of the basic tools has the shears or saw on an extension tube or wood pole. These longer versions can be helpful, since they may eliminate the need for a ladder in some pruning situations. Pole pruners usually operate with a lever handle and metal rod cutting action or with a pulley and rope mechanism. Saws on the ends of poles are usually curved so that the saw hooks onto the branch as it cuts, preventing slipping. Some all-in-one tools have a saw and a pruner on one pole. The poles may be made of wood, fiberglass, or tubular metal (remember, though, that using metal poles near high-voltage power lines can be dangerous). Some poles telescope to give a shorter or longer range, as desired.

A knife and a rasp are useful to have around when pruning. They can smooth jagged edges on large cuts to promote rapid healing.

Chain saws are handy power tools for pruning large limbs. But resist any impulse to climb into a tree with a chain saw for pruning. Chain saws are dangerous tools and should be used only where your footing and balance are secure. Call in a professional for heavy tree work.

It is important to keep all your pruning tools sharp, because plants will callus over more quickly from sharp cuts than from blunt tears.

Disinfecting pruning tools

Bacterial diseases can be transmitted from sick to healthy plants by the tools used for pruning. If diseases like fire blight cause problems in your garden, disinfect the pruning tool with rubbing alcohol after each cut.

than hand shears, but they function best on wood no larger than ¼ inch in diameter. Some models are cordless, with rechargeable batteries, and can run up to 35 minutes between charges.

Pruning saws can cut thick branches. Small curved saws are good for branches up to 2 inches thick. The teeth on a pruning saw are angled back (rather than straight, as on a carpentry saw). The angled teeth cut green wood without binding and cut on the backward instead of the forward stroke.

Some straight-edge saws have teeth on both sides of the blade. One side has coarse teeth, which are useful for larger branches; and the other side has fine teeth, used for smaller cuts. However, a saw with teeth on both sides can sometimes inadvertently damage other branches in tight pruning situations.

Bow saws have thinner blades cut more quickly than pruning saws. But they are too wide to fit in tight places.

Keep the metal clean, dry, and lightly oiled to prevent rust. The beveled edges on the teeth require some attention when sharpening. Place the saw between two boards in a vise to keep the blade from bending while you work on it. Start sharpening at one end and follow the existing bevel. File the leading bevel of one tooth and the trailing bevel on the next simultaneously. File every other tooth from one side; then reverse the saw and file the remaining teeth from the other side. Use steel wool

PRUNING TECHNIQUES

Pruning is an important part of keeping your garden in shape. These pages show how to use some of the basic pruning techniques.

Where to prune

Plant growth proceeds from buds, especially the terminal bud. Removing a terminal bud by pinching or cutting will force growth through a lateral or latent bud.

A bud-scale scar indicates where this year's growth began as the terminal bud broke dormancy in spring. Flat, triangular vegetative buds unfurl as new leaves and branches. Plump flower buds become flowers and then fruits.

When pruning, cut back to a bud that points in the direction you want growth to flow. Never cut back to a place between buds, because the stem will rot and disease can enter the plant. (Grapes are an exception to this rule. Cut grape vines back to a node between buds, since the hollow grape stem calluses over better at the node.) Cut to ¼ inch above the bud. Don't cut too close or too far away from the bud. The blade of the pruning shears should cut at the angle of desired growth.

Wide-angle scaffold branches are strong, but narrow-angle scaffolds are weak and should be removed.

Pruning techniques

Cutting back some plants, either all the way to the ground or only partway, stimulates new growth.

Heading back removes the growing tips of branches. Repeated heading back gives the plant a full, dense, sculpted look.

Pinching is a type of heading back. It removes the terminal bud, forcing growth back into the lateral buds. Pinched plants become more dense. Pinching off some of the flower buds on a plant diverts energy to the remaining buds to make larger flowers.

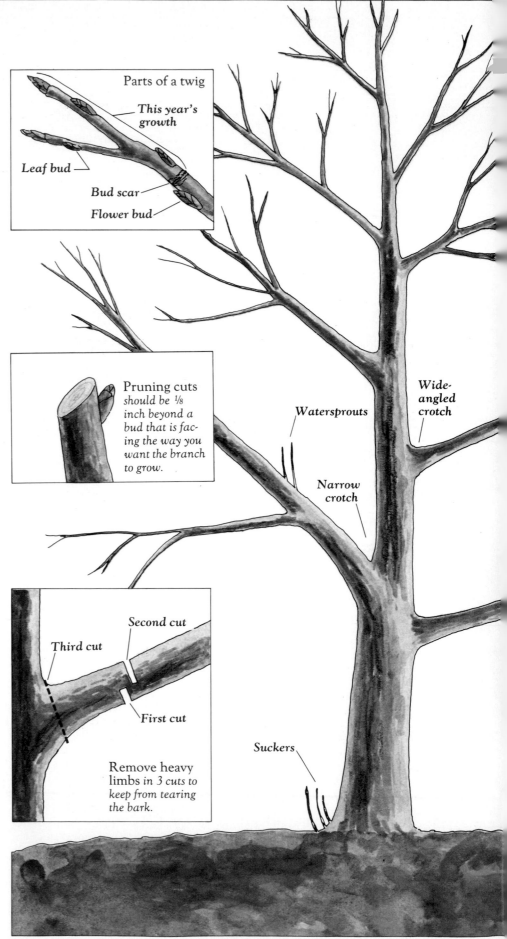

Parts of a twig

This year's growth

Leaf bud

Bud scar

Flower bud

Pruning cuts *should be ⅛ inch beyond a bud that is facing the way you want the branch to grow.*

Wide-angled crotch

Watersprouts

Narrow crotch

Second cut

Third cut

First cut

Remove heavy limbs *in 3 cuts to keep from tearing the bark.*

Suckers

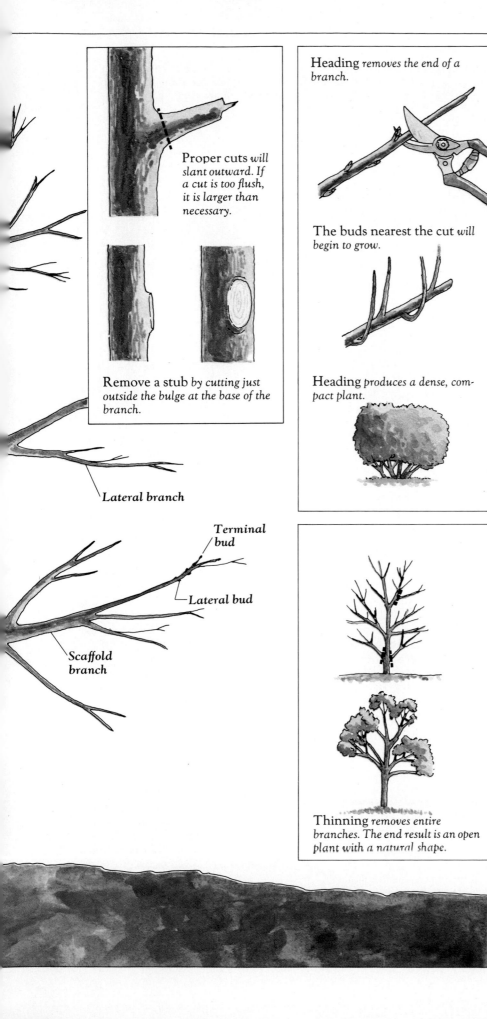

Proper cuts *will slant outward. If a cut is too flush, it is larger than necessary.*

Remove a stub *by cutting just outside the bulge at the base of the branch.*

Lateral branch

Terminal bud

Lateral bud

Scaffold branch

Heading *removes the end of a branch.*

The buds nearest the cut *will begin to grow.*

Heading *produces a dense, compact plant.*

Thinning *removes entire branches. The end result is an open plant with a natural shape.*

Shearing removes many growing points at once. Plants for which shearing is appropriate then release many buds from dormancy at the same time, resulting in dense growth with a sculpted look.

Thinning takes out entire branches, giving a lighter, more open, natural look. The energy that would have gone to the thinned branch will be distributed among the other branches, causing them to grow longer. When wind is a problem, thinning branches can help reduce the wind load of the plant.

Suckers should be removed, especially when they come from roots below a bud union or a graft, since the sucker will be of a different form than the scion.

Deadheading is the removal of the spent flowers on plants such as roses, rhododendrons, and dahlias. It increases flower production. If the plant is thwarted in efforts to produce seed, it puts extra energy into producing more flowers.

How to prune

Make thinning cuts close to the trunk or larger branch. If you are using a scissors-type hand pruner or lopper, lay the blade against the trunk. Most cuts should be made with the pruner "upside down," with the blade cutting upward. When cutting with a saw, make a similar close cut just outside the *collar* (the slight swelling at the base of the branch). Don't cut into the collar.

Prune large branches with three cuts. Make the first a few inches to a foot from the trunk. Cut from the bottom of the branch, about a quarter of the way through the branch. The second cut is from the top of the branch, about an inch beyond the first. The third cut removes the stub.

If there is any danger that falling branches might take off smaller branches below, cut the branches back piece by piece, starting with the end.

PRUNING ORNAMENTAL TREES

When and how to prune depends largely on the type of tree you have and the effect you wish to achieve through pruning. Here are some suggestions for pruning ornamentals.

Pruning at planting

Prune branches as needed to balance the top of the tree and make it more attractive. You don't have to make the top shorter, but you should thin out any weak or crossing branches. If you live in a windy area, thin the entire top to reduce the force of the wind on the tree.

A properly shaped ornamental tree has these characteristics: the trunk is straight and tapered, and the shape is balanced, with well-spaced scaffold branches coming off the trunk at a wide (45° to 90°) angle. Branches set at a wide angle to the trunk are much stronger than those set at a narrow angle. Also, branches are stronger if they are substantially smaller in diameter than the trunk.

Pruning during development

Shaping the tree is important at this point, so think of your long-term plan and become aware of the tree's natural growth pattern. Trees grow in one of two basic patterns: excurrent and decurrent.

Excurrent trees naturally develop a strong, dominant leader that is always in control of the tree's growth. Conifers, liquid amber, and tulip tree are examples. The leader is vigorous enough to remain the highest growing point on the tree. Never top off the leader of an excurrent tree.

Decurrent trees have a spreading, more rounded shape. Lateral limbs may grow as vigorously as the leader and may even outgrow the leader. Several major branches develop from the trunk over the years, creating a sprawling shape. The apparent leader or any branch of such a tree can be topped, headed back, or thinned.

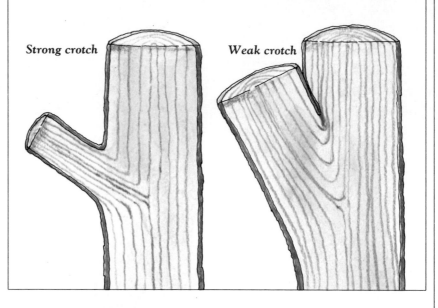

Crotch angle and branch size *determine strength of a branch. Branches are stronger if their crotch has a wider angle. They are also stronger if they are considerably smaller in diameter than the trunk, rather than the same size.*

Strong crotch   **Weak crotch**

Keep in mind the function of the tree in your landscape. If you want branches that children can climb on, leave the low branches. But if you want to be able to walk under the tree as it develops, remove branches below a height of 7 or 8 feet. Leave some low temporary branches to nourish the trunk as it develops, but head them back to keep them from fully developing; then cut them off when the trunk is 4 to 6 inches in diameter.

In the third and fourth years of pruning, select the scaffold branches in decurrent trees. Select branches that radiate from the tree symmetrically and that are properly spaced vertically. The correct spacing may be 12 inches for a Japanese maple but 24 to 36 inches for a large oak. Eliminate all shoots that don't assist in building this framework.

Pruning mature trees

When approaching a mature ornamental tree, prune in this sequence:
1. Remove any dead, damaged, diseased, or infested branches.
2. Remove any crossing or competing branches and prune off watersprouts.
3. Remove any low-hanging branches that might be hazardous to people.
4. Shape the tree to its appropriate natural form.

Thinning out may be advisable as a tree matures to allow more light into the tree or to allow light through the tree, perhaps to a house window or to plants under the tree. Thinning (rather than heading back) will retain the natural shape and beauty of the tree.

Some trees need little pruning, such as birch, liquid amber, and some broadleaf evergreens (Oregon grape and holly, for example). Others can withstand extremely heavy pruning. Eucalyptus and redwood trees have extraordinary recuperative powers and can regenerate even when cut back to the ground.

Nonflowering ornamental trees can be pruned at any time of the year, except in subzero weather. Winter pruning stimulates vigorous spring growth and results in a larger tree, but it also causes more watersprouts. Late summer pruning, although more difficult because the tree is in leaf, reduces vigor. Prune in the summer if you don't want the tree or shrub to respond with vigorous growth.

Excurrent trees *(left) keep a dominant leader as they grow. Don't prune the leader in these trees.* **Decurrent trees** *(right) lose their dominant leader and become round-headed.*

Proper scaffold spacing *has branches evenly spaced both vertically and around the trunk.*

Prune pines *by breaking off part of the candle in the spring.*

Spring-flowering trees, such as crabapple and hawthorn, should be pruned for cut flowers while flowering and then shaped immediately after bloom. They will form next year's flowers on wood grown through summer and autumn.

Summer-flowering trees, such as golden rain tree, should be pruned in winter or early spring.

Pruning conifers

Conifers usually need little pruning. They should be pruned cautiously, since most will not produce latent buds in older wood behind the foliage area.

Conifers are of two types. One type has branches radiating from the trunk in whorls (spruce, fir, and most pines). This is known as determinate growth. The other has branches radiating in a random fashion (arborvitae, hemlock, juniper, and yew) and is said to have indeterminate growth.

If you prune to behind the foliage on determinate conifers, the branch will die. And once lower branches are gone, they will not grow back. Prune determinate species by heading back new growth to a bud. For pines, prune by pinching the candles. If you pinch off half the candle as it is expanding, the branch will grow only half the size. For spruce and fir, prune the new growth back halfway to increase density. Don't prune the leader of most determinate conifers or you'll destroy the natural shape of the tree.

The indeterminate types, with many latent buds all along the branch, can generally be sheared without unfortunate consequences.

Prune most conifers after the new growth is completed in late spring or early summer. Juniper and cypress can be pruned safely at any time, though early spring to late July is best. A flush of new growth will conceal the cut marks at these times. Regardless of when and how much you prune, be sure to give conifers lots of water at pruning time.

PRUNING FRUIT TREES

Don't be afraid to prune your fruit trees. Unpruned trees become too bushy, lose their vigor, and produce smaller fruit. You can't kill fruit trees by pruning incorrectly, and you can correct any pruning mistakes as the tree grows.

Once you learn a few simple rules about which branches will bear fruit and how to shape the tree, you are ready to perform the yearly pruning that your fruit trees need. In general, you should do most pruning during the dormant season, but light pruning can be done in the summer to restrain excessive growth.

Vase shape. *Three or four scaffold branches are spaced only inches apart on the trunk.*

Delayed open center. *Three or four scaffold branches are spaced a couple of feet apart.*

Pruning young trees

The first pruning provides an opportunity to start determining the eventual shape of the tree. The buds will sprout in spring and grow in the general direction they were pointing. The bud nearest the end of each stem will grow more vigorously than those below it. Cut back to buds that are facing the direction you want the branch to grow.

A branch coming off the trunk at nearly a right angle is much stronger than a branch growing at a more upright angle. If a tree does not form good branch angles (cherries, in particular, do not), you can tie weights or splints onto young branches to force them in a better direction.

Retain some of the low branches for the first few years. Although these will not figure in the shape planned for the mature tree, the extra leafy growth will help develop trunk strength.

Three training styles

Vase pruning shapes a tree to a short trunk and three or four main limbs, each with several lateral branches. This style creates an open center that allows light and air to reach all the branches and promotes fruiting on the interior and lower branches. Vase pruning

also helps keep tree height low for easy care and harvesting. This shape is particularly recommended for apricots, peaches, nectarines, and plums. Apples and pears are often pruned to a vase shape. This style is also appropriate for any trees in containers.

Modified central leader pruning shapes a tree to one tall trunk with several major limbs branching off at different levels. This results in a strong form that will support heavy crops and survive stormy weather. The center of the tree is shaded, though, and will not produce much fruit. The taller tree is also more difficult to prune and harvest. Pecan, walnut, and other large trees are usually pruned to a modified central leader. Dwarf trees can also be trained in this style because their small volume does not inhibit interior fruiting.

Delayed open center pruning attempts to combine the virtues of both vase and central leader pruning by providing the strength of a central leader and the sunny center of a vase shape. Semidwarf apples, other medium-size trees, and fruit trees planted in lawn areas can be shaped in the delayed open center style.

Modified central leader. *A tall trunk supports several scaffold branches.*

Developing a vase shape

Follow this sequence for vase pruning:
1. At planting, cut off the central stem 2 to 3 feet above the ground. Prune any side branches back to two buds.
2. During the first dormant season (a year after you plant the tree) remove the leader and direct growth to three or four strong scaffolds. Choose branches that radiate evenly around the trunk. Maintain about 6 vertical inches between the branches, and keep the lowest scaffold at least 18 inches off the ground. Leave some

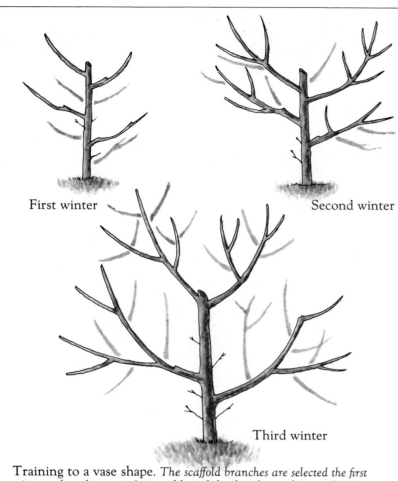

First winter

Second winter

Third winter

Training to a vase shape. *The scaffold branches are selected the first winter, when the tree is 1 year old, and developed over the next 2 years.*

small branches on the lower trunk to encourage trunk strength. Prune back scaffolds to one-third of their length.

3. During the second dormant season prune off aggressive new shoots but leave twiggy growth, which will be the fruit-bearing wood in most trees. Choose and encourage additional scaffolds if needed.

4. During the third dormant season prune to remove any broken limbs or crossing branches, but don't do any more major pruning until the tree has produced a good-sized crop.

Pruning mature trees

Once the basic shape of a tree has been developed, make pruning decisions according to which branches bear fruit. Most trees produce fruit on short branches, or *spurs*, which will bear fruit for several years. Prune each year to remove excessive growth and crossing branches; cut out a portion of the older fruiting wood each year.

Here are some suggestions for pruning specific trees:

Apple. Train standard-size trees to a vase shape and dwarf trees to a central leader. Fruit is produced on short spurs that last 5 to 10 years, and sometimes as long as 20 years. Prune lightly to remove one-tenth of the older wood each year.

Apricot. Prune to a vase shape. Fruit is produced on the previous year's stems and on spurs that last 3 to 4 years. Prune out one-fourth of the older growth and cut one-half of the previous year's stems.

Cherry. Train cherries to the central leader system. Fruit is produced in clusters on small spurs that last for 10 to 12 years. Sweet cherries need to be topped to keep the tree at a manageable size.

Remove only weak and crossing branches in yearly pruning. Sour cherries are smaller, bushier plants and should be pruned to increase branch length.

Citrus. Mature citrus should not be pruned except to remove broken or twisted branches. They produce a great many shoots at pruning cuts, which results in a broom effect. Citrus may be bush or tree in form, depending on variety. Fruit is borne on 1- or 2-year-old wood.

Peach and nectarine. Train to a vase shape. Fruit is produced on the previous year's long stems and on short-lived spurs. Prune back each of last year's stems to one-half its length. Annual pruning is more critical for peaches and nectarines than for any other fruit type.

Pear. Train to a modified central leader with five or six scaffold branches. Fruit is produced on small, long-lived spurs. Prune lightly when of fruiting age.

Plum. Plums are divided into two groups: Japanese (table plums such as Santa Rosa and Satsuma) and European (prunes). They are distinguished by the length of their fruiting spurs. Japanese spurs are 3 inches long. European spurs are up to 3 feet long. Both types bear fruit for 6 to 8 years. Some fruit is also produced on the previous year's growth. Remove one-third of the new wood each year by thinning and shortening. When a branch has produced fruit for 8 years, select a new lateral and remove the old branch.

Thinning fruit

Developing fruits should be thinned out on many types of trees. Cherries, citrus, figs, pears, and prunes are the exceptions and do not need thinning. Thinning results in fewer but larger fruits, but it should be done before the fruits are half-grown. Thin apricots so that the fruits are 2 to 3 inches apart; plums, 3 to 4 inches; nectarines, 4 to 5 inches; peaches, 5 to 6 inches; and apples, 8 inches apart, or one fruit per spur.

PRUNING BERRIES AND VINES

Pruning is needed on most vines and berry bushes to promote larger crops of fruit or flowers. Pruning also plays an important role in training and controlling the vigorous growth of many vines. But even less rampant species may need thinning to produce large fruits.

Pruning cane berries

Blackberries, boysenberries, loganberries, and raspberries are cane berries. New branches, called *canes*, sprout from the root system and grow up during one year and then produce fruit the next year. Canes that have fruited once will not fruit again. Pruning cane berries is mainly a matter of removing canes that have already fruited and then training the canes that are going to fruit next.

After the vines have fruited, cut off the old canes at ground level. Some growers paint identifying color marks on the base of each new cane as it appears in spring to make identification easier at pruning time.

The plants will produce a large number of new canes each year. But if all of these are allowed to mature and produce fruit, the crop and the individual fruits will be small. So when growth resumes in spring, select the five largest canes from last year's growth and remove the others.

During the spring, cut back the canes that you have selected to produce fruit to a length of about 3 feet. The canes will also have side branches, called *laterals*; cut the laterals back to 12 to 18 inches.

Some types of raspberries are called *everbearing*. This type produces a small crop in the fall on the tops of the new canes. Cut off the part of the cane that bore fruit. The rest of the cane will bear fruit the following spring and then die. Prune the lateral branches of everbearing raspberries back to 6 or 8 inches during early summer to encourage bushiness, larger crops, and larger fruits.

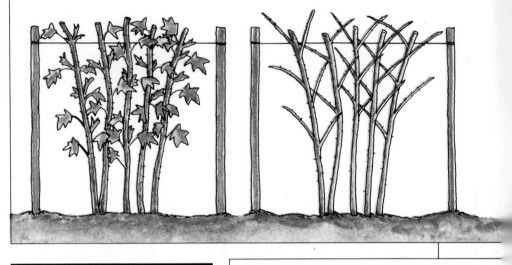

Pruning cane berries. *After harvest, remove the canes that bore fruit and tie 5 new canes to the wire. Head them back to about 3 feet high.*

That winter, prune the lateral branches back to 12 to 18 inches.

Pruning blueberries, currants, and gooseberries

These three bush berries bear heavily with little pruning.

Blueberries need cross-pollination, so plant more than one variety that blooms at the same time. Each winter, remove branches that are more than 3 years old.

Currants produce best on a plant with six to eight trunks. Don't prune for the first few years except to shape the plant, remove suckers (straight, vigorous shoots that come from near the base of the plant), and remove damaged branches. Fruit is borne on wood 2 or more years old, with 2- to 3-year-old wood producing the most fruit. Remove 4-year-old branches each spring.

Gooseberries bear on 1-year-old wood and on short side branches on older wood. Any branches that are 3 years old or more will not bear fruit and should be removed. Thin the bush when planting and each year thereafter to encourage an open shape that will make harvesting among the thorny branches easier.

Pruning grapes

The first few years after planting, prune to encourage the formation

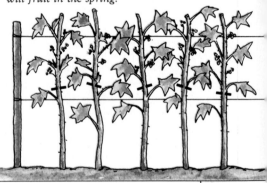

Everbearing raspberries *fruit on the ends of this year's canes. Cut off the portion that has fruited. The bottom of the cane will fruit in the spring.*

of a strong trunk. Before planting, cut the roots back to 6 inches and the stem to three buds. The first winter after planting, cut off all new growth except the strongest branch. Cut that branch back to three buds and tie it to a vertical support. The following spring, when sprouting shoots from the three buds are 12 to 14 inches long, tie the strongest shoot to the vertical support. Tie the two other shoots to a wire about 30 inches off the ground or to another type of horizontal support. Train one shoot in each direction.

When pruning grapes, cut through the stem near a bud where the stem is not hollow. Cutting a

Spur-pruned grapes *are pruned to 2 buds. Each of these grows and bears grapes. The stronger is pruned to next year's spur, and the weaker is removed.*

Cane-pruned grapes *must have longer canes left. Prune some to 10 buds and some to 2 buds. The latter will produce canes for next year's fruiting.*

stem in the hollow area can allow rot into the plant.

Grapes are produced each year on new growth, but only on new growth that sprouts from a stem that is 1 year old (last year's new growth). The new shoots that come directly from the trunk or other old branches will not produce fruit.

A simplified view of grape pruning is that half the previous year's growth should be cut off and the other half cut back to two buds per branch.

There are two basic types of grapes, and they need to be pruned differently. Most wine grapes (except for Thompson seedless) and muscadines should be spur-pruned. Spur pruning cuts back the stems to two buds every year. Thompson seedless and many American varieties, such as Concord, should be cane-pruned. Cane pruning leaves several long stems on the plant each year.

To spur-prune, look for the branches that fruited last year. If you pruned back to two buds per stub last year, then there will be two branches coming off each stub or spur. Pick the stronger of these two branches and cut it back to two buds; remove the other branch.

Train the main branches that come off the trunk so that the fruiting spurs are about a foot apart along the stem.

On grapes that must be cane-pruned, the first few buds on a stem will not produce fruit; so if you cut the stems back to 2 buds each year, you would never get any fruit. When the young vine has a large enough trunk (usually after the second year), cut back the side branches to 2 buds. These buds will produce two long canes. Every year thereafter, cut back one cane to 2 buds, and cut the other back to 10 buds. The cane with 10 buds will bear fruit. After a cane has borne fruit, cut it off. From the branch where you left 2 buds you will get two new canes: one you can cut back to 2 buds, and one you can cut to 10 buds and allow to fruit.

Pruning ornamental vines

Most ornamental vines become unmanageable if they are not trimmed. If faced with a neglected vine, trim it back to three or four main stems and trim back the side branches to two or three buds. The vine will put out a surge of new growth on the remaining stems.

Plant ornamental vines at least a foot away from house foundations. After planting, select three to five shoots and cut them back to half their original length. This will encourage new growth and vigor.

English ivy and other nonflowering vines can be pruned or sheared at any time in moderate climates and from early spring to midsummer in cold areas.

Ornamental vines flower either on the current season's growth or on the previous season's growth. Vines blooming on the current season's growth should be cut back to a basic framework or to the ground in winter. Vines blooming on the previous season's growth should be pruned after flowering.

Pruning wisteria

Wisteria tends to make long twining branches. To produce an attractive vine with many flowers, it must be pruned heavily each year. Choose one main trunk the first winter and remove any other shoots that come from the ground. Cut this trunk at the level you would like the lowest branch to appear. A few lateral branches will grow the next summer. The second winter, continue to shape the main framework of the vine, removing unwanted lateral branches and cutting others where you wish to force more growth.

Once a lateral branch is established, prune any growth from it back to two or three buds. This spur pruning forms short, thick branches (called spurs) that produce flower buds rather than shoot buds. To force more new growth, prune the new growth back to about 6 inches long during the summer. The more frequently this pruning is done, the more lateral branches will appear.

PRUNING SHRUBS AND HEDGES

Shrubs and hedges need pruning to keep them in shape. If they are not thinned, cut back, or sheared as necessary, many shrubs will become overgrown thickets, crowding and growing into one another. A vigorously growing shrub will benefit from having its size reduced by about a third each year.

Some shrubs are grown for the beauty and color of their stems. The red-osier dogwood (*Cornus stolonifera*), which has red stems, is an example. Remove a third of the oldest stems each year to encourage new stem growth.

When to prune flowering shrubs

The first thing to know before pruning a flowering shrub is whether it blooms in the spring or in the summer.

Spring-blooming shrubs, such as forsythia, bloom on the previous season's wood. Buds are formed in June or July, but they remain dormant until early spring. These shrubs can be pruned while they are blooming or a week or two after the flowers drop. Don't prune in autumn or you will cut off the wood and buds forming for next spring's flowering. New growth that develops during the summer can be controlled by pinching.

If you wish, you can cut branches as soon as the flower buds begin to swell in spring and put them in water indoors to force early blooms.

Summer- and fall-blooming shrubs bloom on the current season's wood. Summer lilac (*Buddleia davidii*) is an example. Prune these shrubs in early spring, after frost is no longer likely and before plant growth begins. Prune for shape, thinning out whole branches as necessary. Heavy pruning results in more vigorous regrowth and more flowers.

Deadhead rhododendrons *by breaking off the spent flower. Be careful of the buds under the flower.*

To increase blooming *in rhododendrons, pinch the tips of new growth in the spring.*

Deciduous shrubs, those that lose their leaves in winter, have a strong ability to renew themselves. Each spring these shrubs send up numerous new shoots, and proper pruning is essential to keep them from becoming overgrown. If you want them to grow vigorously, prune them while they are dormant; early spring is usually the best time. But if they are large enough, and you would like to restrict their growth, prune them after the spring flush of growth is over—usually toward the end of June.

Broadleaf evergreens often grow slowly, developing compact forms that need little pruning. The best time to prune these shrubs is just before a period of fast growth, usually in early spring.

How to prune shrubs

Deciduous shrubs. First remove long shoots that spoil the shrub's shape or that are broken, diseased, dead, or crossing other branches. Then thin out by cutting older branches back to the ground.

You can follow a 3- or 5-year pruning cycle with deciduous shrubs. Removing about a third or a fifth of the mature wood each year will keep the plant open and allow new shoots to become major branches. The 3-year cycle of pruning old wood will produce more new shoots; the 5-year cycle is best for some slow-growing shrubs such as lilac and spiraea.

Broadleaf evergreens. The removal of dead, broken, and diseased branches is usually the main task when pruning these shrubs. Reshaping may be necessary if the shrub has grown to block other plants or a window.

Flowering shrubs. Any flowering shrub putting out numerous flowers can be encouraged to produce fewer but larger flowers if some of the flower buds are removed. This practice is called *disbudding*. For the largest flowers, leave one flower bud at the tip of each branch.

Once the flowering season has started, you can prolong blooming by removing the spent flowers.

Start new hedges *by planting in fall or spring. The first year, don't prune at all. This allows the plants to develop larger root systems.*

The second year, *cut the plants back to 6 inches high. This forces growth low on the plant and fills it out to the ground.*

As the hedge grows, *shear it lightly whenever it makes 4 inches of new growth. The shearing is necessary to keep it compact.*

Mature hedges *should be sheared back to leave only about ¼ inch of new growth. Leaving some new growth keeps the hedge more attractive.*

new growth about 1 inch. Additional new shoots with flower-bearing potential will appear.

Azaleas bloom on lateral auxiliary buds and on the terminal bud. The buds are located underneath the bark along the stem. You can cut anywhere on an azalea branch and still be near a bud. The bud just below the cut will break into new growth. Tips of azalea plants can be pinched back or sheared to make the plant bushier. For the most impressive flower display, shear azaleas lightly after flowering.

Camellias should be pruned in spring after flowering. For the largest flowers, disbud in midsummer by saving only one bud per developing cluster, or one for each 2 to 4 inches of branch. Nip off the buds or dry them up by puncturing them with a pin, allowing air to get into the bud. If you pinch back the terminal bud of a camellia, the plant responds with only one replacement branch. To get more branches, cut back to where the current year's growth ends.

Pruning hedges

Plants suitable for hedges can tolerate heavy pruning. To develop a healthy hedge, let the hedge plants grow undisturbed the first season. Vegetative growth will strengthen the developing roots. The following season, prune to 6 inches high to force growth at the bottom of the plant. After that, shear off about ½ inch whenever the hedge has grown 4 inches. This allows it to grow as rapidly as possible but keeps it filled out. When the hedge reaches its desired height, slow its growth by shearing off all but ¼ inch of new growth at each pruning.

Small-leafed hedges (boxwood, yew) can be sheared; large-leafed hedges should be pruned by hand, one branch at a time.

Shape the hedge narrower at the top and wider at the bottom so sunlight can reach the bottom foliage and promote growth.

This practice, known as *deadheading*, forces plant energy into producing more flowers rather than into forming seeds on the spent flowers.

Some flowering shrubs, such as azaleas and rhododendrons, require more grooming than pruning. Use your fingers to remove aging flowers and to pinch back green growth. Because rhododendrons and azaleas differ in the placement of their flower buds, grooming is slightly different for each.

Rhododendrons bloom only on the terminal buds, just above the leaf rosette of branches. After the flower withers, remove the faded flower trusses by bending them over while twisting them gently. Hold the stem in your left hand and turn the faded truss with your right. Be careful not to damage the bud under the spent flower. Next year's flowers will emerge from that bud.

When sticky new growth appears, a flower forms on its end. If you want to double the number of flowers next year, pinch back the

PRUNING ROSES

The general principle of rose pruning is that cutting off old wood produces new wood and more blooms each year.

The severity of pruning differs. Prune more severely for larger (but fewer) flowers, for a smaller bush, or if a plant is weak. Heavier pruning leaves fewer buds to share the food stored in the dormant roots, so each bud will grow more vigorously. The degrees of pruning are defined according to the number and length of canes that are left:

■ *Severe* pruning leaves only 3 or 4 canes, each 6 to 12 inches long.

■ *Moderate* pruning leaves 5 to 12 canes, each 18 to 24 inches long.

■ *Light* pruning cuts back about a third of the plant.

Severe pruning is the prevalent practice in harsh climates, where the exposed bud union must also be protected from frost, usually with a protective mulch. (Some varieties, such as 'Peace', will not tolerate heavy pruning.)

Prune moderately throughout the flowering season to restrain the plant, disbud to get larger but fewer flowers if desired, and remove spent flowers.

Types of roses

Roses are categorized according to whether they bloom on wood produced in the current or previous year. Most modern continuous-flowering roses bloom on the current season's wood, but many older roses and species roses bloom on the previous year's wood.

Roses that bloom on the previous year's wood should be pruned after flowering, before new shoots emerge. Most of these roses produce flowers in spring and are not repeat bloomers.

Most roses in modern gardens are continuous-blooming varieties that produce flowers on the current season's growth. This group includes most of the modern hybrid tea, floribunda, and grandiflora roses. They should be pruned when the plant is dormant but when the buds have begun to

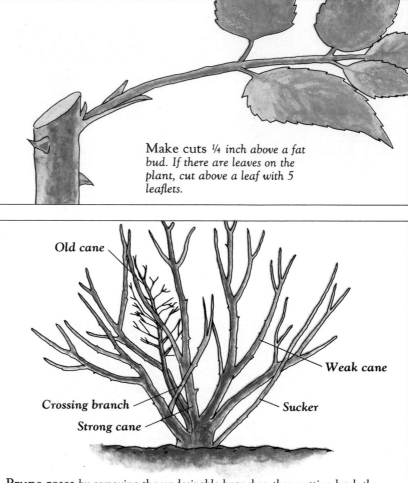

Make cuts ¼ inch above a fat bud. If there are leaves on the plant, cut above a leaf with 5 leaflets.

Old cane

Weak cane

Crossing branch

Sucker

Strong cane

Prune roses *by removing the undesirable branches, then cutting back the canes you are saving to make the plant lower and reduce the number of buds.*

Moderate pruning *leaves a plant a couple of feet tall.*

Severe pruning *leaves a plant only about 1 foot high.*

swell. The time will be January in the mildest climates and after the last frost in severe climates.

Pruning roses

Here are some guidelines for pruning the most prevalent type of roses to produce good flowering.

1. Remove dead or frost-damaged wood down to the nearest healthy dormant bud. Cut until you reach healthy wood, which is cream-colored.

2. Cut out any weak, spindly, or deformed twiggy growth. Remove canes pointing in toward the center, to open up the plant. Where branches cross, remove the weaker one. Remove any suckers that

Climbers *should be pruned to about 5 canes. Don't shorten the canes; bend them at the tips.*

originate from below the bud union by cutting or breaking them flush with the stem. Remove old canes that produce much twiggy growth (old wood has darker bark than new wood).

3. For most plants, thin to 3 to 5 canes that are 8 to 24 inches long. Cut the excess canes back to the bud union. Make cuts to outward-facing buds to create a pleasing vase shape.

In general, the more vigorous the plant, the less you prune. Vigorous roses have new canes ¾ inch in diameter. You can leave 6 canes on strong plants. Cut canes that you leave back by about a third if the rose is vigorous and back to 2 or 3 buds if it is weak.

If the rose is new or weak, remove the flower buds as they form the first year to build the strength of the bush. When you remove roses for cut flowers, leave at least 2 sets of leaves that have 5 leaflets each. This allows new flowers to be produced on long, vigorous stems.

Miniature roses need little pruning. Prune only to maintain their shape or to keep them small.

Climbing roses

Most climbing roses flower on year-old wood. Don't prune them for 2 or 3 years, except to remove dead wood. They need this amount of time to establish mature canes for flowering.

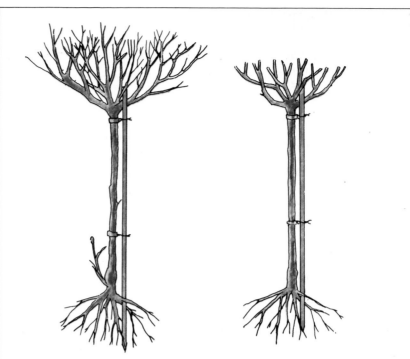

Tree roses *should be pruned to maintain their tree shape. Remove suckers from the trunk and base of the plant. Thin out the head, and shorten canes to strong buds that are pointed in the direction you want the cane to grow.*

Long canes grow from the bud union. Don't tip these canes. The long canes don't flower, but flowers appear the next year on the laterals of these canes. Prune back to 3 to 5 young canes. Prune the laterals on these canes back to 2 or 3 buds.

Pruning climbers with pliant canes is easiest if you untie the rose from its trellis or other support and lay it on the ground. Use soft ties to refasten the climber to its frame.

Some varieties of climbing roses, such as 'Don Juan' and 'Golden Showers', are unusual in that they flower on both old and new wood. Prune laterals back to 2 buds after flowering and head back the new canes by a third.

Rambler roses are favorites of some rose fanciers because they produce copiously on year-old canes, but they need constant, heavy pruning each year.

Specially shaped roses

Standards, or *tree roses*, are bush-type roses that have been grafted for effect onto trunks that are 3 or 4 feet tall. To keep the trunk unbranched, rub off sprouting buds that develop along it. Prune to keep the top symmetrical and to remove any dead, crossing, or diseased canes. Remove any suckers that emerge from the root stock or along the trunk.

Hedge and border roses are vigorous, bushy plants, such as the pink 'Fairy' rose or the taller 'Nevada'. Plant border roses about 2 feet apart and hedge roses 3 to 4 feet apart. Cut them back to 8 to 12 inches for bushy, low-growing plants. Each winter, remove about half of the new wood until the rose reaches its desired height. Varieties that flower on the current season's wood are pruned in winter; those blooming on older wood are pruned after flowering.

MOWING LAWNS

Proper mowing is essential to a healthy lawn. It promotes growth and keeps the lawn looking its best. Because the growing habits of different types of grasses vary, be sure to give your lawn the correct treatment. Some guidelines on when and how to mow are given below.

When to mow

Lawn grasses are of two basic types: cool-season and warm-season. The characteristics of each type are described on page 48. The cool-season grasses grow most vigorously in spring and autumn and become dormant in the heat of summer. Warm-season grasses grow vigorously in the heat of summer but become dormant in cool weather.

There is a direct relationship between grass height and root depth. Roots will grow deeper if the proper grass height is maintained. Deep roots promote growth of a healthy, dense lawn that can withstand heavy use and discourages the proliferation of weeds and disease. Grasses mown too low can produce a shallow-rooted lawn susceptible to disease and weed infestation, and the leaf surface area will not be sufficient to feed the roots.

If grass has been allowed to grow too tall, don't mow to the correct height all at once. Weak stems that have been shaded may burn and turn brown when suddenly exposed to bright sunlight. Gradually lower the height over several mowings to give the grass time to adjust to the change.

In general, the more you feed a lawn, the more frequently you have to mow. Heavy nitrogen feeding in the spring, especially, increases the need for mowing. Feed only enough to keep the grass a healthy green color. Cool-season grasses usually deteriorate during hot weather. Feed heavily in the fall to help the grass fill in holes and thin spots. Extra nitrogen in the fall is more likely to increase thickening and spreading rather than lengthening of the grass blades.

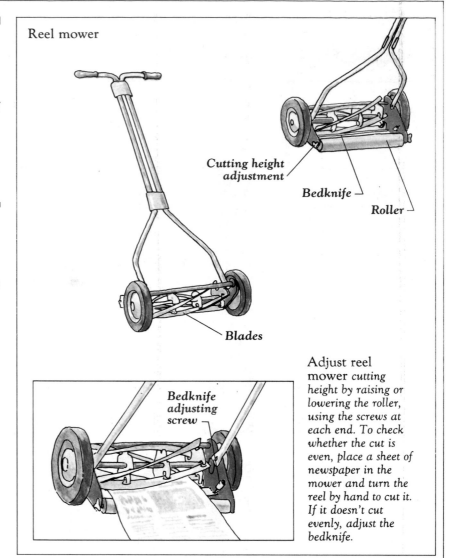

Reel mower

Cutting height adjustment

Bedknife

Roller

Blades

Bedknife adjusting screw

Adjust reel mower cutting height by raising or lowering the roller, using the screws at each end. To check whether the cut is even, place a sheet of newspaper in the mower and turn the reel by hand to cut it. If it doesn't cut evenly, adjust the bedknife.

Grass clippings provide nutrients to the lawn. Don't remove them after mowing unless they sit on top of the grass. If they are short and dry enough to filter into the turf, they can be left, since they decompose quickly. Clippings do not contribute to thatch, which consists of undecomposed stems and roots, not grass blades.

The accompanying chart tells the best height for several common grasses. After determining the correct height for your grass, mow your lawn when the grass is about a third higher.

Lawn mowers

There are two basic types of lawn mowers: reel and rotary. Reel mowers can be manual or powered by engines. All rotary mowers are power mowers, using gas or electric engines.

Reel mowers shear the grass with a scissorlike action that produces a very clean cut. They can cut very low and are preferred for grasses such as hybrid Bermudagrass and bentgrass, which need to be maintained at a height less than 1 inch.

Rotary mowers cut with a high-speed rotating blade. The rotary mower is generally more versatile and easier to handle and maintain than the reel type. But rotary mowers cannot make as sharp or clean a cut as a reel mower. Rotary mowers should not be used to mow lawns lower than 1 inch or they'll scalp the grass.

Rotary mower

Adjust rotary mower *cutting height by raising or lowering the wheels. Sharpen the blade a couple of times during the season. Balance it by filing metal from the back of one end.*

Cutting height adjustment

—Discharge chute

Check balance *of a blade by centering the hole on a pencil.*

The propeller action *of the blade develops a suction that throws clippings out the discharge chute.*

Sharpen *the blade with a file. Only the last couple of inches cut the grass. Sharpen it to the very end, at a 60° angle. Check the balance after sharpening. If the blade is out of balance, the mower will vibrate badly.*

Sharpen mower blades regularly. Dull blades leave crushed and un-cut grass, giving the lawn a ragged appearance. You can easily sharpen rotary blades at home. First disconnect the spark plug wire, then remove the blade. Use a file or grindstone to sharpen the edge of the blade that comes in contact with the grass; sharpen at a 45° angle. Blades on reel mowers should be sharpened at a shop that specializes in lawn mowers.

Mowing tips

Before mowing, always go over the lawn and remove rocks, wire, sticks, nails, and any other debris that might be there. A rotary lawn mower can turn these objects into lethal missiles.

Power mowers are dangerous. Always keep your hands and feet away from the blades while the mower is running.

Mow only when the lawn is dry. Mowing a wet lawn clogs the mower and produces uneven mowing. Wet clippings can mat and suffocate grass.

If you are using a reel mower, alternate mowing patterns to prevent a washboard effect and to reduce compaction. Make wide turns when changing direction, since sharp turns cause uneven cuts in the grass.

Both types of mowers can be adjusted for the mowing height your grass requires. Place the mower on a level surface. On reel mowers, measure the distance from the surface to the reel bed-knife. Correct to the desired height with a screw adjustment near the roller. On rotary mowers, measure from the edge of the skirt to the surface. Adjust the height by moving the wheels up or down. Or measure the height of the grass after mowing and adjust the mower up or down one setting.

Clean the mower with a light spray of water after use. Wipe dry and spray lightly with a penetrating oil. Use a knife or screwdriver to remove caked grass from the bottom of a rotary mower. Make sure motor oil of reel mowers is at the proper level. Never fill gas tanks or oil the mechanism while the mower is on the lawn because any spilled gas or oil can kill the grass it comes in contact with.

RECOMMENDED MOWING HEIGHTS	
Grass	Mowing height (inches)
Bahiagrass	1½–3
Bentgrass	¼–½
Bermudagrass	
Common	½–1½
Hybrid	½–1
Centipedegrass	1–2
Fescue	
Chewing	1–2
Red	1–2
Tall	2–3
Kentucky bluegrass	1½–2
Ryegrass	1–2½
St. Augustinegrass	1–2½
Zoysia	½–1

WHEN TO HARVEST VEGETABLES AND FRUITS

To the experienced gardener, harvesting at the right time for peak ripeness and flavor may be second nature. But to the beginner, it is not obvious that a zucchini should be harvested when it is 8 inches long rather than 2 feet. Here are some guidelines for harvesting several of the most commonly grown vegetables and fruits.

Vegetables

Beets. Young beets 2 inches in diameter are more tender than 4- to 5-inch beets. Greens from thinned beets are delicious when steamed; prepare the same way you would prepare chard or spinach.

Bell peppers. Wait until fully convoluted pepper shape forms. Bell peppers can reach the size of a large apple. Mature peppers will turn red if left on the plant for 2 or 3 more weeks. Red bell peppers are sweeter than the immature green ones and have a different flavor.

Broccoli. Harvest the green bud cluster while the buds are still tight, before there is any yellow flower color.

Brussels sprouts. Heads form under each leaf. Harvest from the bottom up as the heads reach full size and are still firm. Break off the leaves as you go.

Cabbage. Harvest when heads are solid but before they split. Check firmness by pressing the center of the head.

Carrots. Harvest spring carrots before hot weather arrives; harvest fall carrots before the first moderate frost. The small carrots that you thin during the growing season are delicious.

Cauliflower. Pick when curds are still firm but heads are 6 to 8 inches or more in diameter. If blanching (whitening) of the curd

Corn is ripe when the end kernels split and release milky juice if pressed.

Peas form distinct bulges and the pods feel full when ready to pick.

is desired, tie outer leaves above the head as it forms.

Corn. Corn is ready to pick when a kernel spurts milky fluid if punctured by your fingernail. Ears should be firm and full; the silk should be dry and dark. Eat at once, since flavor and tenderness deteriorate rapidly after picking.

Cucumbers. Harvest most slicing varieties when 1½ to 2 inches in diameter and 5 to 8 inches long. Pick when green; yellow cucumbers are overripe and bitter.

Eggplant. Harvest when 6 to 8 inches long, depending on the variety. Most eggplants become rich purple and have a high gloss. When the eggplant is ready to harvest, its skin is soft enough to break with a fingernail. Immature eggplants will have less flavor; overly ripe ones will be bitter and have poor texture.

Green pole beans. Harvest pods when the seeds make bulges but the skin is still smooth and shiny. Check seed package instructions for variations.

Lettuce. Leaf varieties ('Black-seeded Simpson', 'Oak Leaf') are

ready when individual leaves are large enough to pick. Harvest butterhead when the loose head has formed and head lettuce when the head is firm.

Onions and garlic. Harvest green onions when they are the thickness of a pencil. For bulb onions and garlic, remove flower heads to encourage bulb formation; harvest when tops have died back and are completely dry and brown. Withhold water in the final 2 weeks.

Peas. Snow peas are best when harvested young; pick when pea seeds just begin to show through the walls of the flat pods. Other peas are ready as soon as the peas reach full size. Feel the pods to see when they are full. Some pea plants produce full-sized peas with edible pods, such as 'Sugar Snap'. Harvest as they reach 4 inches long and finger thickness.

Potatoes. Harvest new potatoes when plants flower. New potatoes are small and sweet, with a thin skin, but do not store well. For full-sized tubers that can be stored through the winter, harvest after

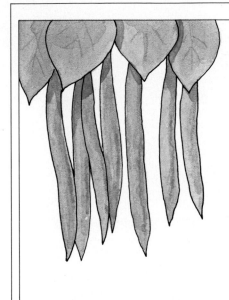

Beans *are most tender if they are harvested while the pod is still shiny.*

Watermelon, *when ripe, says "thunk" instead of "thank" when tapped, and its underside turns white.*

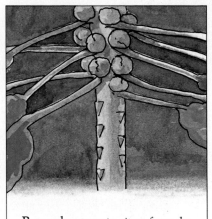

Brussels sprouts *ripen from the bottom up. Harvest the lowest sprouts as they reach full size.*

the vines have yellowed and died back. If the soil is loose, harvest by hand; otherwise use a flat-tined fork to avoid damaging the tubers.

Radishes. Harvest when roots have enlarged, while they are still crisp and succulent, before they become woody and split.

Spinach. Spinach is a cool-weather crop; it becomes tough and will bolt to seed in warm weather. You can pick as much as half the foliage on a spinach plant at one time. Spinach takes longer to mature in very cool weather, so take only a few leaves at a time from one plant. Break off the outer stalks while they are still young and tender.

Squash. Zucchini and other summer squash should be harvested when about 8 inches long. They lose tenderness as they grow larger but are still good for stuffing. Winter squash should remain on the vine until mid-October so the fruit wall thickens well for storage. They are ripe if a thumbnail cannot penetrate the skin.

Tomatoes. Allow tomatoes to ripen to uniform bright red (for most varieties). In hot weather, pick in the pink stage and allow to fully ripen indoors (heat slows down the coloring process, so a red tomato in hot weather may be overripe).

Harvest all fruit before the first frost. Store green ones in a frost-free place, wrapped individually in newspapers, until they ripen.

Fruits

Color, firmness, and flavor help to determine harvest time for fruits. Most fruits are ripe when the stem breaks loose from its branch as the fruit is lifted gently. If you have trouble breaking the fruit loose, let it ripen another couple of days.

Apples. As the ripening season progresses, test apples every few days for tenderness, color, and taste. The seeds turn brown when the apple is ready for eating.

Apricots. Harvest when fruits are soft and fully colored and have the characteristic apricot aroma. Apricots are particularly sweet when fully ripened on the tree.

Blackberries. Mature fruit is plump, juicy, sweet, and dull in color. The fruit slips easily off the stem. Harvest every 2 or 3 days.

Cantaloupes; melons. Harvest when the stem slips easily from the fruit. Ripe 'Crenshaw' and 'Casaba' melons will have an enticing aroma at the blossom end. The underside of watermelons turns from whitish to yellowish. When

tapped, mature watermelons give a dull thud but immature watermelons give a metallic, ringing sound.

Cherries. Harvest when fruit is somewhat soft and full-flavored. Pick with stems on so the fruit won't deteriorate. Cool after harvesting.

Grapes. As grapes mature and sugar content increases, cluster stems turn from green to brown. Berry color alone is not a good guide of maturity. Remove clusters with scissors or hand shears.

Peaches; plums. Peaches and plums are best left on the tree until ready to eat. Test for characteristic flavor and aroma.

Pears. Harvest while still firm and somewhat green; allow to ripen in a cool place. If allowed to ripen on the tree, texture becomes gritty.

Raspberries. Harvest when they develop full reddish color and slip easily off the stem.

Strawberries. Harvest when color is uniform and ripe red, and fruit is firm but beginning to soften slightly. Harvest with green caps to retain firmness and quality (pinch stem off about 1/4 inch above cap). Eat or refrigerate immediately, but use within 5 days. Don't wash until ready to eat.

SUPPORTING PLANTS

*Many plants can't be grown without support.
Each type of plant requires a different
support system, from a stake for a tree to an
arbor for a grapevine.*

Many plants look better if they are supported. Some are trees that need temporary support until their root systems grow large enough to support them. Some are flowers that have such large blooms that their stems can't hold them up without help. Others are plants that sprawl or climb trees in nature but look nicer or bear better if supported on a trellis or an arbor.

Supporting trees

Trees may need to be staked for three reasons: to support or straighten the trunk, to anchor the roots, or to protect the trunk.

Trees that are allowed to grow in one spot from seedlings seldom need support at any point in their lives. Many nursery trees, however, are pruned to look like miniature versions of mature trees, with all the branches coming from the top third of the trunk and the bottom two-thirds bare. The lack of branches on the lower portion keeps the trunk from expanding as it should. Then, to make the trunk nice and straight, it is tightly tied to a stake from the time it is very small. In addition, the trees are often grown packed tightly together. This is done partly to save precious space in the nursery, but

When long cucumbers, such as these Armenian cucumbers, are grown hanging from a trellis, they grow straight.

also to make the trees grow taller than they would if the sun could reach all their leaves.

All these practices lead to a slim, weak trunk that cannot support the weight of the top of the tree. When a newly purchased tree is cut from its stake, it usually flops to one side, sometimes far enough to touch the ground. The tree must be supported in the landscape until the trunk grows strong enough to hold itself upright.

But this support should be seen as a temporary crutch, not as a permanent aid. One aim in staking the tree should be to encourage the trunk to grow strong. This can be done in two ways. One way is to allow temporary branches to grow from the trunk. These can be headed back to keep them small until they are no longer needed. These branches encourage the trunk to grow in girth and to grow thicker at the base, tapering toward the top. This taper makes the trunk strongest where it needs strength. The branches will also help to protect the trunk while its bark is thin by keeping animals and people away from it.

The other way to encourage the trunk to grow strong is to allow it to move in the wind. Tie the tree to the stake at only one point, as low as possible, so that it flexes and bends in the wind. This bending stresses the trunk, causing it to grow thicker and stronger where it is stressed, much as exercising

your muscles make them larger and stronger. If the trunk is so weak that it will not remain upright when tied at only one point, tie it at several points to a flexible pole, such as a ⅛-inch iron rod, then tie this pole to the stake at one point. The pole will support the trunk but still allow it to bend.

Often, the trunk is strong enough to support the tree but the root system is too small to hold it upright. This is especially the case in a windy location. In this instance, a few short, stout stakes will brace it until its roots grow into the native soil and anchor it. If the wind is not too strong, thinning out the top of the tree so that the wind doesn't have so much to push on will substitute for staking.

Here, too, the staking is a temporary measure. Your aim is to help the tree root quickly so that the bracing can be removed. There are three things you can do to aid the formation of a strong root system. One is to allow the tree to bend a little in the wind. Bending stresses the roots as well as the trunk, causing them to grow thicker and stronger. To allow the roots to be stressed, tie the tree to the stake with flexible ties. These can be nylon ropes or wire rope with compression springs in them. Compression springs are available from hardware stores; they allow the wire to stretch a little, then become firm.

Arbors can add grace and beauty, as well as shade, to a garden. Woody vines need strong supports.

A second thing you can do to aid in the formation of a strong root system is to backfill the planting hole with unamended soil. Recent research has established that trees and shrubs establish in the native
soil more quickly if the soil that is used to fill the hole in which they are planted (the *backfill* soil) is not improved by added organic matter. Roots grow well in improved backfill soil, but they do not leave it easily to grow into the native soil. And a tree is not firmly established in a location until its roots are well into the native soil.

The third thing you can do to help the roots grow strong is to feed and water the tree correctly. If you live in an arid climate, check the root ball regularly after it is planted, and water whenever it is only slightly moist. You will find that the tree requires frequent watering for a few weeks after planting, but then the need for water drops. This happens when the roots begin to spread through the soil so that they are getting water from a larger soil volume. At this point, gradually change your watering practices so that you water deeply and thoroughly but infrequently. Allowing the soil to dry out somewhat between waterings

encourages the roots to explore more widely and deeply for water.

Stakes can serve a third function for young trees: they can protect the trunk. Until the bark grows thick and tough, it is susceptible to tearing. Since the sap flow is through the thin tissue between the bark and the wood, a tear in the bark reduces the flow of sap, stunting the top of the tree to some extent. Three or four conspicuous stakes around the trunk keep lawn mowers and tricycles from endangering it.

Supporting flowers and vegetables

Support systems for flowers should, of course, hold up the blooms. In addition to this obvious function, they should be inconspicuous and convenient to use. Since each flower has its own architecture, there are a multitude of staking systems available. A flower with a single stem, such as gladiolus, is best held up by tying it to a single stake. But to use a single stake for every bloom on a large football mum would require a forest of stakes.

If your flowers are in a cutting garden that is hidden at the rear of the lot and not meant to be seen,

the appearance of the stakes is unimportant. But the most beautiful flowers are usually in the most conspicuous locations, where they can be admired, and their beauty should not be detracted from by a mechanical support. The easiest way to make a staking system inconspicuous is to hide it in the flower foliage. This means that the system should be as small as possible and made of thin, green parts that look like plant stems. If ties are a part of the system, they should be thin and green also.

To stake flowers properly, the flower stalk must be supported from the time it begins to form until it blooms. This means frequent readjusting on the part of the gardener. A support system that does not need adjusting (such as pea brush) or needs a minimum of adjusting (such as a wire cage), requires much less fussing with than a system that necessitates tying every few days.

Support systems for vegetables are usually more functional than support systems for flowers. (Although more and more vegetable gardens are being designed with concern for their appearance as well as their yield.) Their aim is to increase the yield of perfect fruit

Top: Wooden trellises, like this A-frame, are excellent space-saving supports for cucurbits such as melons and pumpkins. You will need to train the vines up the frame and hang heavier fruit from cloth slings.

Bottom: Tomato cages are a good compromise between no training at all and the constant pinching and tying necessary for pole training.

and to make picking easier. One aim is to save precious garden space. Cucumbers or melons growing on a trellis produce much more fruit per square foot than if they were sprawling on the ground.

Storage is also a concern. Most vegetable support systems are large because vegetable plants tend to be large and heavy. They are usually not discarded at the end of the season. If storage space is limited, ways to store the support system must be considered when the system is designed. If a trellis can be taken apart for storage, or if it is weatherproof and can spend the winter in the garden, storage won't be a problem.

Supporting vines

Vines are adapted to using other plants for support in nature. Instead of spending their energy forming wood to hold themselves up, they can concentrate on producing more leaves, flowers, and fruit. Although some vines are annuals, most are woody perennials and will grow to the size of a small tree if given proper support.

Annual vines, such as sweet peas and morning glories, are useful for hiding a structure or a view quickly. In one season, they can cover a wall 8 feet high. They are not very heavy and can be supported by strings or small sticks.

Woody vines, such as wisteria and grapes, grow more slowly, at least for the first few years. But eventually they can cover the side of a large building and weigh hundreds of pounds. Structures to support woody vines must be strong. They should be built as sturdy as a house, with a solid foundation and strong members. Since they are exposed to weather, and are difficult to repaint when covered with vines, they should be of rot-resistant wood, such as redwood or cedar, or be made of pressure-treated wood. Vines are often grown on an extension of the house, such as an arbor or a trellis. In planning a deck, a grape arbor can be planned to cover part of it. The grapevine will shade the deck, and perhaps the house, in the winter, then drop its leaves and let light through in the winter.

STAKING NEWLY PLANTED TREES

Young trees may need both support and protection. You can use stakes to hold up their trunks or anchor their roots and to protect them from damage. If a tree is planted in an exposed area, it may need protection—especially from lawn mowers—until its bark has grown thick enough to protect it. Older trees that have been transplanted to a new location may need support while their roots grow into the surrounding soil. And the trunks of trees grown in containers may not be able to support the weight of their tops without support.

Some trees, particularly conifers, rarely need staking. But others, especially large trees, may not have a big enough root system to anchor the tree in the ground; stakes will keep them from being blown over by high winds. Sometimes thinning out top branches may be sufficient to reduce the weight and wind load on a tree.

Provide support for trees only when they need it. Moving in the wind helps a young tree build strength as it grows. Staking should be only temporary. A year after planting a deciduous tree, inspect it for strength. If supporting the trunk was the reason for staking, undo the ties to see if the trunk can stand upright; if it can, remove the ties and stakes. If anchoring was the reason for staking, rock the tree in the ground to see if it is firmly rooted; if so, remove the stakes. A tree that still needs staking after 2 years should be dug out and replaced. Its roots are probably circling and kinked, and not spreading into the native soil. Such a tree will never be strong and stable.

Check staked trees periodically to be sure the loop is not too tight, causing damage to the bark and cutting off the flow of nutrients. Also observe whether chafing of the tie material is causing any damage. Loosen or replace ties as necessary.

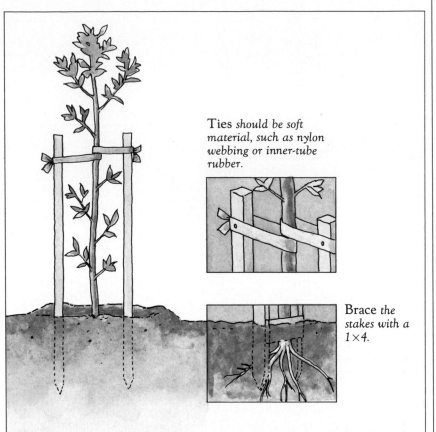

Ties *should be soft material, such as nylon webbing or inner-tube rubber.*

Brace *the stakes with a 1×4.*

Support trees *with 2 stakes. Tie the tree in only one spot, as low on the trunk as possible. Cut the stakes off just above the tie.*

Three stakes *provide trunk protection as well as support.*

How to stake a tree

If the trunk is not strong enough to hold up the tree, it needs to be staked. Two stakes will provide better support; but if you have to use only one, place it between the plant and the prevailing wind direction. If you're using two, place the stakes so that a line between them will be perpendicular to the prevailing wind. Using two stakes, both with ties around the trunk, will help keep the trunk from rubbing against its support.

The stakes should be only tall enough to hold the tree upright. Tie the tree only at one level. The stake should penetrate 18 inches into the ground; add that 18 inches to the distance between the ground and the tie point when you calculate the total stake length needed. Insert the stake so it presses tightly against (but doesn't go through) the root ball.

Place the ties as close as possible to the tops of the stakes to prevent rubbing against the trunk. If you are using a single stake, make the tie in a figure-8 pattern so the trunk is less likely to rub the stake. Use rubber, nylon webbing, polyethylene tape, tire cording, or some other suitable tie material. Wire, even when covered with garden hose, harms the trunk if left on too long. Use rustproof tacks or staples to hold the tie firmly on the stake.

A cross brace made of a 1-by-4-inch board at the bottom of the

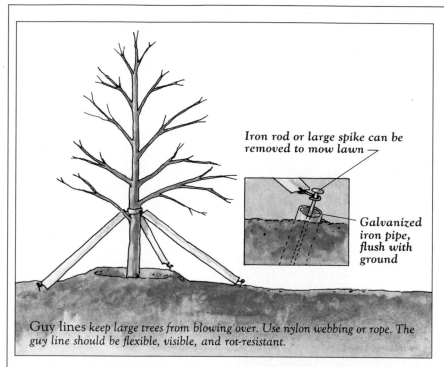

Iron rod or large spike can be removed to mow lawn →

Galvanized iron pipe, flush with ground

Guy lines *keep large trees from blowing over. Use nylon webbing or rope. The guy line should be flexible, visible, and rot-resistant.*

Protect trees *with 3 or 4 stakes. Paint them white for visibility, or tie rope between them.*

stakes will help keep the stakes upright in extremely windy locations.

Staking to protect a tree trunk

Drive 3 or 4 short (about 1 foot long) stakes 6 inches into the ground. Space the stakes a foot away from the tree and equidistant from each other. The aboveground part of the stake should be clearly visible. Join the stakes with nylon rope, or twine with pieces of cloth tied to it to make it visible. Another approach for maximum visibility is to run a wire through a plastic pipe between the stakes.

Staking to anchor tree roots

Roots may not grow fast enough to anchor the tree, or the top may develop a dense head of foliage that the roots can't hold upright, especially in wind. Heavy rains or frequent irrigation, particularly in loose soil, may also make a young tree vulnerable to wind. The top may need thinning (not heading) to reduce its wind resistance and its weight.

Support stakes will anchor the tree. Or, if you are using three stakes to protect it, simply use stronger and longer stakes and tie the tree to them about one-third the distance up the trunk.

Using guy lines to support large trees

Large trees transplanted into a landscape may need support for the first year to keep them from blowing over. But stakes can't provide enough support for large trees. Use three guy lines instead, spaced equidistant from each other and 5 to 10 feet from the trunk of the tree. Nylon webbing or nylon rope makes excellent guy lines. Attach the lines to a collar, made of a soft material such as 3-inch nylon webbing, around the tree's trunk. At ground level, you can fasten the wires to pins inserted in sunken pipes. You can easily remove the pins for grass mowing or other maintenance. Or you can attach the guy lines to 2-by-2-inch or 2-by-4-inch stakes or to stakes or pins buried in the ground.

Propping up heavily laden fruit trees

Some fruit trees, such as apples, may need props to hold up branches if they bear heavily. (Proper pruning of the tree can reduce the need for supports.) If you think you will need to prop a tree, do so as soon as the fruit begins to swell. Use a 1-by-6-inch board with a notch in one end.

The board should be somewhat longer than the distance from the branch to the ground. Place the notch under the branch and about two-thirds of the distance from the trunk. Push the board under the branch until the branch begins to lift. The board should be leaning toward the tree at about a 20° angle. If the soil is too hard to anchor the end firmly, dig a shallow hole for the board.

Supporting shrubs

Shrubs seldom need support. If one does, place a single stake near its center and wrap twine around several branches and the stake.

TIPS FOR SUPPORTING TREES

■ Make the stakes as short as possible but tall enough to hold the tree upright.

■ Tie the trunk at just one level, near the tops of the stakes, to allow the tree to flex both above and below the tie.

■ Use tie materials that will not damage the tree trunk by chafing or girdling.

■ Use stakes and ties for as short a time as possible.

Supporting Flowers

Many flowering plants need support, especially when they are in full bloom. These include tall plants, plants with floppy stems, plants that produce heavy blossoms, and sprawling plants. For support, you can use stakes or wire cages, depending on the plant's needs. Be sure to fasten the stems to the support gently to prevent damage to the plant.

Ties

Many different materials can be used as ties; just be sure the tie won't damage the plant's soft stems. You can use twine, twist ties, insulated wire, polyethylene plastic tape, rubber strips, wire inside a piece of garden hose or bicycle-tire tubing, wide elastic bands, cloth strips, and many others. To keep the tie from sliding on the stake, tap small nails into the stake on each side of the tie or staple the tie to the wood.

Stakes

Use bamboo canes or 1-by-1-inch stakes as supports. Make sure the stake will be tall enough to support the mature plant. Insert the stake at planting time so you won't damage the roots by punching through them later. Before insertion, sharpen the bottom of the stake and wet the soil so the stake can be pushed in easily. As the plant blooms, there is a danger that a person bending over to smell the flower can be poked in the eye by the end of the stake, which is difficult to see from above. As the plant begins to bloom, cut off the top of the stake so it is below the level of the flower.

How to support flowers

Many devices are sold in garden centers and through garden supply catalogs. Most of these work well and are simple to use. If you want to make your own supports, here are a few ideas:

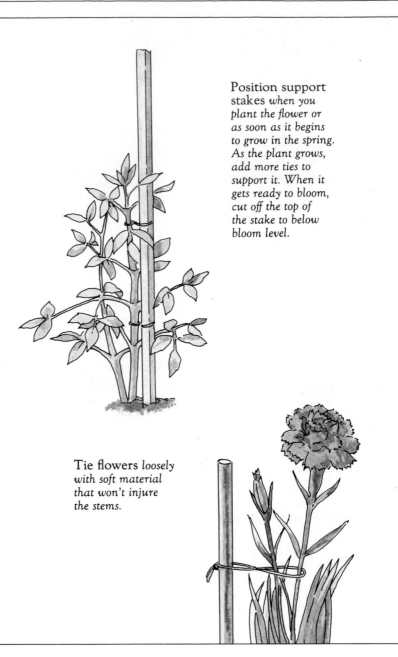

Position support stakes *when you plant the flower or as soon as it begins to grow in the spring. As the plant grows, add more ties to support it. When it gets ready to bloom, cut off the top of the stake to below bloom level.*

Tie flowers *loosely with soft material that won't injure the stems.*

Wire cages. Galvanized wire cages with 4-inch or 6-inch mesh are good for short plants with many stems. These are similar to tomato cages, but smaller. As the plant grows, the foliage grows through and hides the cage.

Woody prunings. Bushy herbaceous flowers can be trained on pruning clippings from trees or shrubs. Cut the woody prunings to a length of about 16 to 20 inches and insert them around the plant when it is 8 to 10 inches high. The developing foliage will hide the supports.

Wire hoops. Tie a ring of heavy wire to 2 or 3 stakes as the plant begins to grow in the spring, or when you plant it. As the plant grows, slide the hoop up the stakes. If the plant has many flower stalks, crisscross the hoop with a few pieces of string or lighter wire to keep the flowers from leaning on one edge.

Pins. Ground covers can be anchored with pins you make from foot-long sections of 16-gauge wire. Star jasmine, when trained as a ground cover, responds well to this treatment.

To contain
several flower
heads, *tie a single
loop of twine around
all of them and
around a stake. Add
more loops as the
flowers grow.*

A wire cage,
*similar to a tomato
cage, supports dense
masses of foliage.
As the plant grows,
the foliage hides
the cage.*

Pea brush—*dry
sticks or prunings
stuck in the ground
among flowers—
supports climbing
flowers, such as*

*sweet peas and
nasturtiums. Place
the brush early, as
soon as the flowers
begin to grow.*

Plants that need support

Tall plants that produce flowers
on a single stalk, such as delphinium, hollyhock, and gladiolus, may
need to be staked. When setting
out the plant, place the stake an
inch from the stalk or bulb. Shove
the stake as far into the ground as
necessary for stability. Tie the
flower stalk to the stake as soon as
it begins to develop. If you wait too
long, it can develop a bend that
will never straighten out. Tie the
stalk to the stake in a loose figure-8
pattern. As the stalk grows, add
higher ties.

Plants with many floppy stems,
including asters, coreopsis, and
carnations, may need support.
These bushy plants can often be
staked with pruning clippings; simply place a circle of branches
around the plant when it is 8 to 10
inches high. Peonies may be supported with low wire-basket cages.

Plants with heavy blooms, such
as chrysanthemums, may also need
to be staked. Insert a single stake at
planting time; then gather the developing stems around the stake.
Or you can place additional stakes

in a circle around the plant and
gather the stems into the circle
with twine around the stakes. For
dahlias, insert a stake 2 inches
from the tuberous root at planting
time. If many stems emerge, insert
3 more stakes around the first
stake, about a foot away, and tie
twine around the stakes at intervals to support the stems.

Sprawling plants can be supported with stakes and wire or twine or
with wire cages. You can use a wire
hoop taped or tied to 2 or 3 stakes
to support flowers that have a
great many stems.

SUPPORTING VINES

Vines can cover an unsightly wall or fence, grow over an arbor or other structure to provide shade, or be trained on a trellis to provide color in the garden.

How vines cling

Climbing vines cling to supports in three main ways:

■ Some vines, such as moonflowers, *twine* around a support. The vine stem may twist or spiral around supports, around itself, and around other stems of the vine. These vines climb well on thin, vertical supports. They are particularly attractive climbing a string or pole.

■ Other vines wrap *tendrils* around a support; these include passion vine, grapes, and sweet pea. Tendrils are modified leaves along the stem that reach out and wrap around string, wire, stakes, the plant itself, or other plants. These vines need small supports to cling to, such as wire or lath, since their tendrils usually can't encircle objects larger than a couple of inches in diameter.

■ Some other vines cling with *holdfasts*. These can be disk-shaped

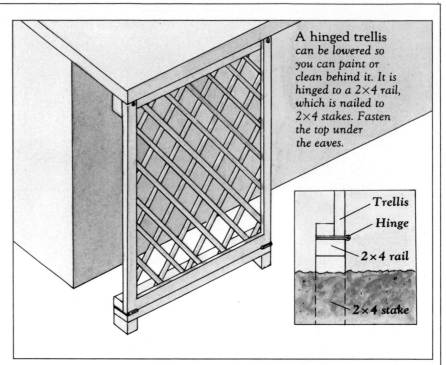

A hinged trellis *can be lowered so you can paint or clean behind it. It is hinged to a 2×4 rail, which is nailed to 2×4 stakes. Fasten the top under the eaves.*

Trellis — Hinge — 2×4 rail — 2×4 stake

suckers, hooking claws, small roots, or tendrils with disks that attach themselves to the support. Boston ivy and Virginia creeper are common examples. These vines will climb almost anything, including smooth walls.

Nonclimbing vines, such as some kinds of jasmine and climbing roses, must be given support by the gardener. They must be tied to a trellis, fence, or other structure.

Twining vines, *such as these moonflowers, look graceful climbing strings.*

HOW VINES CLING		
Vine	**How it clings**	**Leaves**
Bittersweet	Twining	Deciduous perennial
Boston ivy	Holdfasts	Deciduous perennial
Bougainvillea	Must be tied	Evergreen perennial
Carolina jessamine	Twining	Evergreen perennial
Clematis	Twining	Deciduous perennial
Climbing hydrangea	Aerial rootlets	Deciduous perennial
Climbing roses	Must be tied	Evergreen perennial
Common jasmine	Twining	Evergreen perennial
Creeping fig	Holdfasts	Evergreen perennial
English ivy	Holdfasts	Evergreen perennial
Grape	Tendrils	Deciduous perennial
Honeysuckle	Twining	Deciduous perennial
Japanese honeysuckle	Twining	Evergreen perennial
Moonflower	Twining	Annual
Morning glory	Twining	Annual
Nasturtium	Twining	Annual
Passion vine	Tendrils	Evergreen perennial
Potato vine	Twining	Evergreen perennial
Scarlet runner bean	Twining	Annual
Star jasmine	Twining	Evergreen perennial
Sweet pea	Tendrils	Annual
Trumpet creeper	Aerial rootlets	Deciduous perennial
Trumpet vine	Tendrils	Evergreen perennial
Virginia creeper	Holdfasts	Deciduous perennial
Wisteria	Twining	Deciduous perennial

Methods of supporting vines

Vines can be trained in many ways. Examine your landscape to see what the possibilities are. Here are some suggestions:

■ When training a vine flat against a wall, use spacers to allow for some air circulation in back of the vine; this will help prevent plant disease and damage to the house paint. (English ivy and other plants that cling with rootlets will damage paint.) Vines planted close to a wood wall will also trap moisture,

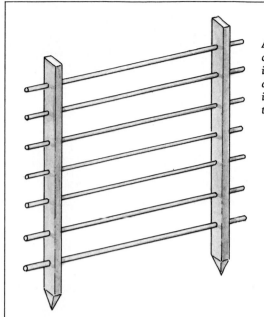

A ladder trellis *can be made of ¾-inch or larger dowling. Drill holes in 2×4 or 4×4 posts to receive them.*

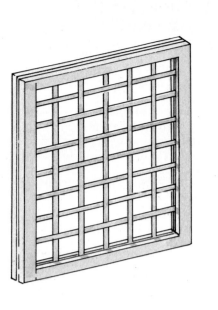

A basket-weave trellis *of lath is sandwiched between 1×2 or 1×4 boards. This lightweight trellis can be mounted anywhere.*

Support heavy vines, *such as grapes and wisteria, with a substantial arbor. To keep it from becoming too massive, prune the vine back to a basic scaffold each winter.*

can weigh hundreds of pounds. When building trellises for these vines, make the supporting framework strong enough to hold their weight. Every few years, prune the vine heavily in early spring or just before a period of rapid growth to remove some of the excess wood that accumulates. Establish a basic structure of woody vines and laterals that cover the trellis or arbor well, and prune back to that structure. In early spring you can prune heavily, even removing all the leaves from evergreen vines, without damage.

Vines in trees

Vines may look beautiful climbing into a tree, but a vigorous vine can grow over the top of the tree and shade it. When this happens, the tree drops its leaves in the shaded portion and can even die. It's better to keep vines from climbing trees, or to restrict them to the main trunk by pruning them every year. However, training a vine into a dead tree is often a way to extend its usefulness for several years. If a favorite tree is weakening and you are afraid you might lose it, plant a wisteria, some ivy, or a grapevine at its base. In about three years, the vine will be well into the tree. If the tree lives, remove the vine or restrict its growth to the trunk.

keeping the wall damp and promoting dry rot.

■ Twining vines, such as morning glory, are attractive trained to vertical strings along the side of the house. Tie the strings to nails or dowels in the eaves at the top, loop them around nails in a board at the bottom, then tie the string to itself with a slip knot. Later, as the string stretches, you can take up the slack by sliding the slip knot up the string. Train one or two vines to each string. To keep the trellis neat, don't let the vines cross from one string to another.

■ To hide old stumps or unsightly snags, cover them with fast-growing annual vines. Moonflower,

morning glory, or scarlet runner bean can completely cover a stump in only a few weeks.

■ Make a hinged lath frame that can be lowered from a wall so you can clean or paint the wall or have access to the vine.

■ Tie lightweight vines with twine, rubber bands, polyethylene tape, or plastic- or paper-reinforced wire ties (twist ties). For heavier vines, use insulated wire, rubber tree ties, or elastic bands.

Trellises for heavy vines

Some vines, such as English ivy, wisteria, and grape, can grow to be tree-sized plants. After 5 or 10 years, their trunk and branches

SUPPORTING VEGETABLES

Only some vegetables need to be supported when they mature; climbers, mainly beans and peas, are the most obvious. Tomatoes are easier to pick and are less susceptible to sun scald if supported. Support is not essential for other sprawling plants such as squash or melons, but they will develop more and cleaner fruits in small spaces if they are given support.

When wind is a problem, the tall-stemmed plants in the cabbage family, particularly broccoli and Brussels sprouts, can easily be blown over, especially if the ground is wet. Stake supports are advisable under these conditions.

Climbing vegetables

Beans. Pole beans are twining plants, and as the name implies, their most common support is a pole. (Bush beans don't need support.) Most beans can grow to cover a 7-foot pole, so be sure to use one that is long enough. Because beans may slide to the bottom of a smooth pole when shaken by the wind, use a rough pole, wrap the pole loosely with jute twine, or drive small nails into the pole to keep the beans from sliding.

Make a hole in the ground with a crowbar, then force the pole into the hole. Plant 10 beans around each pole; thin to 4 or 6 after they germinate. For greater strength, tie three or more poles together at the top to make a bean "teepee."

Peas. Peas hold to their support with *tendrils*—modified leaves that wrap tightly around small objects. The two most common supports for peas are brush—dead branches stuck in the ground—and some sort of fence. A pea fence is supported by fence posts; it can consist of woven wire fencing, chicken wire, or smooth wire strung between the posts.

Tall peas need supports about 5 feet high. Low peas grow well without supports, but harvesting will be easier if the plants are trained on a fence about 2 feet high. Build the fence or put the brush support in place first, then plant peas in rows on each side of it. You may have to place the young vines on their support at first, but from then on they will climb without help.

Tomatoes. Tomatoes are the all-time favorite among vegetable gardeners. The support must keep the fruit away from slugs and snails, allow the foliage to shield the fruit from sun scald and cracking, and allow good air circulation. Here are some strategies you can use for growing tomatoes:

■ Don't support them at all. Allow each vine about 25 square feet in which to sprawl. The tomatoes will be more difficult to pick, and many will be lost to sun scald, insects, and slugs, but the vines will grow and bear well.

■ Tie the vines to a single stake. The stake should be at least 2 by 2 inches square and driven well into the ground. Plants of the large varieties of tomatoes can weigh over 50 pounds, so they need strong support. Place one plant at the base of each stake and allow only one or two vines to develop from each plant. Tie the vines loosely to the stake with soft rags or twine every foot or so. Pinch off the sprouts that grow at the base of each leaf. About 4 weeks before the first fall frost, begin pinching off newly formed blossoms, since fruit set from these blossoms won't have time to ripen. This method takes regular attention but develops a high yield (per square foot) of large fruit.

■ Tomato cages are cylinders of wood or wire used to support the plant. Several commercial models are available, but you can easily make your own from welded wire fencing or concrete reinforcing wire. For a large tomato variety, make the cage 24 inches in diameter and 60 inches high. In cool climates, you can wrap the cage in plastic (creating a greenhouse effect) to encourage rapid development. Tuck any emerging stems back into the cage, except when

Tomato cages *must be made of wire mesh large enough to reach through.*

Stake tomatoes *and train them to 1 or 2 vines for the highest production. Tie them at 1-foot intervals.*

you want to prune excess vegetative growth. Make sure the wire cage has 4-inch-square holes so you can reach through to remove the tomatoes easily. The wire may be sold as hog wire or fencing wire in 50-foot rolls, 4 to 6 feet high. Although some fencing is thick enough to be self-supporting, a 2-by-4-inch stake driven 2 feet into the ground and extending 4 feet up the cage gives needed stability in the wind. Concrete reinforcing

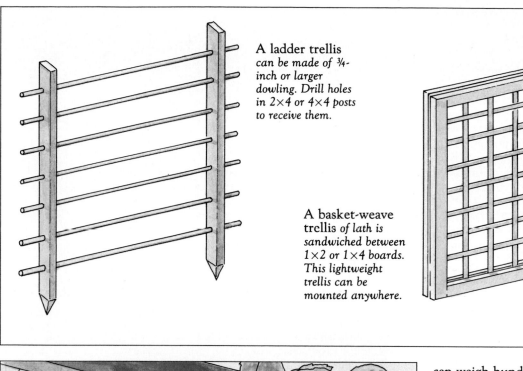

A ladder trellis *can be made of ¾-inch or larger dowling. Drill holes in 2×4 or 4×4 posts to receive them.*

A basket-weave trellis *of lath is sandwiched between 1×2 or 1×4 boards. This lightweight trellis can be mounted anywhere.*

Support heavy vines, *such as grapes and wisteria, with a substantial arbor. To keep it from becoming too massive, prune the vine back to a basic scaffold each winter.*

keeping the wall damp and promoting dry rot.

■ Twining vines, such as morning glory, are attractive trained to vertical strings along the side of the house. Tie the strings to nails or dowels in the eaves at the top, loop them around nails in a board at the bottom, then tie the string to itself with a slip knot. Later, as the string stretches, you can take up the slack by sliding the slip knot up the string. Train one or two vines to each string. To keep the trellis neat, don't let the vines cross from one string to another.

■ To hide old stumps or unsightly snags, cover them with fast-growing annual vines. Moonflower,

morning glory, or scarlet runner bean can completely cover a stump in only a few weeks.

■ Make a hinged lath frame that can be lowered from a wall so you can clean or paint the wall or have access to the vine.

■ Tie lightweight vines with twine, rubber bands, polyethylene tape, or plastic- or paper-reinforced wire ties (twist ties). For heavier vines, use insulated wire, rubber tree ties, or elastic bands.

Trellises for heavy vines

Some vines, such as English ivy, wisteria, and grape, can grow to be tree-sized plants. After 5 or 10 years, their trunk and branches

can weigh hundreds of pounds. When building trellises for these vines, make the supporting framework strong enough to hold their weight. Every few years, prune the vine heavily in early spring or just before a period of rapid growth to remove some of the excess wood that accumulates. Establish a basic structure of woody vines and laterals that cover the trellis or arbor well, and prune back to that structure. In early spring you can prune heavily, even removing all the leaves from evergreen vines, without damage.

Vines in trees

Vines may look beautiful climbing into a tree, but a vigorous vine can grow over the top of the tree and shade it. When this happens, the tree drops its leaves in the shaded portion and can even die. It's better to keep vines from climbing trees, or to restrict them to the main trunk by pruning them every year. However, training a vine into a dead tree is often a way to extend its usefulness for several years. If a favorite tree is weakening and you are afraid you might lose it, plant a wisteria, some ivy, or a grapevine at its base. In about three years, the vine will be well into the tree. If the tree lives, remove the vine or restrict its growth to the trunk.

SUPPORTING VEGETABLES

Only some vegetables need to be supported when they mature; climbers, mainly beans and peas, are the most obvious. Tomatoes are easier to pick and are less susceptible to sun scald if supported. Support is not essential for other sprawling plants such as squash or melons, but they will develop more and cleaner fruits in small spaces if they are given support.

When wind is a problem, the tall-stemmed plants in the cabbage family, particularly broccoli and Brussels sprouts, can easily be blown over, especially if the ground is wet. Stake supports are advisable under these conditions.

Climbing vegetables

Beans. Pole beans are twining plants, and as the name implies, their most common support is a pole. (Bush beans don't need support.) Most beans can grow to cover a 7-foot pole, so be sure to use one that is long enough. Because beans may slide to the bottom of a smooth pole when shaken by the wind, use a rough pole, wrap the pole loosely with jute twine, or drive small nails into the pole to keep the beans from sliding.

Make a hole in the ground with a crowbar, then force the pole into the hole. Plant 10 beans around each pole; thin to 4 or 6 after they germinate. For greater strength, tie three or more poles together at the top to make a bean "teepee."

Peas. Peas hold to their support with *tendrils*—modified leaves that wrap tightly around small objects. The two most common supports for peas are brush—dead branches stuck in the ground—and some sort of fence. A pea fence is supported by fence posts; it can consist of woven wire fencing, chicken wire, or smooth wire strung between the posts.

Tall peas need supports about 5 feet high. Low peas grow well without supports, but harvesting will be easier if the plants are trained on a fence about 2 feet high. Build the fence or put the brush support in place first, then plant peas in rows on each side of it. You may have to place the young vines on their support at first, but from then on they will climb without help.

Tomatoes. Tomatoes are the all-time favorite among vegetable gardeners. The support must keep the fruit away from slugs and snails, allow the foliage to shield the fruit from sun scald and cracking, and allow good air circulation. Here are some strategies you can use for growing tomatoes:

■ Don't support them at all. Allow each vine about 25 square feet in which to sprawl. The tomatoes will be more difficult to pick, and many will be lost to sun scald, insects, and slugs, but the vines will grow and bear well.

■ Tie the vines to a single stake. The stake should be at least 2 by 2 inches square and driven well into the ground. Plants of the large varieties of tomatoes can weigh over 50 pounds, so they need strong support. Place one plant at the base of each stake and allow only one or two vines to develop from each plant. Tie the vines loosely to the stake with soft rags or twine every foot or so. Pinch off the sprouts that grow at the base of each leaf. About 4 weeks before the first fall frost, begin pinching off newly formed blossoms, since fruit set from these blossoms won't have time to ripen. This method takes regular attention but develops a high yield (per square foot) of large fruit.

■ Tomato cages are cylinders of wood or wire used to support the plant. Several commercial models are available, but you can easily make your own from welded wire fencing or concrete reinforcing wire. For a large tomato variety, make the cage 24 inches in diameter and 60 inches high. In cool climates, you can wrap the cage in plastic (creating a greenhouse effect) to encourage rapid development. Tuck any emerging stems back into the cage, except when

Tomato cages *must be made of wire mesh large enough to reach through.*

Stake tomatoes *and train them to 1 or 2 vines for the highest production. Tie them at 1-foot intervals.*

you want to prune excess vegetative growth. Make sure the wire cage has 4-inch-square holes so you can reach through to remove the tomatoes easily. The wire may be sold as hog wire or fencing wire in 50-foot rolls, 4 to 6 feet high. Although some fencing is thick enough to be self-supporting, a 2-by-4-inch stake driven 2 feet into the ground and extending 4 feet up the cage gives needed stability in the wind. Concrete reinforcing

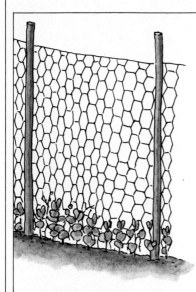

Peas or beans *could be trained on this simple support. The same arrangement works for plants in the ground.*

Pea brush *is an old-fashioned way to support peas. The brush is stronger if it is tied in bunches, as shown here.*

Pea fencing *can be made of chicken wire. Plant a row of peas on each side and help them get started on the wire.*

This cucumber trellis *is self-supporting. It can be hinged at the top for easy storage. Make it large enough to reach into easily, since the cucumbers hang down inside.*

Pole beans *climb rough poles most easily. Tie the poles together at the top for strength. This teepee is also an inviting playhouse for a child.*

wire is made of thicker wire, but since it is not galvanized, it will rust. But a cage made of it will last for several years. Short cages will work well for bushy or *determinate* tomatoes; taller cages accommodate vining or *indeterminate* types.

Sprawling vegetables

Melons and squash are usually grown sprawling on the ground, but their vines can also be tied to wood or wire supports. If well supported, the neck of the vine next to the fruit can withstand more weight than most gardeners expect. Fruit that might tear a stem can be supported with slings made of rags or old nylon stockings.

Vining cucumbers will climb on strings and on wood or wire racks. Bush cucumbers hug the ground; their fruit can be kept off the ground with low ladder- or lattice-type supports.

Vegetables with tall stems

Use a single stake and twine to hold broccoli, Brussels sprouts, and cauliflower plants upright in windy locations. Place the stake between the plant and the direction of the prevailing wind.

PROTECTING FROM WEATHER

Nature has a particular climate and germination time for every plant. Part of the gardener's art lies in growing plants outside the regions to which they are adapted. Here are some techniques for stretching the natural boundaries of plant growth.

Cold, sun, heat, wind, and rain define the limits of our gardening activity, unless we garden in the controlled environment of a greenhouse. A gardener must be aware of changing weather conditions as the cycle of the seasons progresses. To some extent, you can modify outdoor conditions by protective devices, including shade barriers against sun or coverings against frost. However, such measures must be heroic to ensure the safety of plants inappropriate for your region. After you select plants suitable to your locale, you must find a favorable site in the garden for their sun and shade needs.

The elements often put sharp restrictions on plants. Each plant has a cold and heat range beyond which it won't flourish. If you push a plant to the edge of that range, wind can intensify the environmental stress. Wind requires a plant to draw up proportionally more water to transpire through its leaves. Wind and rain can devastate plants by knocking them over, breaking branches, and washing away soil. Stress from cold, heat, wind, and rain can leave a plant in a weakened condition, unable to rally effectively against insect or disease attack.

A piece of corrugated fiberglass roofing forms a miniature greenhouse that allows these tomato seedlings to be set out weeks earlier than would be possible otherwise.

Weather and plant selection

A wise gardener will take the time to choose plants appropriate for the weather conditions of the region. Inappropriate plants can be a problem, especially among our mobile populace (as when a Chicagoan transplanted to Phoenix attempts to recreate a lush midwestern lawn in the desert).

The intensity of summer sun and heat and the extent of frost and hard winter freezes will determine what perennial plants can flourish at your homesite. Your local Cooperative Extension Agent can furnish a list of such plants for your region. Similarly, the number of days between your last spring frost and first autumn frost will determine your growing season for annual flowers and for vegetables.

Weather and plant siting

The amount of sun or shade a plant needs is a major concern. Locate shade-loving plants under trees or in sheltered areas. Shade-loving impatiens flourish, for example, in a flower bed under the drip line of an oak tree, but they will wither in bright sun.

Avoid mixing drought-requiring and water-loving plants in the same setting. For instance, avoid shading a water-loving azalea with a drought-requiring oak, which

will succumb to crown rot in the damp, cool environment needed by the azalea.

The effects of cold

Coolness, even without frost, can damage some plants. Gradually acclimatize seedlings and plants raised indoors to cool outdoor conditions in a warm environment. Cold frames, hotbeds, and lath houses perform this role in spring.

The last frost in the spring and the first frost in the fall are likely to be *radiation* frosts. Radiation frosts occur on clear, still nights as the heat of the soil is radiated to the dark sky. Either wind or a cloud layer will usually prevent a radiation frost. A clearing night following a day of rain is especially likely to engender the first frost of the fall.

If you can protect tender plants against this first frost, you may get several more weeks of growth from them. The easiest protection against a radiation frost is a covering. An old sheet or a piece of cardboard is often all that is needed. Plants in containers can be moved under the eaves, which will offer them enough protection.

Another technique for preventing frost damage is to employ heat sources. Many small heat sources are more effective than a single large one. Use charcoal, jellied alcohol, heater cables, or electric lights. For many home gardeners, a simple and practical solution involves using heater cables or a single incandescent electric bulb at the base of favorite plants, with the plant covered by plastic.

Watering adequately helps protect a plant during frost and cold. If a plant has adequate soil moisture to replace moisture transpired through its leaves, the plant will be less likely to suffer damage. In a hard-freeze region, water the garden until the ground freezes. After the ground freezes, mulch plants so that frost will not penetrate deeply into the ground. Use mulches of chopped leaves, wood chips, straw, evergreen boughs, and pine needles. Watering and mulching can reduce the desiccating damage caused by winter winds drawing water from leaves, warm sun stimulating leaves to transpire, and frozen soil withholding its water (as ice) from the roots.

Periodic thawing and freezing of the soil can heave small plants out of the ground. Once frozen, it's better if a plant stays frozen until spring. Alternate freezing and thawing of water-filled cells causes cells to burst. Tree bark sometimes suffers injury, splitting vertically, when sun warms the tree cells on the outside. The warm cells then refreeze quickly, causing tension between the outer and inner bark that splits the tree.

Snow accumulating on branches in cold weather can crack trees or break limbs. Prevent this problem with judicious pruning to remove weak tree crotches. Shake the snow from branches of low-branching trees if you see the tree is in danger, especially from wet snow and ice in a windy period.

The effects of sun and heat

Bright sun and excessive heat, especially if accompanied by wind, can dry plants quickly. Even if the ground is moist, plants may be unable to draw up enough moisture through their roots to balance the moisture transpired from their leaves. The plant wilts as a defensive mechanism. When water is inadequate, the water needed to hold cell walls rigid is not present and the plant collapses. Usually, if

A coldframe protects young seedlings from excess heat and cold or too bright sun. On warm days, and as plants become stronger, you can prop open the cover.

the soil is moist, the plant will recover without damage after the period of stress.

However, plants don't always escape unscathed, especially if the soil is dry. Leaves burn at their edges or shrivel up entirely. The bark of dark-colored trees may develop sun-scald roughness, a vulnerable opening for future fungal or bacterial invasion.

Shade-loving plants, which often also like a moist soil environment, frequently suffer stress in times of heat and bright sunlight. Water your camellias, rhododendrons, and azaleas attentively in these circumstances because their shallow roots dry out quickly.

The effects of wind and rain

Rain can wash out soil, pack soil, dirty plants, break stems, ruin flowers, and create conditions favorable to disease. Rain with wind is more than twice as damaging. Wind alone can do physical damage to plants, cause excess water loss, dry out soil quickly, and blow fungal spores to new host plants.

Some of wind's havoc is more subtle. Much damage can occur

because of winds blowing incessantly over evergreen plants in winter. In winter the deciduous plants drop their leaves, partly to protect themselves in the absence of water. Some plants, such as the California buckeye, drop their leaves in summer during the dry period. Evergreen plants can transpire some water through their leaves in winter, but the amount will be reduced because at cold temperatures growth slows and eventually ceases. But warm winter sun can stimulate leaves to transpire while the groundwater remains frozen. Wind makes further demand on the moisture of these leaves. Incessant winds draw moisture from the leaves, requiring the plant to draw up moisture from the ground if possible. This will be difficult if the ground is frozen. Leaf burn, scorching, sunburn, and windburn describe the appearance of leaf damage around the tip, edges, or on the entire leaf, which may turn brown, shrivel up, and fall. In extreme cases the entire plant will perish.

You have several defenses against these harmful conditions. The most important defense is to choose plants that are well suited to your region. Protect plants from winter winds with screens or site the plant away from the wind. Wrap the bark of trees that are subject to damage. Prune plants to be more compact so they offer less wind resistance. Move plants in containers to more protected locations. Be aware that container plants freeze and thaw more quickly than plants in the ground.

Not all wind flow through your garden is harmful. In fact, if you allow some wind to pass through your garden, pockets of cold air won't collect. Dammed air is naturally cooler and frostier than flowing air. When wind approaches, break its flow with permeable barriers, such as loose hedges, rather than with absolute dams, such as solid walls. The force of the wind is like that of a wave of water hitting a barrier. If the barrier is solid, the wave tumbles turbulently over the top. If the barrier has openings, such as the space between pilings on a jetty, the force of the wave diffuses. Wind will travel over or through your windbreaks in the same manner. Deciduous trees and shrubs can be shade protectors in summer and allow wind passage in winter. Evergreens, forming a solid, impenetrable mass, trap cold air and increase frost damage. Ideally, a middle ground must be found between sufficient air flow to reduce frost and not enough wind flow to create desiccating conditions. Rhododendrons and azaleas are especially sensitive to winter windburn damage from continuous, dry winds.

Often the most difficult weather situations combine stressful conditions. Summer thunderstorms can bring on a cluster of potentially damaging weather factors. Hard rains and high winds, especially when they occur together, can do physical damage to plants. The weight of water on limbs may endanger a tree that can withstand wind alone, without the weight of water. Prune trees to develop strong crotches that can withstand wind and water stress. Be sure that trees are staked or guyed during the rainy season. Gradual water saturation of the ground will weaken the root hold and make the tree subject to blowing over.

Top: These cloches are panes of glass held together with patented clips. This type can be joined at the ends to form long tunnels.

Bottom: A simple unheated greenhouse extends the gardening season by a month or two. In mild climates, they allow gardening all year long.

GETTING A JUMP ON SPRING

You can get a jump on spring by starting seeds well before the weather is warm enough for planting directly in the garden. You can plant seeds indoors, or outdoors in a cold frame, hotbed, or individual covers to get an early start. These simple structures will provide warmth and protection for the developing seedlings.

Coordinate your planting date with the estimated last spring frost date for your area (see page 40). It should take about 6 to 8 weeks for germination and seedling development before plants will be ready to be moved into the garden.

Building a cold frame

A cold frame is a box with a transparent, usually sloping, top. It collects heat from the sun during the day and retains warmth at night. Typical early spring weather is ideal for cold-frame use; the days are warm and sunny, but the nights are still too cold for unprotected young seedlings.

A cold frame built in the garden usually has no bottom. A layer of garden soil or planting mix is used for starting the seeds. The sides can be made from wood, bricks, hay bales, or any other material that can support the top and provide some insulation. Paint wood surfaces or treat with a copper sulfate preservative to reduce rotting.

You can use an old sash window as the top for a cold frame. Fiberglass, plastic sheeting, or other transparent materials can also be used. Since you will need to open the top often to provide ventilation, make sure it fits tightly but won't be difficult to open. A typical cold frame is 3 feet wide and 6 feet long; the back is 18 inches high and the front is 12 inches high.

In order to take full advantage of available sunlight, locate the cold frame so that the sloped top faces south. Placing it against a south wall will increase heat accumulation. A cold frame should be equipped with a thermometer.

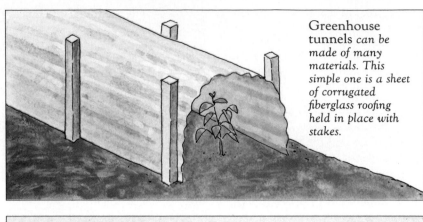

Greenhouse tunnels can be made of many materials. This simple one is a sheet of corrugated fiberglass roofing held in place with stakes.

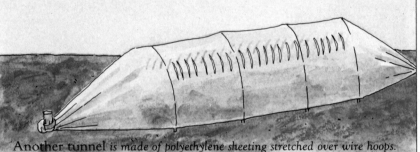

Another tunnel is made of polyethylene sheeting stretched over wire hoops. A commercially available type has slits in the sides and doesn't need ventilating.

Individual plant covers can be made of plastic jugs with the bottom removed.

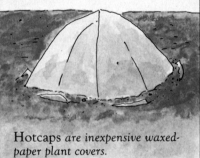

Hotcaps are inexpensive waxed-paper plant covers.

Building a hotbed

A hotbed is simply a cold frame with a heat source. Steam, hot water, hot air, electricity, or decomposing manure can be used to provide heat. An electric heating cable that can be plugged into a household socket is the easiest system to install.

Heating cables are available in a variety of sizes. The cables are described according to length and wattage. A 30-foot 200-watt cable is typical. In an average area you should use 12 watts of heating power per square foot of hotbed. If you live in a very cold area you may want to double the watts per square foot.

Use small pegs to hold the cable in place while you wind it back and forth across the bed to provide an even distribution of the heat. Cover the cable with a piece of hardware cloth to protect it; then cover the hardware cloth with 2 inches of sand.

Manure gives off heat as it decomposes. To heat a hotbed with manure, dig a pit under the box and fill it with a foot or more of manure. You can use whatever manure is available, but it should be fresh. Bagged manure is usually

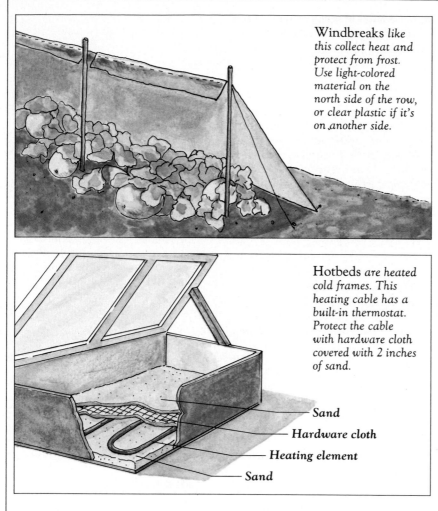

Windbreaks like this collect heat and protect from frost. Use light-colored material on the north side of the row, or clear plastic if it's on another side.

Hotbeds are heated cold frames. This heating cable has a built-in thermostat. Protect the cable with hardware cloth covered with 2 inches of sand.

— *Sand*

— *Hardware cloth*

— *Heating element*

— *Sand*

already decomposed and will not produce much heat. Put several inches of topsoil on top of the manure, and pack slightly. The manure may take a few days to begin producing heat.

Using cold frames and hotbeds

Starting seeds in a hotbed, or in a cold frame in milder climates, has several advantages over indoor germination. When indoors, plants are in an environment that is always warm. A seedling that gets warm days and cool nights will be sturdier. The low humidity inside a house is also detrimental to good seedling development.

In cold climates a cold frame can be used to harden seedlings that have been germinated indoors. Hardening plants is accomplished by placing them for a few days in a location that is cooler and perhaps sunnier than the germination area.

Most seedlings that have developed indoors need to be toughened before planting outdoors or they will be shocked by the abrupt climate change.

Ventilation is essential to release excess heat and moisture. Plants will overheat if a cold frame or hotbed is kept closed on a sunny day. If the weather seems warm, prop the box open during the day and close it at night. Thermometers will help tell if the box is too hot or cold, but daily checking and adjustment is the best control method.

An insulating cover, such as a rug, blanket, or piece of plywood, can be placed over the cold frame to help conserve heat at night.

Individual covers

You can create individual covers around plants in the ground to capture sun warmth and to protect vulnerable seedlings from wind. See other frost-protection ideas on page 136. Individual covers need to be checked regularly and opened or ventilated when heat builds up inside.

Make "hotcaps" of plastic by forming a cone stapled to a stake, or buy commercially available hotcaps of waxed paper. Hotcaps collect sun warmth during the day and prevent loss of that warmth at night. They also raise the humidity level and reduce wind flow.

Fashion corrugated fiberglass panels into greenhouse tunnels by bending the panel and then wiring the bottom together or by holding the panels in a bent tunnel shape with stakes.

Cut the bottoms from translucent plastic milk containers to make individual covers; the hole at the top will provide ventilation. Cut off part of the handle if you want to push a stake through the carton to anchor it.

Stretch long sheets of plastic over a rigid wire frame that is set up along a row of plants. Cover the ends with nylon netting to make them birdproof.

Cover transplanted seedlings with plastic margarine tubs to protect from sun, wind, and predators in their first days after planting.

Form plastic sheeting, reinforced with wire, into cylinders or long semicircular tubes that can cover rows of plants.

Make A-frames of clear plastic stretched over wood. Large A-frames can cover a whole row of plants. A-frames that are hinged at the top are easy to store for reuse.

Reflective surfaces, such as aluminum foil, white fabric, or white paint, increase the heat and light that fall on a plant. Use reflectors to speed and strengthen development of young seedlings and to help ripen crops that need more heat or light than the local climate provides.

Make a low lean-to of paper, fabric, or another light-colored material on the north or upwind side of a vegetable row. The lean-to shouldn't shade the plants. It reflects light and heat, and blocks wind.

PLANNING A GREENHOUSE

A greenhouse is an ideal environment for plants. Temperature, humidity, and light can be controlled to suit the plants, and the greenhouse provides protection against weather. Lights, heaters, coolers, and watering systems can all be controlled by electric timers, freeing the greenhouse owner from much time-consuming work.

Designing a greenhouse

Size, cost, available space, and time considerations will all play a part in your design decisions. Permanent units are available in many different sizes and shapes, ranging from window-sized attachments and small freestanding units for apartment patios to large commercial units with all-automatic heating and watering. Heaters and other accessories can be added later to upgrade any unit. Gardening magazines are a good place to find the addresses of companies selling plans, kits, and prefabricated units.

Leave room to expand. Most greenhouse owners find they don't have enough space to do all they'd like to do.

Climate factors

If you live in a climate with moderate summers, choose the sunniest location possible. If you live where the summers are very hot, build your greenhouse next to a tree or building that can provide some shade and protection from the afternoon sun. You will especially want sun for your greenhouse during the winter, so keep in mind the lower angle of the sun in winter and make sure that the greenhouse will not be in the shade. Trees that lose their leaves in winter will not obstruct sunlight after their leaves have dropped.

If your site is especially windy, you'll want a sturdy frame, well-fitted windows, and weatherstripping to keep out drafts.

Types of greenhouses

Greenhouses can be freestanding or attached. Freestanding units have ample interior space and are easy to expand, but utilities to service them can be costly to install and maintain. Attached greenhouses are positioned against a building, such as a house, garage, or shed. These lean-tos are generally cheaper and easier to build and maintain than freestanding greenhouses, and utilities may be readily available from the adjacent building. You save on construction costs, of course, for the already-completed wall. Lean-tos sometimes allow direct entrance to the house, which can be an incentive to use the greenhouse in bad weather. In some settings, a lean-to can double as a garden room or a passive solar space-heating unit for the house. But lean-tos also have some disadvantages; they often have less light and space and cannot be expanded as easily as freestanding units.

Glazing

Greenhouses can be covered with glass, plastic film, or fiberglass. Glass is expensive, but it is still the preferred glazing for permanent greenhouses because it is strong and durable. Larger panes permit better light transmission and will present fewer heat-leaking joints than smaller panes do. When sunlight hits glass at a right angle, 90 percent of the light passes through to the inside. Other glazing materials are not able to transmit light as effectively.

Polyethylene and other plastic films are the least expensive glazing materials. Because polyethylene must be changed each year, it is usually used with temporary greenhouses or greenhouses that have only seasonal use. Some new and tough plastic films can withstand up to 5 years of use, but they are subject to tearing and wind damage even before the plastic degrades from sunlight's ultraviolet rays.

Fiberglass panels are a familiar material for patio coverings. For a greenhouse, use the most translucent fiberglass available. Sunlight

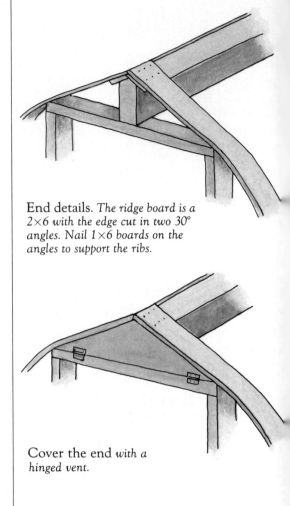

End details. *The ridge board is a 2×6 with the edge cut in two 30° angles. Nail 1×6 boards on the angles to support the ribs.*

Cover the end *with a hinged vent.*

passing through fiberglass panels produces a soft, shadowless light. The rigidity and durability of fiberglass are impressive. Unlike glass, it can withstand a blow without breaking. Sunlight's ultraviolet rays erode the surface of fiberglass, exposing the glass fibers and roughening the surface. This rough surface catches dirt. After a few years, the amount of light that passes through the fiberglass is reduced considerably.

Vinyl and acrylic panels can also be used for greenhouses. Evaluate new glazing products according to their cost, durability, and ability to transmit light.

Framing

Metal and wood are the principal framing materials used for large

This simple greenhouse has ribs made by cutting 20 strips 4 inches wide by 8 feet long from a sheet of ¼-inch exterior-grade plywood. Nail them to the ridge board, which is supported on 2×4 door frames.

The foundation is 12 feet by 8½ feet. It is made of two 1×8 boards cleated together and staked to the ground.

greenhouse units. Plastic ribs or bent PVC sprinkler pipe can support some small units. Metal frames may be aluminum or galvanized iron; both are strong and weather-resistant. Iron is stronger, but aluminum is lighter and easier to work with. Aluminum is virtually maintenance-free, but galvanized iron needs occasional painting. Because metals transmit heat readily, winter heating may be more costly for metal-frame units.

Wood is attractive and easy to work with when constructing a homemade unit. Redwood and cedar are the most durable woods. While regular repainting will reduce rotting, all woods will eventually rot. Wood does not transmit heat as readily as metal, so wood-frame greenhouses will be slightly less expensive to heat during the cold winter months.

Heating and cooling

The amount of heat your greenhouse will need depends on the climate and on the needs of the plants you'll be growing. If your winter climate is severe, plan some insulation devices for the greenhouse. Place blankets or rigid panels on the greenhouse during the coldest periods. Using insulating blankets during daylight hours will restrict light, but a lowered light level is preferable to cold damage.

Your greenhouse can be an effective passive solar collector if you have some way to store the heat. Water is an excellent medium for collecting and storing heat. Some greenhouse gardeners place their benches over metal drums of water. Paint the drums black to absorb maximum heat.

Gas and electric heating units can provide supplemental heat.

Gas systems are generally more complicated and costly to install, and electric heaters are more costly to operate. Electric heating cables laid on the benches will keep soil in the pots warm but will not increase the temperature inside the greenhouse. Cables will encourage faster rooting of cuttings and quicker germination and growth of seedlings, even in summer when no other heating is needed.

Arrange a ventilation system with openings near the floor and an outlet at the high point in the roof to create a flow of air through the greenhouse. You may want to install a fan system to assist this ventilating air flow when heat builds up.

PROTECTING PLANTS IN WINTER

Winter is a perilous time for garden plants. Leaves become scorched if plants cannot obtain enough moisture. Sudden temperature changes can cause the bark on trees and shrubs to split, and alternate freezing and thawing can break plant roots. Plants that are not adapted to cold weather can freeze and die.

Good planning is the key to protecting your garden from cold and frost damage. If you anticipate the need for mulches or other protective devices, get them ready in the fall.

Protecting against winter scorch

What many people assume to be frost damage on trees and shrubs is often actually scorch caused by a lack of available water. This happens when the soil is frozen and cannot yield water. Wind on a sunny winter day is especially damaging to plants.

Give plants a thorough watering in the fall, so that the soil is moist when it freezes. Mulching the ground around plants reduces soil freezing and makes it easier for roots to continue functioning during cold weather. Shade plants during the winter with snow fencing, lath, or other covers.

Winter bark scald

A sudden temperature change as the sun emerges from behind a cloud and warms the bark of a tree on a cold day can kill the bark. Sun scald is most likely to occur on the southwest side of the trunk on sunny days.

Paint the trunk with whitewash or white interior latex paint, or shade it with burlap, tree wrap, or a board for protection.

Protection against frost heaving

Cycles of alternate freezing and thawing of soil may cause plants to be shoved up out of the ground,

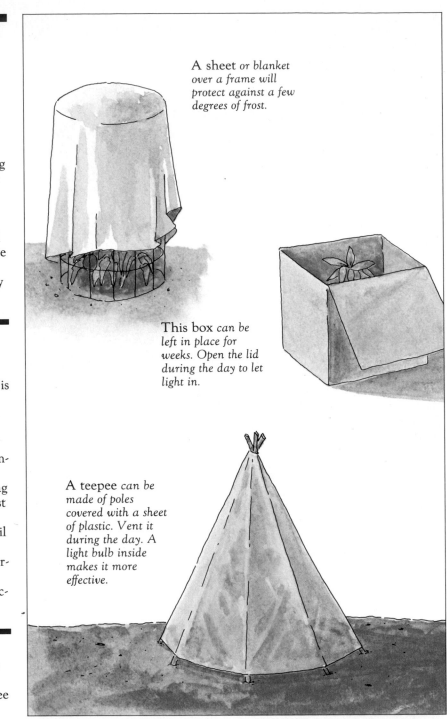

A sheet *or blanket over a frame will protect against a few degrees of frost.*

This box *can be left in place for weeks. Open the lid during the day to let light in.*

A teepee *can be made of poles covered with a sheet of plastic. Vent it during the day. A light bulb inside makes it more effective.*

breaking and exposing some of the roots. This is known as *heaving*. Small, shallow-rooted plants are particularly susceptible to heaving.

Mulch plants with straw or sawdust to keep the soil from thawing until spring. Apply the mulch after the ground is frozen.

If a plant has heaved, keep it covered and frozen until spring approaches and the ground can be worked to permit replanting.

Protection against cold damage

Some plants are damaged by extreme cold. Choose plants that are not normally damaged by cold in your area. Tender exotics can be grown almost anywhere with enough attention, but the extensive care needed may not be worth the extra trouble.

A wire frame *filled with leaves, straw, or snow will protect small plants from cold and drying out. Build the frame in the fall, but don't fill it until necessary.*

A simple lath structure *protects plants from winter sun scorch. Snow fencing can be rolled out over a frame.*

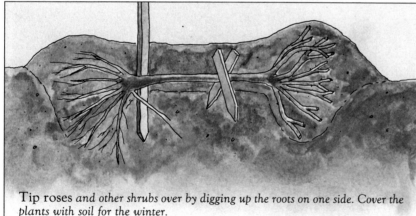

Tip roses *and other shrubs over by digging up the roots on one side. Cover the plants with soil for the winter.*

even if they are not broken. Protect small plants with boards leaning teepee-fashion over them. Spreading shrubs, such as boxwood, can be tied into shape with twine in the fall so the weight of the snow doesn't cause them to open and deform.

Salt injury

Road salt thrown onto foliage or absorbed through the roots causes a browning on the side of the plant that faces the road. New growth in the spring will be normal, but stunting and eventual death will occur if salt accumulates in the soil. There's nothing you can do about salt on the foliage. Leach excess salts from the soil in the spring with long irrigations unless spring rains are heavy.

Frosts

Frosts are a dangerous enemy to gardeners in moderate climates. Unusually early or unusually late frosts can catch gardeners by surprise. Protection against frost usually only aims to keep the air around a plant a few critical degrees warmer than the air for a few hours. Here are some ways to protect plants against frost damage:

■ Cover plants with a cardboard box, a basket, a sheet of plastic, or a blanket. An electric light bulb under the cover makes it even more effective.

■ Cover a large plant or whole bed with a piece of plywood mounted on posts.

■ Cover small plants with glass or plastic jugs with the bottoms removed.

■ Put a kerosene heater or lantern under fruit trees. Heat from the flame will warm the air around the branches.

■ Move container plants under an overhang.

■ Place many small heat sources throughout the garden. This can be done with strings of electric light bulbs, electric heaters, kerosene lamps, or small piles of charcoal briquettes in a hubcap or broiler pan. Each source will heat the plants within a few feet of it.

After the first hard freeze in the fall, untie plants that are trained up on supports or trellises, lay them on the ground, and cover with mulch. If a shrub (such as a rose) can't be bent over to lie on the ground, dig up the roots on one side, tip the plant over, and cover it with soil or a heavy mulch.

Shovel snow onto short plants as an insulating cover. Build wire cages around taller plants and fill them with snow, straw, or dead leaves for insulation.

Frost cracks

During very cold weather, wood freezes and expands, causing explosive cracks. These cracks usually occur where there is some rot or other weakness in the wood. As the weather warms, cracks usually close and heal over, but they may open in the same place the following winter.

Paint the exposed edges of bark with a pruning sealer to keep them from drying out. If the bark is loose, nail it back to the trunk. If the same crack opens every winter, put long bolts through it to hold it together.

Snow damage

Shake snow and ice off limbs that are near the breaking point. Excessive buildup may deform plants

PROTECTING PLANTS FROM SUN, WIND, AND RAIN

Young plants and plants recently moved to a new location are particularly susceptible to damage from strong sunlight, wind, and rain. But even established plants can suffer from extreme weather.

Put landscape plants where they will not need temporary shading structures every summer. Plants that cannot tolerate hot sunlight should be planted under trees, under patio shade structures, or on the east or north side of the house. Larger shrubs or vines trained on a trellis may also provide shading for more sensitive plants planted under them.

Protection from the sun

Too much hot sun can damage plants either by scalding tissues or causing dehydration.

Temporary shading devices can be used to protect germinating seedlings and young transplants; they can be removed when the plants become accustomed to their environment. One to three weeks of shading is usually enough.

- A shingle shoved into the ground can shade a single plant.
- A newspaper tent can shade several plants.
- Wooden A-frames covered with burlap or cardboard can shade a whole row of plants.
- A cardboard box can provide emergency shade for a stressed plant.
- A wire cylinder draped with burlap makes a handy movable screen.

The trunks of young trees may scald when exposed to intense sunlight, especially trees with dark bark. You can reduce sun scald by painting the trunk with whitewash or white interior latex paint, or by wrapping the trunk with burlap or a similar material.

You may need to provide shading for some individual fruits and vegetables as they mature. Sun scald on melons can be avoided by shading the fruits with newspaper for the last few weeks before harvest. Tomato plants trained on a

A tent shelter *can be made of shingles or wooden flats.*

This lath shelter *is a frame sitting on 4 stakes.*

Shingles *make quick, easy shelters for transplants. Place them on the southwest side of the plant.*

A board on bricks *provides shade for seedlings.*

cylindrical wire cage produce fruit in the shaded interior and are less likely to have scalded fruit than plants grown on stakes.

Protection from wind

Wind can damage plants by drying them out, by breaking branches and tearing leaves, and by increasing the damaging effects of high or low temperatures. The most effective windbreaks are permeable and allow some air to pass through. The turbulence caused by wind surging over a solid barrier can be just as harmful to plants as the unimpeded wind.

Hedges are excellent windbreaks when mature, but they may need temporary structural assistance when young. Lath screens, perforated plastic sheeting, and burlap are all good materials to use for constructing temporary windbreaks.

If your homesite needs a large windbreak, choose deep-rooted trees. Some shallow-rooted species are fast growers, but they may blow over during heavy wind, especially if the ground is wet. A local nursery should be able to help you select trees with a good combination of fast growth, deep roots, and sturdy branches that will not break off easily.

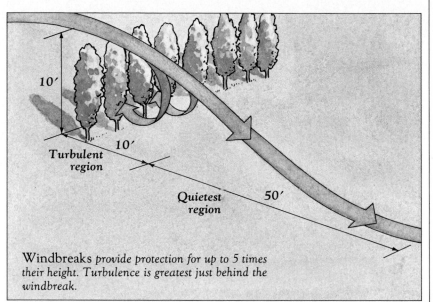

10′

10′
Turbulent region

Quietest region 50′

Windbreaks *provide protection for up to 5 times their height. Turbulence is greatest just behind the windbreak.*

Whitewash *protects young tree trunks from sun scald by reflecting the sun's heat.*

The most common garden injury caused by wind is the drying out of soil and roots. The evaporation of water from topsoil and leaf surfaces is greatly accelerated by wind action. Plants that were soaked the day before can dry out and wilt in several hours of heavy winds. Young or fleshy plants such as vegetables are particularly susceptible to dehydration by wind. Give your plants plenty of extra water during windy times.

Planting vegetables in alternating rows of tall and short plants can protect the smaller plants against wind damage. A temporary windbreak of sunflowers, corn, or staked tomatoes can be planted along one or two sides of a vegetable garden to provide protection for the smaller plants.

Very young vegetables can be planted between tall mounded rows of dirt, covered with bottomless paper bags, or protected by other small structural windbreaks.

Preventing wind damage to trees

Wind damages many trees that could have been protected by proper preparation. A young tree that has grown considerably during the summer may need to be thinned before heavy fall winds arrive. Removing several branches to create a more permeable top growth with reduced wind resistance may mean the difference between a snapped trunk and a healthy tree.

Trees should be encouraged to form deep roots. If a tree is watered frequently and lightly, the roots will naturally tend to grow close to the surface. If the tree is watered less often but thoroughly soaked, the water will penetrate deep into the soil and the roots will be encouraged to grow deeper in search of the water.

For information about staking and guying trees, see page 120.

Protection from rain damage

Rain can damage plants by splashing mud, by causing erosion or drainage problems, and by beating blossoms. Container plants can be moved under protective overhangs while in bloom. Mulches placed on top of bare soil will absorb the impact of falling rain and prevent much of the mud splashing and erosion problems.

Sprinklers in the yard can cause the same types of damage as rainfall, so mulches are recommended for areas that are irrigated by overhead sprinklers.

Water falling on fruits and vegetables that are close to maturity can cause splitting. Cherries and tomatoes are particularly likely to split if watered from above.

TO PROTECT PLANTS FROM SUN, WIND, AND RAIN

■ **Keep plants well watered. Give extra water on hot or windy days.**
■ **Use mulches to conserve soil moisture and prevent rain splash.**
■ **Protect young plants with screens or shading devices.**
■ **Thin tops of young trees to reduce wind drag.**

CONTROLLING WEEDS

Different weeds in different types of plantings pose different problems. Each situation calls for a specific technique of weed control. But the best weed control is the one that prevents their growing in the first place.

Weeds are plants that someone considers undesirable.

Any more rigorous definition wouldn't satisfy everyone. Historically, the tomato was a weed, thought to be poisonous, before it became our favorite home vegetable. Bermudagrass constitutes a prize lawn in some settings and a despicable invader in others. Dandelions, raised as a green in some gourmet vegetable gardens, are anathema in most American lawns. English daisy is a pleasing ornamental to some lawn owners but a bane to others, who prefer the undisturbed green carpet of grass. Kudzu, imported as an erosion control and ornamental plant, has become a dirty word throughout the Southeast.

The list could go on and on. Though definitions of weeds are subjective, home gardeners will have a firm understanding of what they mean by weeds.

The damage weeds cause

The most obvious damage that weeds cause in the home setting is that they are unattractive; they are to our gardens what dust is to our house. But there are other, less obvious reasons for controlling weeds in your garden.

The seeds from this dandelion will germinate to become a new generation of weeds. The best way to prevent future weeds is to control present weeds.

One other reason is that weeds compete with desired plants for space, water, nutrients, and light, reducing the yield in a vegetable garden or the number and size of flowers in a flower garden. Some vegetables, such as onions, will be stunted if their early growth includes competition with weeds.

A few weeds are in a class by themselves because they are toxic. These include poison oak, poison ivy, and stinging nettles. Other weeds, such as ragweed, contribute to the discomfort of people with allergies.

Weeds in the garden or in wild areas near the garden can serve as alternate hosts for pest insects and diseases that damage garden plants. As examples, the weed datura serves as a host for tomato hornworm and some wild cruciferous plants host the clubroot disease that damages cabbage family plants.

Kinds of weeds

To control weeds, it's important to make their acquaintance.

Some weeds are *annuals,* completing their life-cycle in one year or less. Such weeds can often be controlled when they germinate or as they mature, either with cultivation or with chemicals. A *biennial* weed lives for two seasons, producing seeds in the second year. *Perennials* live for three or more years.

Some perennials are difficult to eliminate. They may have long tap roots (dandelion) or invasive underground stems (Bermudagrass) that cultivation never eliminates entirely.

Weeds fall into one of two botanic groups. They may be *grassy* weeds, such as crabgrass, with long stems and relatively narrow leaf blades. Or they may be *broadleaf* weeds like the dandelion, with net-veined, relatively wide leaves.

Preventing weeds

Prevention is the first strategy in weed control. Weeds thrive when they find an open space in the lawn or garden. Maintaining a vigorous lawn or shading and crowding out weeds in a well-managed garden reduces the weeding job.

The saying "seeds one year mean weeds seven years" captures the wisdom of preventing weeds from going to seed in your garden. The average weed produces 25,000 seeds during its lifetime. Some of these will germinate right away, but others can lie in the soil for years, to germinate when the soil around them is disturbed.

Like other plants, weeds need sunlight to survive and thrive. Mulches of organic material or black plastic suppress weeds by blocking necessary sunlight.

When bringing materials into your garden, be sure to check them for potential weed seeds. A mulch of straw or hay will cause endless weeding problems if there are many grain or weed seeds in it.

Weeds are easiest to control in bare ground. Before you put in a garden or a landscape project, be sure all the weeds are dead. Just cutting them off with a hoe often leaves live roots and millions of seeds in the soil, ready to sprout and grow. This is especially important if you are putting in a ground cover or perennial flower bed, where you won't want to dig around the roots of the plants.

Killing weeds

Since the beginning of agriculture, the hoe has been the basic tool of gardening. Hand hoeing or cultivating is effective in some situations. But hoeing is slow, hard work. Hand pulling of weeds is also effective with some weeds on a small scale, but it is discouraging if you have many weeds. Hoeing or hand pulling will not kill weeds with long roots, such as the dandelion, or which sprout from underground stems.

Herbicides

Herbicides are another strategy in weed control. Herbicides—chemicals that kill weeds—work in several ways.

The most effective way to kill weeds is with a *fumigant*, a gas that penetrates the soil, killing all living tissue. Fumigants kill seeds, insects, and disease organisms as well as weeds. They also kill any roots, and are difficult, dangerous, and time-consuming to apply.

Preemergence herbicides kill germinating seeds, eliminating the young plant before it emerges from the soil surface. *Postemergence herbicides* kill plants that are growing.

Some postemergence herbicides are *contact* killers, killing plant parts covered by the spray. Contact herbicides affect only the aboveground part of the plant, which is sufficient to kill some weeds but not those with long taproots or underground stems.

Top: Oxalis is a persistent perennial. Although the top of the plant is easy to kill, the corms—the bulblike objects—resprout readily.

Bottom: Chickweed has invaded this bed of carnations. Weed control in crowded beds is difficult; it is easier to prevent the weeds than to kill them later.

Systemic herbicides travel through the plant, moving from the leaves to the stems and roots, killing the entire plant. Systemics are the only way to eradicate some persistent perennials with taproots or underground stems.

Selective herbicides kill certain plants but not others. For example, 2,4-D kills broadleaf weeds in the lawn without killing the grass.

Nonselective herbicides kill all plants they contact. Glyphosate is a nonselective herbicide. It can be used to kill all the plants in an area, or for spot treating if the weed can be isolated.

Nuances of chemical weeding

The effectiveness of herbicides is relative, depending on many variables. Sometimes it is difficult to kill selected weeds and not kill desired plants, if the two are growing together. For instance, broad-leaved weeds in dichondra are more difficult to kill than broad-leaved weeds in a lawn because the herbicide will also kill the dichondra, which itself is has broad leaves. The dose of chemical, relative maturity of the plant (younger weeds are easier to kill than older weeds), air and soil temperatures (which affect the speed of chemical reactions), and possible waxiness or hairiness of plant leaves are variables that affect the art and science of applying herbicides.

Weed control around trees and shrubs

Weeds in lawns and in vegetable or flower gardens receive ample discussion in this chapter, but how should you control weeds around trees, shrubs, and ground covers?

Use preemergence herbicides, such as dichlobenil, around roses, shrubs such as camellias or azaleas, and around trees. The herbicide, applied in early spring, prevents weed seeds from germinating. This strategy is effective for all weeds except those that overwinter and grow from roots or underground stems.

Hand removal of the occasional weed is often practical around trees and shrubs. The shade of

Dense plantings are almost weed-free. Both the lawn and the border in this picture are planted densely enough that weeds can't get started.

large plants usually weakens the ability of weeds to survive. Cultivate shallowly so as not to damage shrub or tree feeder roots.

Besides hand removal, you can use a contact weed killer or a translocator, such as glyphosate, for stubborn weeds. Be careful that the spray does not fall on the trees and shrubs, or they too may be killed. Some shrubs and trees are so sensitive to herbicides that it is best to avoid using herbicides around them. Yews are an example.

Controlling weeds in ground covers

Invasive weeds can be a vexing problem in ground covers, especially if the weed is a difficult perennial, such as quackgrass or Bermudagrass. If the ground cover planting is new, some ground will probably be bare and weeds may be in a flush of growth.

If you have the opportunity, postpone putting in a ground cover until you control weeds at the site. In a weedy setting, it may be advisable to fumigate or kill all vegetation with a systemic. (For nonchemical alternatives, such as smothering with black plastic or deliberate sprouting and then killing, see pages 144.) When your soil is clear of weeds and the ground cover is in place, mulch with an organic material, such as bark, wood chip, or straw, or with black plastic, until the ground cover becomes vigorous enough to crowd out and shade over competing weeds. Prevent further germination of weed seeds in a ground cover with a preemergence herbicide. Avoid further cultivation of the soil, because each soil disturbance brings more weed seeds to the surface to germinate.

PREVENTING WEEDS

Weed control is one of the most important jobs in a garden. It can become a time-consuming and backbreaking chore unless preventive steps are taken to control weeds before they become established. Preemergence herbicides can kill weed seeds as they sprout. Healthy lawns and shrubbery will crowd out young weeds before they can get started. Mulches will prevent seeds from receiving the light they need. And a single application of soil sterilant can prevent weed growth in patios and parking lots for more than a year.

Remove existing weeds

The first—and most important—step in preventing weeds is to remove the weeds that are already in the garden before they produce seeds. Weeds are prodigious creators of seed. One stalk of oat grass may produce 250 seeds. A tumbling pigweed plant may produce several million seeds.

Most of the weeds in your garden came from seeds that formed in your garden; only a small part of them came from outside. If you can keep weeds that are now growing in your garden from going to seed, next year's weeding chores will be minimal. Weed your yard carefully one time, removing every weed you find. Then use the preventive measures described below. After that, go through the garden once a week, killing every weed you find. With most of the weeds controlled, this weeding tour will become quicker and quicker each week. In the next growing season, you should find only a few weeds on each week's tour.

Prevent weed seed germination

Use mulches to prevent light from reaching the soil surface. (See page 26 for information about mulching.) The lack of light will prevent weed seedlings from growing. Cut down any existing weeds before applying the mulch.

You can use any of a number of materials to create a mulch. Spread organic materials under plants to create a mulch that conserves moisture and prevents weeds. Apply organic mulches at least 3 inches thick to prevent weeds from germinating. Use materials from your own yard, local agricultural refuse, or packaged ground wood or bark products. Be sure the mulch itself is free of weed seeds.

Black plastic mulches are very effective against weeds and will last for years if protected against exposure to the sun. When possible, put the plastic in place before planting and then cut slits to plant through. In a vegetable garden, cover the edges of the plastic mulch with soil or rocks to prevent wind damage to the plastic. Spread fir bark, sand, or decorative rocks over the plastic in an ornamental garden.

Cover the soil with plants

Whether in lawns or in gardens, weeds have difficulty establishing themselves in areas where garden plants are vigorous. Competing plants struggle for available sunlight, so a thick canopy of desirable plant material will discourage weed growth in the garden.

Feed your lawn to keep it thick and healthy so the grass can prevent weed seeds from germinating and can crowd out those that do germinate. Plan your vegetable garden so that the mature plants will have overlapping leaves. This will provide maximum production and minimum weeding. For vegetables that grow slowly, plant radishes or lettuce in the bare spaces so that they, rather than weeds, will occupy the ground.

Ground covers are particularly effective at stopping weed growth. Plant low-growing ground covers, such as creeping thyme or Corsican mint, in the flower bed and between shrubs. Use deeper ground covers to keep large areas of ground free of weeds.

Keep the ground dry

If you live in a region where it rains every week during the summer, it won't be possible to keep your ground dry. But if you live in a dry-summer region, you have some control over how water is applied to your garden. Most weed seeds won't germinate in dry soil. If you can water only the garden plants, and not water the ground between those plants, you won't have weed problems there.

The easiest way to accomplish this is to use a watering technique that doesn't wet all the ground. Sprinkling, either by hand or with a stationary sprinker, spreads water over the entire soil surface. Furrow irrigation wets only the surface adjacent to the furrows. Basin irrigation wets only the soil in the basins. And drip irrigation wets just a very small spot under each emitter. A drip system throughout the garden can cut weeding to a minimum.

Preemergence herbicides

Some weed killers are made specifically to kill seedlings as they sprout. These preemergence herbicides do not kill plants that are already growing. Because they affect seedlings only as they emerge from the protective seed coat, preemergence herbicides can be used to prevent weeds among existing plantings.

Preemergence herbicides attach to soil particles as soon as they touch them. They are usually sprayed or spread on weed-free soil, then watered in well. The herbicide moves only an inch or less into the soil, then attaches to soil particles and goes no deeper, no matter how much water is applied. The herbicide remains in the surface inches of soil for several weeks, killing all seeds that sprout.

If the soil is tilled during this period, the effect is diluted or lost. Before applying preemergence herbicides, remove the existing weeds and till the soil. If you plant in protected soil or otherwise disturb it, the ground that is disturbed may allow weed seeds to sprout.

Spot-treating *before weeds to go seed prevents many future weeds.*

Mulches *can be used to kill existing weeds or prevent new ones from growing. This plastic mulch will kill all the weeds under it.*

Preemergent herbicides *form a protective barrier at the soil surface. Seeds that germinate there are killed.*

Time your application of pre-emergence herbicides to coincide with weed germination. Many spring weeds germinate as the soil reaches a temperature of about 50°F. If you take the temperature of your soil every week, you will know when to apply these herbicides to achieve the best effect.

Spread preemergence herbicides on lawns in the early spring to kill crabgrass and other weeds as the seeds sprout. If you live in a mild-winter region, apply them again in the fall to kill the winter weeds.

Apply preemergence herbicides to flower beds and shrubbery areas in fall and spring to control both warm- and cool-season weeds.

Use these herbicides in recently cultivated areas where new seeds have been brought to the surface.

Soil sterilants

Some weed killers have a residual effect that can last for several years after a single application. These are called *soil sterilants;* they will prevent all plant growth in the treated area. Use soil sterilants on patios, driveways, and sidewalks and along fence lines. Apply the chemical carefully, and avoid adjacent plantings. Don't apply it on soil that contains roots of garden plants or trees, or where runoff or erosion might carry it onto garden plants.

Keep weed seeds out of the garden

Many weed seeds will blow into your garden. Some cultural practices will reduce the number of seeds that get into your yard.

Do not use any mulching materials or imported topsoil that might have weed seeds in it. Agricultural refuse is usually full of weed seeds, and the nutritional value of manures or other materials may be offset by the nuisance of extra weeds. Imported materials may also carry types of weeds that would not otherwise find their way into your yard.

If you really want to use barn-yard refuse, put the materials in a large pile for several weeks or months before applying it to the garden areas. The heat generated by the decomposing materials will kill most of the weed seeds. For directions on making hot compost, see page 24.

If areas adjacent to your garden have weeds on them, seeds are likely to blow into your yard. Spray these areas with weed killers, or cut down the weeds before midsummer when the seeds begin to form. Plant hedges to filter wind from areas that cannot be mowed or sprayed.

Use lawn clippings as a mulch only if they are free of both weed seeds and stems that could resprout, such as stems of Bermuda-grass and other runners.

KILLING WEEDS

Two approaches may be used to kill existing weeds. You can kill them in place and let them dry up where they are, or you can remove them physically. In many cases it is necessary to do both. Small weeds, or weeds in areas where appearance isn't important, can be killed in place. This is usually easy and quick to do. Seedlings and annual weeds can be pulled, cultivated under, or hoed out without killing them first. Removing the crown of the plant (where the top and roots meet) usually kills these plants. Many perennial weeds, both green and woody, must be killed before being removed. They will resprout from bulbs, roots, or underground stems left in the soil.

Killing weeds in place

Weeds are killed in place with herbicides. Based on how they kill weeds, there are two types of weed-killing chemicals: *contact herbicides*, which kill weeds on contact, and *systemic herbicides*, which are absorbed by the weeds and move down through the plants to kill their roots.

Contact herbicides kill any plant tissue they touch. One drop of contact herbicide on a leaf will make a dead spot the size and shape of the drop. They are effective against young weeds and annual weeds but don't work on perennial weeds, which will resprout from the roots. Contact herbicides act quickly, killing the weeds in a day or so.

Systemic herbicides are absorbed by the plant and travel throughout it, killing all parts at one time. They act slowly, taking from a few days to a couple of weeks to kill the plant. They are most useful against difficult-to-kill perennials and woody plants.

Within these basic categories there are further divisions that indicate which weeds a particular chemical will control. Some weed killers are *selective*—they differentiate between grassy plants and broad-leaved plants. This means that some weed killers will kill the broad-leaved weeds, such as dandelions, in a lawn but will not harm the grass. Other selective herbicides will kill grass plants but won't affect broad-leaved plants. Use selective grass killers to kill grassy weeds among ground covers, shrubs, or other broad-leaved plants. Apply selective broad-leaved killers to kill broad-leaved weeds in lawn areas. The most common selective broad-leaved herbicides are 2,4-D and MCPP.

Application equipment

When applying herbicides, avoid getting any of the chemical on desirable plants. Spray only in calm weather to avoid drifting spray, and use the size or type of equipment that can be carefully controlled in order to confine application to the intended area.

The three most common types of applicators for herbicides are *hose-end sprayers, tank sprayers,* and *fertilizer spreaders.*

Hose-end sprayers are jars that connect to the end of a garden hose. Put the chemical in the jar, turn the hose on, and the chemical will be siphoned out of the jar and mixed with the water coming through the hose. Some sprayers are preset to deliver a certain ratio of water to chemical; others are adjustable.

Tank-type sprayers spray with pressure from a hand pump. Put in the chemicals and water at the desired ratio, pump up the unit, and spray with a hand-controlled nozzle. Tank sprayers have a smaller capacity and a softer spray than hose-end sprayers, but they allow more precise application control.

Apply granules with a fertilizer spreader. If you are treating a lawn, use a dropper spreader for the most accurate coverage. Beware of old rusty spreaders that may not be calibrated to distribute the chemical evenly. If you are spreading granules across a ground cover or other rough area, use a broadcast spreader.

Many herbicides are packaged with built-in applicators. These chemicals are used directly from the can or bottle. Some are pressurized sprays or jet-stream applicators driven by compressed gas;

When hoeing weeds, *slice or scrape the weed just below ground level.*

In groundcovers, *apply herbicides with a paint brush to avoid harming garden plants.*

others contain small hand-operated pumps. These applicators are convenient for small jobs, since they can be used immediately with no mixing or cleanup. But they are usually too slow for large jobs.

Killing brush

Some herbicides are especially formulated for killing brush, such as poison ivy and brambles. Apply them while the leaves are actively

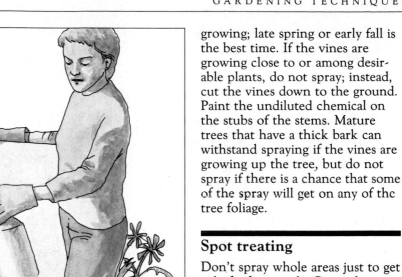

Use a shield *to protect garden plants when spot treating in crowded areas. A piece of cardboard makes a quick, disposable shield.*

growing; late spring or early fall is the best time. If the vines are growing close to or among desirable plants, do not spray; instead, cut the vines down to the ground. Paint the undiluted chemical on the stubs of the stems. Mature trees that have a thick bark can withstand spraying if the vines are growing up the tree, but do not spray if there is a chance that some of the spray will get on any of the tree foliage.

Spot treating

Don't spray whole areas just to get rid of a few weeds. Control occasional or scattered weeds with spot treatments. Do not leave your tank or hose-end sprayer filled and ready for occasional use, though. Buy small amounts of premixed herbicides in aerosol cans or finger-pump sprayers.

Removing weeds

Weed seedlings can be killed by simply stirring the soil with a cultivator or tiller. Larger weeds must be cut off at ground level and raked up. A hoe is the tool usually used for this task, but any other specialized tool can be used.

When a hoe is used for weeding, it is a cutting tool. Keep it sharp. To sharpen a hoe, file the blade at a 45° angle, then run the file flat across the back of the blade to remove the burrs. A hoe should be sharpened after every couple of hours of weeding, or more often in rocky soil. To cut a weed off, pull the hoe toward you, almost parallel to the ground. Cut off the weed just under the soil surface. If it's necessary to remove the roots of any weed to kill it, don't use a hoe unless you kill it first with a systemic herbicide. If you hoe properly, you will dig up very little soil. Weeding with any type of cutting or pulling tool is easier if the soil is moist. During dry weather, water the ground before weeding. In dry weather, you can leave small weeds on the surface to die. But during wet spells, rake them up to keep them from rerooting.

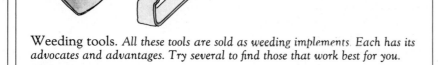

Weeding tools. *All these tools are sold as weeding implements. Each has its advocates and advantages. Try several to find those that work best for you.*

WEEDING THE LAWN

The best defense against lawn weeds is a healthy lawn. Proper watering, feeding, and mowing will produce a thick, vigorous lawn that discourages weed seeds from germinating and crowds out the weeds that do manage to germinate. See pages 72, 86, and 112 for instructions on lawn care.

Control weeds before starting a lawn

Remove any weeds and eliminate as many of the weed seeds in the soil as possible before planting a lawn. If you will be laying sod rather than seeding your new lawn, the sod will smother most of the annual weeds that sprout from seeds. But the more tenacious perennial weeds will come right through it.

Water the soil to promote germination of weed seeds. Use herbicides or shallow cultivation to kill the weeds as they sprout. After a few cycles of this treatment, a substantial portion of the weed seeds in your soil will have germinated and died.

Controls for the major lawn weeds

The accompanying drawings will help you identify the most common lawn weeds. *The Ortho Problem Solver* can further identify these and other species not described here. If you are not sure, take samples to a local nursery or your Cooperative Extension Agent for positive identification.

Annual bluegrass (*Poa annua*) is a narrow-leaved annual that grows fastest during the cool weather of spring and fall. It dies in the summer. The key to control is preventing reseeding. Apply preemergence herbicides in early August and again in September.

Bermudagrass (*Cynodon dactylon*) is an extremely persistent narrow-leaved perennial with vigorous deep roots and underground stems. It grows best during warm

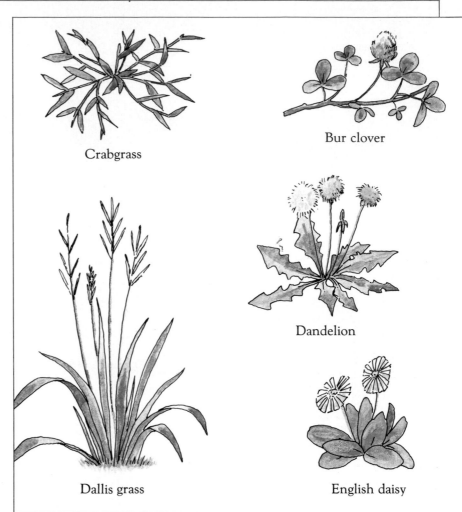

Crabgrass

Bur clover

Dandelion

Dallis grass

English daisy

weather and dies back to the dormant underground stems in freezing temperatures. Bermudagrass has a number of hybrid varieties and is often used as a lawn grass.

Hand digging will not control Bermudagrass. Treat infestations that have spread into desirable broad-leaved plants with a selective contact grass killer. In heavily infested lawns, use a systemic herbicide to remove all growth and then reseed to grow a new lawn.

Buckhorn plantain (*Plantago lanceolata*) and **broadleaf plantain** (*P. major*) are perennial weeds that resprout from the roots each year. Control them with selective herbicides in the spring or fall. They are difficult to control and may need more than one application.

Mouse-ear chickweed (*Cerastium vulgatum*) is a broad-leaved perennial weed that grows in full sun. It

is most likely to be a problem on wet soil and where the lawn is thin. The stems root where they touch the soil, forming a thick mat that crowds out the lawn grass. Apply a selective herbicide in the spring or fall, while the weed is growing actively.

Crabgrass (*Digitaria*) is a narrow-leaved annual. It grows from seeds that germinate in early spring. Crabgrass matures during summer, then produces seeds in the late summer and fall.

Control crabgrass with preemergence herbicides in early spring. Spot-treat individual clumps during the summer. Keep the lawn thick and lush, and set the lawn mower high to discourage crabgrass seedlings.

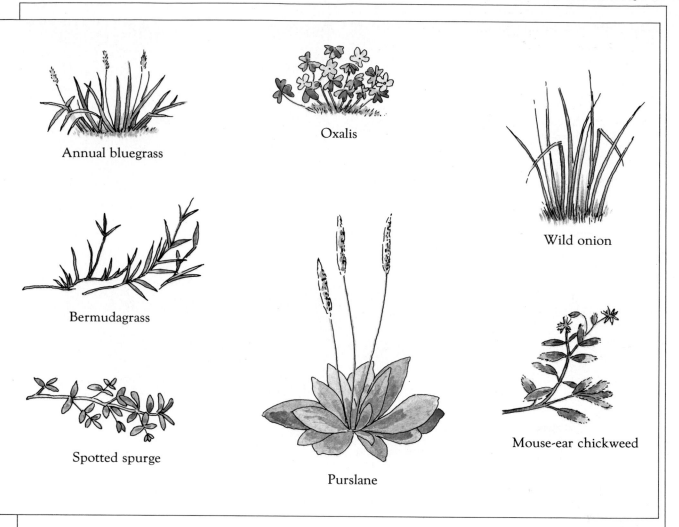

Annual bluegrass

Oxalis

Wild onion

Bermudagrass

Spotted spurge

Purslane

Mouse-ear chickweed

Curly dock (*Rumex crispus*) is a broad-leaved perennial that has a long, thick taproot. It grows best during spring and fall; but because of its taproot, it competes successfully against lawn grasses during hot, dry weather. Control curly dock by spot treating or spraying selective herbicides.

Dandelion (*Taraxacum officinale*) is a broad-leaved perennial that appears mainly in the spring and fall. Control by applying a selective herbicide during spring or fall to prevent it from setting seed. Spot-treat any new plants that appear during the summer.

Dallis grass (*Paspalum dilatum*) is a grassy weed that is a serious pest in the South. Spot-treat with a grass killer to control it.

English daisy (*Bellis perennis*) is a broad-leaved perennial that will grow all year if protected from drought and heat. It is difficult to control and should be spot-treated or sprayed with a selective herbicide in late spring.

Oxalis (*Oxalis corniculata*) is a broad-leaved perennial that grows best during spring and late summer. Selective herbicides will supress but not eradicate it. Spray several times in spring or fall, when air temperatures are 60° to 80°F. A thick, vigorous lawn will smother oxalis.

Purslane (*Portulaca oleracea*) is a broad-leaved annual that thrives during hot weather and grows mainly in sparse lawns. It can be controlled by applying preemergence herbicides in spring, or by treating with selective contact herbicides during the summer.

Spotted spurge (*Euphorbia maculata*) is a broad-leaved annual that grows most aggressively from late spring through early fall. Apply preemergence herbicides in spring for partial control. Treat several times with selective contact herbicides in summer for best results.

White clover (*Trifolium repens*) is a broad-leaved perennial that grows best during the cool weather of spring and fall. It is most noticeable when it flowers during early summer. Control by applications of preemergence herbicides in spring and selective contact killers during the spring or fall.

Wild onion (*Allium canadense*) is a perennial weed that resprouts from underground bulbs each year. It looks like a coarse grass, but has a distinct onion or garlic scent when crushed. Use a selective herbicide, or spot-treat with a systemic. Treat again whenever new plants appear. It may take 2 or 3 years to eliminate the onions from your lawn.

WEEDING THE VEGETABLE OR FLOWER GARDEN

Weeds in vegetable gardens and flower beds compete with desirable plants for water, nutrients, and sunlight. They can dramatically reduce the flower and crop yields. In the vegetable garden, weeds use up the nutrients and water that the vegetables need. Also, many weeds give off chemicals from their roots into the soil that slow the growth of other plants growing around them. This effect has been established in some weeds and is suspected in many others because their presence seems to cause more stunting in vegetables than can be explained by simple competition. In addition, the quality of the vegetables can be dramatically decreased by the presence of weeds. Flowers may not be damaged as severely or noticeably by weeds, but the weeds spoil the appearance of the flower bed and give the setting for the flowers a messy and unkempt look.

Remove weeds before planting

If the area you intend to plant has a large number of weeds growing on it, you may want to begin the weed control program several months in advance. Advice on fallowing is given on page 144.

Use a contact weed killer to kill annual weeds in the bed. The chemical may have some residual effect, so check the label to see how long to wait before planting. If the weeds are small, you can leave them to be tilled in. If they are large, remove them after they have been killed.

If you have perennial weeds, such as Bermudagrass, in the garden area, take more time to prepare the bed. These weeds are hard to eradicate, and small roots left in the soil can resprout and take over the bed in one season. Apply a systemic herbicide before removing any of the top growth. Spray and remove weeds within 5 feet of the planting area to discourage a reinfestation.

Black plastic mulches are a modern favorite. Lay out the plastic first, cover the edges with soil, then plant through holes you cut.

Organic mulches control weeds during the gardening season, then can be dug in at the end of the season to rot and improve the soil. Use weed-free mulching material, spread from 2 to 4 inches deep.

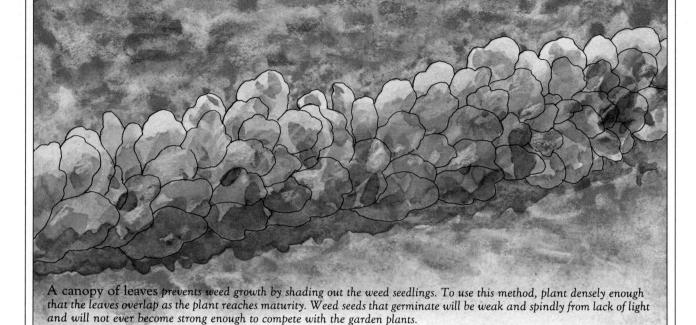

A canopy of leaves *prevents weed growth by shading out the weed seedlings. To use this method, plant densely enough that the leaves overlap as the plant reaches maturity. Weed seeds that germinate will be weak and spindly from lack of light and will not ever become strong enough to compete with the garden plants.*

Weeding the established garden

Be careful not to disrupt the roots of nearby plants when hand weeding. Pinch or cut the tops of weeds whose roots entwine with the roots of a desirable plant. Use your fingernails or scissors, since pulling out the weed would disturb the roots of the plant you want to keep. For weeding tools, see pages 20 and 146. Cut off the weeds at soil level, instead of digging deeply to get them out, because stirring the soil will bring more weed seeds to the surface.

Pick a few weeds every time you visit the garden area. Weeds grow rapidly, and removing a few weeds can quickly turn into a major project. Get into the habit of picking a handful of the largest weeds every few days.

Apply mulches to prevent weeds

Use mulches to kill developing weed seeds and young weeds by depriving them of sunlight. See page 26 for a list of possible mulch materials. Choose a mulch that will not introduce new weed seeds or weed parts into the garden.

Straw is a favorite mulch around tomato plants and strawberries. Straw helps manage weeds, keeps the ground evenly moist and cool, and keeps the fruit from rotting when in contact with damp soil. Dig decaying straw into the soil after the crop has been harvested.

When using black plastic, hold the edges down with soil or stones. Stretch a strip of black plastic along the planting row and cut the plastic where you want to insert the plants. If you plan to plant seeds directly into the bed, place strips of plastic in the space between rows.

Water and cultivate with weeds in mind

Do not water bare areas where weed seeds could germinate. If there are many weed seeds in your soil, consider using a drip system or furrow irrigation to deliver water right to the plant roots.

Cultivation brings more weed seeds to the surface. Use a mulch to avoid cultivating. Or, if you cultivate, try not to disturb more than the top inch of soil.

Exclude weeds with a canopy of leaves

Space young plants so that the leaves of mature plants just barely overlap slightly. The canopy forms shade that discourages weed seed germination. Interplant the bare space between slow-growing vegetables. For example, plant spinach between early pepper or tomato plants set out in the spring; then harvest the spinach as the weather begins to warm up. Plant radishes between any vegetables or flower plants that need interplanting.

Use preemergence herbicides to prevent weed germination

Suppress weeds in a vegetable or flower garden with a preemergence herbicide, which will not affect growing plants but will kill weed seeds as they germinate. Use preemergence herbicides in established plantings to prevent new weeds from sprouting. These herbicides will not affect the taste or safety of vegetable crops. If you apply a preemergence herbicide, don't cultivate the soil or you'll weaken the chemical barrier to germination that the herbicide creates.

CONTROLLING PLANT PESTS

Insects, birds, and animals share our gardens with us. They must be controlled to keep them from taking more than their share. Here is a philosophy of pest control that seeks to accomplish its ends with as little time and effort as possible.

Controlling insects and animals is a necessary garden activity, but not one that most people enjoy. People become gardeners because they love working with the soil and plants, not because they enjoy pitched battles against lower life forms. The wisest stand to take is usually to avoid long campaigns if you can, and to deal with skirmishes quickly and positively.

Long campaigns occur when a pest exists in great numbers in your neighborhood. There are two ways to avoid doing intensive and continuous battle: one way is to keep the pest from building up to great numbers by being alert to population increases and squelching them before they get out of control. The other way to avoid major campaigns is to avoid plants that are desirable to that pest. If you live in an area where gypsy moths are a yearly plague, don't plant oaks or other trees that are attractive to them.

The role of insects

Insects and plants have evolved together. Insects exist in large numbers and will always be present in the garden. In fact, they are the principal pollinators of flowering plants. Only a few of them are plant pests; the rest clean up de-

This lacebug is a true bug. It sucks juices from plants, causing the light-colored areas shown on this marigold.

caying organic matter, drink flower nectar in return for pollinating the flowers, or eat other insects. Insects that eat plants can be divided into two broad groups: those that suck juices from plants, and those that chew on them.

Sucking insects

The damage caused by all sucking insects is similar: leaves turn pale green or yellow—often in blotchy patterns—are small and sometimes distorted, and plant growth slows. In a severe case, the leaves die and fall off, and the whole plant may die. Some sucking insects are more damaging than others, but it usually takes a large number of them to seriously harm a plant. Most sucking insects are found in one of two insect orders: the *homoptera*, or aphid order; and the *hemiptera*, or true bugs. An additional group of sucking pests is the mites. Mites are not true insects but are more closely related to spiders.

The aphid order includes aphids, whiteflies, scale insects, mealybugs, and many other groups. This order includes the most frequent vectors of plant diseases. Leafhoppers, in particular, transmit a great many plant diseases. Most homopterans reproduce prolifically; their key to evolutionary survival seems to be to make young faster than other insects can eat them. They are

often relatively defenseless as individuals, but they are spectacularly successful as a species.

Most homopterans hatch from eggs (although some are born live) as active creatures that look like tiny aphids. In this stage, they are often scattered by the wind to other plants. This stage is also very vulnerable to insecticides. Aphids continue to look like this, only growing larger as they age. But other homopterans go through dramatic changes. Many settle down in a single spot, insert their needlelike mouthparts into the plant, and cover themselves with wax. Among the scale insects, the wax becomes a shell that protects them. The mealybugs and some aphids exude the wax as filaments that form a fluffy covering that looks like cotton. The wax repels liquids, so these insects are difficult to control with general-purpose insecticides; instead, you must use insecticides formulated especially for them. Whiteflies are scalelike as larvae but go through a dramatic change and become winged flies as adults.

Many homopterans don't digest all the sap they take in. They must process a great deal of plant sap to get enough protein to grow, since plant sap contains only a small amount of protein but a lot of sugar. (Maple syrup is made from plant sap.) The excess sap is

exuded as a sweet, sticky substance called *honeydew*. This honeydew drops onto leaves, cars, and patio furniture below the plants. A black fungus called *sooty mold* grows on the honeydew, making leaves look dirty and sooty.

The true bugs also suck plant juices, but they are usually more active than homopterans. They spend much of their time moving from one place to another rather than feeding in a single location. Most bugs can be recognized by the X-shaped pattern that their wings form on their backs.

Mites seem to cause an amount of damage that is out of proportion to their numbers, perhaps by injecting a toxin into the plant when they feed. Only a few mites on a leaf can cause it to become spotted and dry. Many mites (including the common two-spotted spider mite) leave a trail of webbing as they move around the plant. This trail builds up to become a network of fine filaments that catches dirt and makes the plant even more unsightly than it would otherwise be. Mite are tiny and active. Look for them on the bottoms of older leaves. Unless your eyes are very sharp, use a 5-power hand lens to see them. Or shake a leaf over a piece of paper. The mites will fall to the paper where they are more easily seen.

Chewing insects

Chewing insects have mouthparts with jaws, like ours (except that insect jaws work sideways instead of up and down). Some of them

Above left: Spider mites have left trails of webbing behind them, covering these hollyhock buds.

Top: Spider mite damage to marigolds. The stippled look is typical of mite damage.

Bottom: A wire mesh basket protects new plantings from birds. In some areas, birds are the worst garden pests.

live on the outside of leaves, chewing holes in them; some live inside leaves (they are called leaf miners); some live in the soil, chewing on roots; and some live inside stems and trunks (borers). Most of these belong to one of two large orders of insects: the *coleoptera*, or beetle order; and the *lepidoptera*, or butterfly and caterpillar order. Several other orders of insects have chewing mouthparts, but they contain fewer members than the two mentioned here.

Beetles have the distinction of being the largest order of animals on earth. Immature beetles are usually

called *grubs*. They are legless, or nearly so, and often live inside something: the soil, a tree trunk, or a piece of fruit. The adults have a pair of hard, often shiny, wing coverings that meet in a straight line down their back. Ladybird beetles are a familiar example. Both the grubs and the adults chew things; often the grub eats the roots of a plant, matures into an adult, and continues to feed on the leaves of the same plant.

Caterpillars are the larvae of butterflies and moths. The adult forms have mouthparts that work like drinking straws. They sip nectar from flowers and decorate our

gardens with their presence. But the eggs they lay hatch into caterpillars and worms, which are some of our most common and voracious garden pests.

Borers are usually beetle grubs, but some are moth larvae (and a few are fly larvae). They hatch from eggs laid under tree bark, then eat tunnels through the wood. Some live between the bark and the wood (bark beetles), and others bore into the wood itself. Borers and bark beetles disrupt the flow of sap through the tree, causing both roots and branches to slowly starve. They sometimes spread diseases (for example, the elm bark beetle is the vector for Dutch elm disease); and because they are inside the plant itself, they are difficult to control.

Controlling insects

Insects are most easily controlled by gardeners who are alert and knowledgeable. The alert gardener inspects plants regularly for insects. The knowledgeable gardener recognizes insects in the garden and knows which ones are harmless or beneficial, which ones might go away by themselves, and which ones pose a serious threat.

Many insect problems can be avoided by such practices as garden sanitation and choosing plants that

Left: Tomato hornworms are voracious eaters. One this size can strip a plant of its leaves in a week.

Above: Regular inspection is the gardener's first line of defense against insect pests. Check plants for pest outbreaks as well as for general health.

are unattractive to the insects that bother you the most. Serious problems can often be avoided by a single well-timed spraying. If the first few mites in a rosebush are killed, they won't be able to produce the thousands of progeny.

It also helps to keep your plants healthy so they'll withstand insect damage. Proper soil, fertilizing, and watering will enable plants to withstand much damage from insects. Weak, old, and stressed plants are more vulnerable to insect damage.

Controlling animal pests

Larger animals pose a different sort of problem than insects. For one thing, they are higher animals than insects and we are often hesitant to kill them. In many cases, it is illegal to kill them. And sometimes they are our pets!

Warm-blooded animals are often much more clever than insects, further compounding the problem. Birds learn quickly that the scarecrow is not dangerous. Often the

best strategy is to exclude pest animals with barriers or fences rather than kill them. Fences of one sort or another are the most common and effective defense against animal pests.

Repellents work against some animals. Visual, sound, smell, and taste repellents work in some cases, but they must be renewed or changed frequently. Birds and animals learn from experience whether visual or sound repellents are actually dangerous. A blaring radio will keep deer out of the garden only until they learn that the radio is harmless. And deer can distinguish, eventually, which dogs mean business and which are merely barking nuisances.

When an animal needs to be removed, traps are usually effective. With a trap you know what you've caught and that you've caught it. If you don't want to hurt the animal, traps that catch animals alive and unhurt are available in many sizes.

PREVENTING INSECT PROBLEMS

Preventing pest infestations is easier than trying to get rid of pests once they have begun to damage your garden. Vigorous, well-fed plants will repel many pests by themselves. Inspect your garden regularly to locate any potential problems before much damage can be done.

Keep the garden clean

Many insect eggs and larvae, as well as disease organisms, are deposited on flowers and fruits and mature as the plant materials lie rotting on the ground. To keep these pests from spreading, remove dead plant materials from the growing area frequently and keep the area clean.

Many pests find nesting and hiding places in refuse piles and then travel out in search of live plants to eat during the night. To discourage them, keep leaves, pruning clippings, and other trash cleared out of the garden.

Many insects feed on weeds, increasing their populations on the host plants before invading your garden plants. Keeping the garden and nearby areas free of weeds is also a way to control insect pests.

Maintain vigorous plants

Insect damage will be less critical to a healthy and well-fed plant. A vigorous plant produces its own repellents and is less likely to be attacked. If it does get chewed on or damaged, growth momentum will usually allow the plant to outgrow the damage.

Adequate water and food are important. Use well-balanced fertilizers. Plants fed a diet that is high in nitrogen but lacking in other essential nutrients may become large and bushy, but the growth is likely to be soft and less resistant to pest infestation.

Inspect plants regularly

Don't wait until plants are overwhelmed by pests before taking action. Check often for signs of

Garden sanitation *is an important first step toward controlling insects. By picking up refuse and removing weeds, you eliminate the shelter and breeding sites they need.*

Search by flashlight *at night to identify nocturnal pests. Handpick them, or spread bait.*

Examine plants *routinely to discover pests before they multiply and cause serious damage.*

chewed leaves, yellowing or distorted foliage, or other damage.

Take notice of any insects, even if you see only one or two. Look carefully for more of the same pest. Look under leaves and in other areas that you may have overlooked in your first inspection. A few individuals could be just passing through, or they could be the only readily visible members of an impending infestation.

Early diagnosis allows you to treat problems more effectively. If you see pests in your garden, find

out what they are. Check in *The Ortho Problem Solver*, or ask for advice from your local nursery or farm advisor. Learn what to do if a few bugs develop into an infestation.

Conversations with your neighbors or nursery may lead you to expect the appearance of a certain pest in your garden. Use appropriate preventive measures, watch for the pest's appearance in your garden, and be prepared to treat plants if an infestation does occur.

Dormant sprays in the winter kill hibernating insects and smother eggs. They are most effective shortly after the leaves fall, before the weather turns very cold.

Earwig traps can be made of rolled-up newspapers. Empty the insects into a plastic bag each day.

Preventive treatments

If you are aware that a pest may appear on certain plants, you can apply preventive treatments before the pest arrives. Roses, for example, are sure to have aphids on new growth and young flower buds. For this reason many rose fertilizers are combined with a systemic insecticide, which is absorbed along with the fertilizer and distributed throughout the whole plant. When the aphids do come into the garden, the treated rose plant will repel them.

Treat deciduous trees and shrubs with an oil spray in the winter. Dormant oil sprays smother eggs, larvae, and overwintering adult insects.

Barriers can prevent certain pests from reaching plants. For instance, if you know that cutworms are likely to be a problem, put paper collars around transplants to prevent the worms from getting access to their desired meal.

Keep infested plants out of the garden

Look carefully at any new plants before planting them in your garden. Check for any signs of pests or diseases. If you suspect that a plant may have some disease or insect pests (eggs and larvae as well as adults), do not bring it into the garden area until you have treated it and are sure that it is completely free of pests.

Traps

Put boards or rolled-up newspapers in the garden to act as dark hiding places for earwigs and slugs. Destroy pests hiding in traps each morning. Remember to destroy the pests each day, or you are only making a place for them to hide.

Plant resistant varieties

Research is constantly being done on insect resistance in plants, and many resistant varieties are on the market now. When you buy plants, look for varieties that are resistant to the insects that are problems in your garden.

Some plants should not be planted in an area where known pests are particularly destructive. For example, oaks are the preferred food for gypsy moths and should not be planted in areas where gypsy moths are prevalent.

Predators

Birds and toads eat harmful pests. A few active predators help keep pest populations in control.

Encourage birds to visit your garden by providing birdbaths and feeders that are safe from cats. Put out suet or peanut butter to attract birds that feed mainly on insects.

Toads are very productive pest predators. They eat nocturnal bugs and worms and can control these pests in a large garden area. If you have toads in your area, encourage them to stay in your garden by providing half-buried flowerpots in moist, shady spots.

CONTROLLING GARDEN PESTS

A wide variety of pests attack gardens, and there are a number of different control methods. The secret of a healthy garden is often knowing which treatments will be effective against which pests. Sprays, dusts, baits, and physical controls all must be used correctly in order to protect the plants in a garden or yard.

Spraying insecticides

Many pesticides have a residual effect of only a few days, so they are acceptable for use on food plants, but this also means that you must make repeated applications for continued control. In addition, if the chemical doesn't kill the larvae or eggs, you may need to spray several times to control the various generations of a pest. Read the label to see what schedule of repeat applications is recommended for a particular pest.

Contact insecticides

Most insectides kill insects that come in contact with them either by being sprayed, by eating the poison, or just by walking across a leaf that has been sprayed. Contact insecticides are effective against most insects that feed on the outside of plants. Cover all parts of the plant when spraying, including the underside of leaves.

Systemic insecticides

Systemic insecticides are absorbed through leaves or roots and circulated throughout the whole plant, including flowers and fruits. They are ingested by insects feeding on the plant. Systemic insecticides are especially effective against small sucking insects.

In addition to being stomach poisons, most systemics are also contact killers. Spray liquid formulations on infested plants for immediate and future control. If a pesticide is systemic, its label will say so. Never use systemics on food crops.

Baits *are used to control slugs, snails, earwigs, crickets, cutworms, and many other pests. Spread them where the pests spend the day, or surround plants you want to protect.*

Insecticide dusts

Some chemicals are sold already mixed, as dusts. Dusts are always used directly from the package, without mixing. The formulations often contain several chemicals that will control a wide range of pests and diseases.

Baits

Pesticides are sometimes combined with baits to control pests that hide during the day and are hard to control with sprays. Use baits to control snails, slugs, earwigs, crickets, and sowbugs.

Apply baits near where you think the pests are hiding—such as in a dense ground cover—or around the plants you want to protect. Or broadcast the bait across your entire yard. Reapply baits after a heavy rainstorm and once or twice a month during warm weather.

Dormant sprays

Many pests that live on fruit trees can be controlled best when the trees are dormant, after they have lost their leaves in winter. Dormant sprays are oils that coat insects and eggs and suffocate them.

Spray your fruit trees in the fall after the leaves have dropped. Because the oils will damage foliage, do not spray once blooms or leaves have appeared. Don't spray oils during very cold weather.

The effects of weather

Apply pesticides only during calm weather. Wind will blow sprays and dusts, making thorough and accurate coverage impossible. Rain will wash off most pesticides, so

Handpick *small numbers of insects to keep them from multiplying.*

Spraying *spreads liquid insecticides. Cover all parts of the plant, including the bottoms of leaves.*

Dusts *can be applied with a duster, as shown here. Some dusts come in dispenser cartons with a duster built in. Dusts need no mixing or measuring.*

applications may have to be repeated after heavy rainstorms. Sprays applied during hot weather (over 85°F) can burn plants; apply them during the cooler morning or evening hours to avoid foliage damage.

Physical controls

Small numbers of insects can be picked off plants and destroyed or disposed of in plastic bags in the garbage. Handpicking is most successful with large, slow insects on small plants.

Remove aphids with a strong spray of water. Be careful to wash them off both the upper and lower sides of leaves. Once they are knocked off, most of them die or are unable to find their way back to the plant.

You can also wash mites off leaves. Washing reduces the dry, dusty environment in which mites flourish. Spray plants regularly to discourage reinfestation.

Safety rules

Garden chemicals, like household chemicals, should be treated with respect. Always read the label and follow its instructions. You can't see from inspecting a chemical what its uses or dangers are, as you can with a machine. Here are a few basic safety tips:

■ Keep chemicals locked up, beyond the reach of children.

■ Keep the chemicals in their original bottle or can, never in an old food container.

■ When finished with a container, wrap it in newspaper and put it in the garbage. Don't burn chemical containers, especially aerosol cans.

■ Mix chemicals outdoors in a well-ventilated and adequately lit area.

■ Wash the sprayer thoroughly after use. This is especially important if you have been spraying herbicides.

■ Wash your hands thoroughly after using chemicals. Shower if the spray drifted. Launder sprayed clothes.

SUCKING INSECTS

Many insect pests cause damage to plants by sucking vital liquids from leaves, stems, and other parts. Aphids are the most common sucking insect found in home gardens, but others can cause just as much or more damage. To protect your plants, try to eliminate these pests before they become a major problem. Early control is much easier than quelling a full-fledged invasion, so keep a watchful eye out for their presence.

Many sucking insects secrete a sweet substance called *honeydew*. Because they must feed on large amounts of sap to get enough protein to grow, much of the liquid and sugar in the sap passes through undigested. This honeydew drops to leaves (and cars and patio furniture) below them. A black fungus called *sooty mold* often grows on the honeydew. Sooty mold is not a plant disease and does not directly harm the plants, but it is unsightly. It can be wiped off, or it will eventually be washed off the leaves by rain.

Aphids

Aphids, also known as plant lice, are usually gray, green, or black. They infest a wide range of plants and can accumulate in large numbers on buds, the undersides of leaves, or on bark or stems. Spray infested plants with insecticides for immediate control. Use systemic pesticides on plants that have chronic aphid problems, such as roses. Aphids are usually easy to control; many insecticides are effective against them. But they reinfest readily too, so watch for them to return. Ladybugs may control a general outbreak, and they help at all times to keep the aphid population in check.

Mealybugs

Mealybugs are a common problem on houseplants and outdoors in warm climates. They are 1/8 inch long and look like specks of white or gray cotton. Older mealybugs are sluggish, but the young move actively. They cluster in crevices or

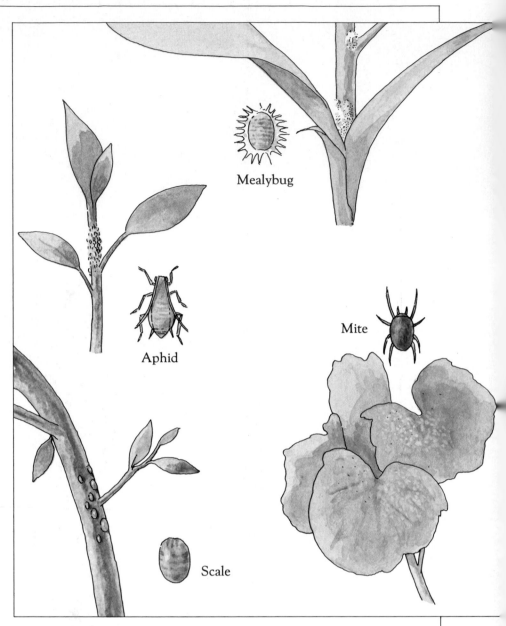

Mealybug

Aphid

Mite

Scale

at branching nodes and are protected by a waxy skin covering. Threads and flakes of wax litter the leaves they are on, giving a messy appearance.

Because of their waxy covering, mealybugs are sometimes difficult to control. Use an insecticide that is formulated for them. You can usually control small infestations on houseplants by daubing the mealybugs with a cotton swab dipped in rubbing alcohol.

Mites

Mites are tiny pests that live mainly on the undersides of leaves. They cause leaves to turn yellow

or brown and have a mottled appearance. Dirty webbing may be visible on the undersides of leaves. If you suspect that a plant has mites, hold a piece of white paper under the plant and tap the leaves sharply. The mites will fall to the paper and appear as reddish brown specks on the white background.

Contact miticides control adults effectively but do not kill eggs. Apply three treatments of contact pesticide at 7- to 10-day intervals to kill new generations as they hatch.

Scales

Scales attach themselves to branches and leaf stems. Different types have waxy, cottony, hard, or

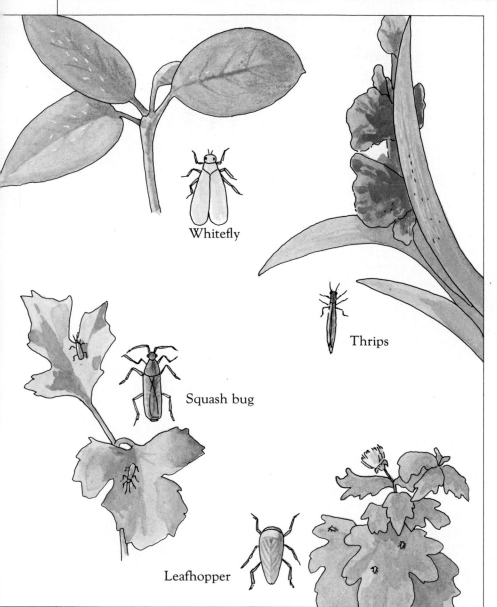

Whitefly

Thrips

Squash bug

Leafhopper

at 7- to 10-day intervals to control newly hatching insects will usually keep them under control, however.

True bugs

Gardeners often refer to all insects as bugs, but there is actually a separate order of insects, the *Hemiptera*, that are the true bugs in the scientific sense. This class includes chinch bugs, squash bugs, stink bugs, and many other pests found throughout the garden.

Apply contact insecticides to infested areas. Keep bugs from becoming a problem by removing garden debris where they can hide and lay eggs. Till the soil thoroughly in the fall to expose eggs.

Leafhoppers

Leafhoppers look like ¼-inch-long green or yellow grasshoppers. They suck juices from the undersides of leaves and prefer to feed on fruit trees, lawns, and vegetable plants. Affected plants have white dots on the leaves, and damaged lawns look wilted.

Control of leafhoppers is difficult because adults move rapidly from garden to garden. Spray contact killers or systemics to eliminate nonflying juveniles and to discourage adults. Spray on a regular schedule if leafhoppers are a constant problem.

soft shells. Large colonies often develop before they are noticed.

A young scale, called a *crawler*, looks like a tiny aphid. Crawlers are active and move around before choosing a place to insert their mouthparts. Then they become immobile and develop a waxy shell.

Because of their waxy shell, scale insects can be difficult to control. The most effective treatment is with a contact spray when the crawlers are active. Watch for crawlers in the spring and spray then. Later in the summer, spray with an insecticidal oil to smother the adults. Systemics are often effective against scales too.

Whiteflies

Whiteflies are tiny, white, winged insects. They explode into the air in large numbers when you shake an infested plant. Their populations build to enormous numbers in warm weather. In areas that have cold winters, whiteflies are mainly greenhouse pests.

Eggs, larvae, and adults are usually present on the same plant. The immobile larvae, which look like tiny transparent scale insects, suck more sap and do more harm than the mobile adults.

Whiteflies have a reputation of being difficult to control. Using a pesticide especially formulated for them and repeating the spraying

Thrips

Thrips look like tiny slivers of wood. They move quickly, with a serpentine wriggle. Thrips suck liquids from leaves and flowers. Foliage that has been damaged by thrips often looks silvery or has silvery streaks. Flower thrips feed on undeveloped blossoms and cause deformations and spots on flower petals.

Remove weeds near the garden where thrips can establish colonies. Spray affected areas with contact killers or systemics. Repeat spraying at regular intervals if infestations are severe.

CHEWING INSECTS

Many of the insect pests in the garden cause damage by chewing leaves and other parts of the plant. They can cause a great deal of damage if not controlled.

Beetles

Almost half of all insects are beetles. They can be recognized by their tough, leathery wings and chewing mouthparts. Some beetles (such as ladybugs) are carnivorous and do not eat plants. Many beetles are nocturnal. Beetle larvae are called *grubs*; they spend the winter in plants or in the soil.

Japanese beetles are a major pest in the eastern part of the country. Adults emerge in June and July, live and feed for 30 to 45 days, and lay eggs in lawns or grassy areas under the soil surface. Arid summers in the West help prevent infestations of this beetle, which prefers a warm, humid, rainy summer. Adult Japanese beetles feed on the flowers, leaves, and fruits of many plants. They chew the tender tissue between veins on tree leaves. Their grubs damage lawns in late summer, until cold drives them deep into the soil.

On food crops, control beetles with contact sprays; on ornamentals, use contacts or systemics. For grubs in lawns, use sprays or granules of contact insecticides. Clean up weeds in fall to reduce the number of places where beetles can spend the winter.

Borers

Borers are the larvae of beetles or moths. They tunnel into tree trunks and plant stems. Vigorous plants are usually able to resist borers, while plants under stress are more subject to borer attacks. Burrowing restricts the flow of nutrients and water in plants and weakens the structure of small plants.

Spray wood and bark with lindane. Cut out and destroy affected stems, or whole plants if the plants are small. Clean up debris around trees in winter to reduce places where they can live through the winter. Burn or destroy any infested pieces of firewood.

Caterpillars

Caterpillars are the larvae of moths and butterflies. They can be smooth, hairy, or spiny. They have voracious appetites and can defoliate an entire plant.

One kind of caterpillar, the larva of the gypsy moth, is in a class by itself because of its destructiveness. The gypsy moth was imported to the United States in the middle of the nineteenth century because of its potential as a producer of silk. It is now the most serious shade-tree pest in the eastern part of the United States.

The larvae emerge from eggs in early spring and may completely cover and defoliate trees. They defoliate oaks first and then move into other trees. Hardwood trees can grow new leaves after defoliation, but conifers suffer more permanent damage.

To control gypsy moth caterpillars, spray the entire tree weekly as needed during the larval period. Destroy egg sacs where visible. Keep trees well watered and fertilized to resist infestations.

Other notable caterpillars include tomato hornworms and green cabbage caterpillars. Look for chewed leaves in your garden that might indicate caterpillar activity. Spray vegetables with a contact insecticide formulated for food crops. Spray ornamentals with contact or systemic insecticides.

Cutworms

Cutworms are fleshy, hairless caterpillars up to 2 inches long that curl up when disturbed. Cutworms feed at night; they are active below ground, at the surface, and among branches. The adults are dark, night-flying moths. Surface cutworms damage early-season vegetables and flowers by feeding on seedlings and transplants. One cutworm can destroy a whole row of plants by chewing the stems at the soil surface.

Cutworms can be controlled with insecticides that are worked or watered into the soil, or with

Japanese beetle

Cutworm

baits. For additional protection, put collars around seedlings. Make the collars out of stiff paper, milk cartons, tin cans, or aluminum foil. They should be at least 3 inches wide. Press them an inch into the ground. Cultivate the soil in late summer and autumn to expose and destroy larvae and pupae. Remove weeds in late summer and fall to reduce places where they can hide during the winter.

Grasshoppers

Grasshoppers can defoliate whole plants, or even whole gardens if present in large numbers. They often infest a garden as adjacent

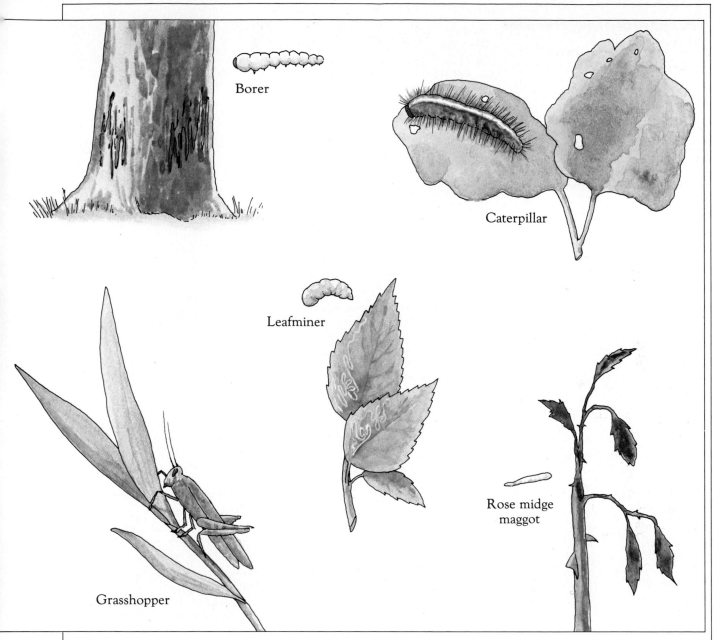

Borer

Caterpillar

Leafminer

Rose midge
maggot

Grasshopper

fields dry up. Some types are solitary and move about in a limited area. Migratory grasshoppers group together in huge swarms that travel hundreds of miles and cause unparalleled destruction when they stop to feed.

If you see or expect grasshoppers, spray your plants with a contact insecticide that has some residual effect.

Leaf miners

Leaf miners are insect larvae that feed inside leaves, between the upper and lower surfaces. They may be the larvae of flies, moths, or beetles. After the larvae hatch, they burrow into the leaf, creating tunnels, blisters, and blotches on the leaf surface. Spray affected ornamentals with systemic insecticides. Contact sprays are not effective because the miner is protected by the leaf.

Maggots

Maggots are the larvae of flies. Root crops, and kale crops like broccoli and cabbage, are commonly affected by cabbage maggots. The maggots chew holes and tunnels in the roots. Affected tissues become pitted and slimy. Dispose of infested plants. Treat the soil with a contact insecticide. You can also interplant radishes among other crops to act as decoys. Maggots will often infest radish roots and leave other plants alone.

Roses in eastern and northern gardens are attacked by rose midge maggots. These maggots cluster in the flower buds and can be very destructive and tenacious. The rose midge has a short life cycle and can produce five or six generations per growing season. Spray flies with a contact insecticide if they are visible. The most important control method is to destroy affected plant parts.

MANAGING ABOVEGROUND ANIMALS AND BIRDS

Birds and animals can cause problems in the garden. Here are some practical strategies for coping with them when they become pests.

Birds

Although birds perform a valuable service in the garden by controlling the insect population, they can also damage plants. Birds often eat freshly planted seeds and destroy young plants while scratching in the soil for insects. They also may eat seedlings, such as pea and ranunculus, and fruits. Birds are particularly attracted to cherries, berries, figs, strawberries, apples, and grapes; they may eat the fruits or damage them by pecking. Even lawns can be damaged by birds pecking for grubs.

Barriers are the most effective protection against birds. Hardware-cloth barriers over seeded areas will prevent birds from digging in soft soil, and chicken wire stretched over frames to make rectangular cages will keep birds away from seedlings. Larger nets of plastic, nylon, or cheesecloth can be used to protect berry bushes or fruit trees from birds. For grapes, tie a paper bag around each cluster; cut a few small holes in the end for air circulation.

Birds can often be repelled if they haven't yet developed the habit of feeding in your garden. But if they have already begun feeding, repellants usually are ineffective. Shiny aluminum-foil streamers fluttering from twine stretched across a garden will discourage birds. An active cat in the garden is also useful for scaring away birds.

Sapsuckers cause a special kind of damage; they drill into trees that have sweet sap to drink from the tree. Trees can tolerate some damage, but excessive sapsucker activity can girdle a tree trunk. Introduction of disease spores by wind or by the bird's bill can lead to heart rot and death of the tree. Sapsuckers are difficult to protect against except on low trees, where an adhesive band or burlap wrap in the pecked area can deter them.

Cats

Besides frightening away nuisance birds, cats also keep down populations of mice, rats, and other rodents in the garden. But most cats like to dig in soft garden soil, disturbing seeds and uprooting seedlings.

Commercial odor repellents keep cats off a specific area. Renew the spray according to label directions. Or place a chicken-wire screen or cage over seedlings or a newly seeded area to deter cats. You can remove the barrier when the plant leaves cover the ground.

Deer

Deer often damage gardens in rural and suburban areas by eating vegetables and flowers and by stripping the new growth off trees and shrubs, especially roses. If food is scarce in winter, deer will eat the bark of young trees, often causing severe damage.

Barriers are the best prevention against deer. Deer can jump high vertically but not horizontally, so a vertical fence must be at least 8 feet high to exclude them. But a barrier 5 feet high and 5 feet wide will work just as well. In practice, homeowners with deer problems have found that a slanted fence is quite effective.

If you don't want to install barriers, choose plants that deer find unpalatable, except when more desirable forage is in short supply. When deer are hungry and plants are flush with new growth, deer will eat almost anything. Your Cooperative Extension Agent can suggest plants for your area.

Repellents are effective, but they must be renewed or changed. Odor repellents, such as human hair or blood meal in a nylon stocking hung from a tree work in some areas. Spray commercial taste

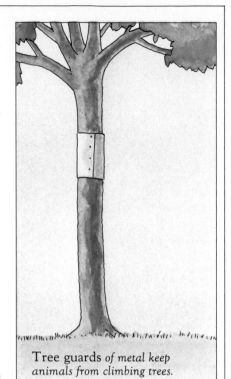

Tree guards *of metal keep animals from climbing trees.*

repellents on vulnerable plants. Noisemakers, blaring radios, and scarecrows will deter deer only until they learn that these devices are not dangerous.

Dogs

Dogs can cause much damage in a garden when they romp through a cultivated area, trampling plants, digging up soil, and depositing urine or droppings.

Commercial odor repellents make an area unappealing to dogs. Renew the spray periodically. Secure gates and sturdy fences will keep most dogs out. The size of the fence and the gate will depend on the behavior, strength, and discipline of the dogs you're trying to keep out. If barriers are not possible, plant in raised beds with paths for the dog to run along. Arrange alternative play areas for pets so that the garden will be less attractive to them.

Rabbits

Rabbits can be a problem because they eat herbaceous plants, especially garden vegetables, and gnaw at the young bark of many trees and shrubs.

Deer fences can be only 5 feet high if they are also 5 feet wide. A slanting fence like this one keeps out deer and is unobtrusive.

Keep rabbits out of the garden with a fence of chicken wire, welded wire, or hardware cloth whose mesh size is 1½ inches maximum. Bury the mesh fence 6 inches under the soil surface and raise it 2 feet or more above the ground. Extend the mesh fence all the way around the perimeter of the area to be protected. As an alternative, place wire cages over the most vulnerable garden plants.

Protect individual trees or shrubs with a 2-foot-high circle of wire mesh around the tree. If the damage occurs during winter in a snowy climate, the barrier must be taller than the snow line.

Raccoons

Raccoons are a nuisance in many rural and suburban settings, whether they are fed deliberately or inadvertently. Pet food and unharvested fruit may attract them. These omnivorous animals forage at night, are agile climbers, and are intelligent and inquisitive; but if trapped, they can be vicious.

A fence is an effective barrier around a vegetable garden. Make the fence of 5-foot-high chicken wire extending 2 feet above 3-foot-high posts. As the raccoon climbs the unsupported wire, its weight will pull it back down. Low-voltage electric fences are also effective. Use two strands, one at 6 inches and the other 12 inches from the ground. To keep raccoons out of

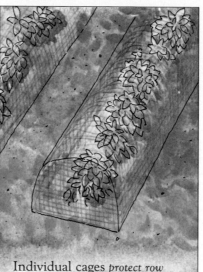

Individual cages protect row crops from birds and animals.

your trees, tie a metal wrap around the trunk. The wrap must be at least 2 feet off the ground and 18 inches high to prevent the raccoons from crawling over it. Prune tree limbs to keep raccoons from climbing onto rooftops or from traveling tree to tree. To prevent foraging in garbage cans, put the cans in a rack or tie them to a fence or other structure to prevent tipping over; fasten the lids securely. The presence of a large, active dog may also keep raccoons away.

Tree squirrels

Tree squirrels damage gardens by digging up newly planted seeds and bulbs. Sometimes they dig up entire plants. These omnivorous creatures survive on seeds, nuts, insects, and bark. They are agile climbers and jumpers, with a 6-foot jumping range.

Chicken-wire barriers are the best protection against squirrels in the garden. Place the chicken wire over newly seeded areas or over seedlings and bulbs; remove it when the plants are large enough to withstand damage. If you want to keep the squirrels out of your trees, wrap a band of metal 18 inches wide around the trunk 4 feet above the ground. Prune back any branches within 6 lateral feet or 2 vertical feet of any other tree, fence, roof, or other perch from which the squirrel could jump into and out of the tree. Squirrels may also be trapped and removed from your area.

Slugs and snails

Slugs and snails eat a wide variety of green plants. They usually leave a slime trail that shines when dry. They can cause great damage to seedlings and to leaves of tender vegetables such as lettuce. Combine several approaches to control snails and slugs.

Use slug and snail controls, in either liquid or pellet form, that contain metaldehyde or mesurol. This material is broken down by rain, so repeat the application every 2 weeks. Begin in early spring to keep large populations from developing.

Clean up vegetation and debris so slugs and snails will have fewer places to hide. This step is essential for long-term control. When you discover their clusters of white eggs in a slimy mass, promptly destroy them.

Protect plants with barriers. You can use a sealed screen barrier for raised beds; the mesh must be small enough to prevent penetration. A 3-inch-high copper wire barrier tacked to a board may hold back snails. You can also use these barriers to hold plants such as strawberries off the ground; this method makes the fruits less vulnerable to damage.

CONTROLLING UNDERGROUND ANIMALS

Underground animals, especially gophers, can be the most frustrating pests for the gardener to control. From the sanctuary of their underground burrows, these animals can do much damage to the garden. You may have to use fences, traps, or poisons to eliminate them. An active cat can help control some of them.

Gophers

Gophers dig tunnels that run a foot or more below the soil surface; they leave crescent-shaped mounds of dirt on the surface as they make new runs. They live and feed almost entirely underground, living alone except during the brief mating periods. They eat plant tops and roots. Gophers can kill shrubs by eating the roots or girdling the underground part of the trunk or stems. Their tunnels can drain irrigated areas and keep water from getting to plant roots.

You can keep gophers out of a raised bed by tacking ¼-inch hardware cloth to the bottom of the wood frame. In open gardens, trapping is the best method of eradication. Search with a long metal probe to locate the main run. Dig down to expose the run and insert two scissors-type or box traps, one facing in each direction. Tie the traps with wire to a stake above the ground. To keep soil from falling on the traps, cover the hole with sod or with a board; sprinkle with soil to block out all light. Check the traps daily. Look for new mounds, indicating recent gopher activity, and set traps when mounds appear. Since gophers are solitary and fiercely territorial, catching one gopher will usually rid your garden of the problem for a while. But the run will be reinhabited by another gopher if there are many gophers in the area.

Poison bait is also effective. With a probe, locate the tunnel, excavate as much as needed, and insert the bait. Be sure that pets can't get to the bait.

Spear-type mole traps *are set on active surface runs. Test a run for activity by flattening it. If it is raised again the next day, set a trap on it.*

Ground squirrels

Ground squirrels are a problem in many gardens west of the Rockies. Especially in the spring, ground squirrels devour tender greens in gardens. After emerging from winter hibernation, they are hungry and may find forage scarce in early spring. Later in the season, ground squirrels feed on seeds, grains, vegetables, fruits, and nuts. They live in large colonies. Often, the only way to control them is to eliminate the colony. This is a job for a pest control contractor.

Barriers and fences are not effective because these agile climbers easily circumvent them. Trapping is the most effective control method. Set the traps near burrow entrances or along pathways used by the animals. Use baits such as peanut butter, nuts, raisins, or cereals. Always wear gloves and protective clothing when removing ground squirrels from traps because they and their fleas may carry disease, including plague. Don't handle live or injured squirrels because they bite, especially when threatened.

Mice

Mice are nocturnal feeders that sometimes eat garden bulbs, freshly sown seeds, tender vegetables, and flowers. They severely damage young trees by gnawing on bark and roots. Mice generally live in grassy or brushy areas, nesting underground in shallow burrows or aboveground in densely vegetated, protected spots. They may also establish nests in thick hay or leaf mulches.

You may have success at keeping mice out of the garden by enclosing it with a fence of fine-mesh (no larger than ¼ inch) wire or hardware cloth extending a foot above and a foot below ground level. Protect young trees by placing hardware-cloth cylinders around the tree base, with the cylinder a foot high and extending several inches into the ground. Wrap tree trunks with a tough plastic, available as tree wrap at some nurseries, to protect them. Keep your garden free of grassy areas or piles of leaves and debris where mice can live. In an unfenced garden, protect valuable plants by encircling the plant with hardware cloth that extends a foot high and is pushed several inches into the ground. Set out traps or poison baits along mouse runways.

Scissors traps are set in main runs. Probe to find the run, then dig down to it and set a trap in each direction. Cover the hole to keep out light and prevent children and animals from examining the traps.

Moles

Moles are small gray or black mammals with smooth, velvety fur. Their eyesight is poor, but their senses of smell, touch, and hearing are well developed. Their large front feet have long trowellike claws for tunneling.

Moles seldom feed on plants, but they damage plants indirectly by tunneling. While searching for grubs, slugs, and earthworms, they dig tunnels, uprooting and pushing up lawn grasses or loosening the soil around roots so that the roots dry out and die.

Their interconnected tunnels are 6 to 8 inches below ground level. To determine whether a tunnel is currently being used, press the ridge down with your foot and then check the following day to see if it has been raised again.

The best way to control moles in the lawn is to reduce their food supply by controlling insect grubs with an insecticide. You can also eradicate moles by trapping them in their tunnels. In the East, you can buy spear-type traps made specifically for moles. In the West,

where the dominant mole species digs a deeper tunnel, scissors-type traps are more effective. For deep runways, explore with a probe and trap as you would for gophers. Poison baits, repellents, and fumigants are generally ineffective against moles.

You can protect raised planting beds with physical barriers such as ¼-inch hardware cloth stapled to the bottom.

Rats

Both the Norway rat and the roof rat cause damage around homes and gardens and may enter houses to nest and forage. In some areas they are major fruit tree pests, eating and fouling fruit. Young rats can squeeze into houses through holes as small as ½ inch. If rats are a problem in your area, you can keep them out of the house by sealing all potential points of entry. Chimneys and air vents are main entry points.

The roof rat flourishes in suburban settings that have abundant

food and nesting supplies, such as ivy and juniper. The Norway rat—also known as the brown, sewer, wharf, or house rat—can be discouraged by good sanitation practices, including management of compost piles to make the compost heat up quickly and thoroughly.

To eliminate rats, it's best to trap them. Bait the traps with beef, bacon, nuts, fish, or carrots, tying the bait to the trigger. Check the traps once a day and dispose of dead rats, using a glove or tongs to remove them. Avoid touching the rats because they host fleas and mites that can transmit disease. Poison baits can also kill rats, but the disadvantage of this method is the risk of stench from a dead rat decomposing in an inaccessible wall space.

Woodchucks

Woodchucks, also known as groundhogs, are a problem in many rural and suburban areas. The woodchuck feeds aboveground on tender vegetables, flowers, and succulent greenery. Woodchucks occasionally have diseases that they can transmit to humans, so always wear gloves and protective clothing when handling these animals.

Fencing can keep woodchucks out of the garden. Surround the area with a woven-wire fence held in place with 3-foot-high stakes. To prevent woodchucks from burrowing underneath, bend the bottom foot of the fence outward and bury it a few inches. To keep them from climbing over the fence, extend the fence 18 inches above the top of the stakes. The weight of the climbing woodchuck will bend the wire out and down toward the ground so the animal won't be able to climb over. Any trapping or shooting of woodchucks must comply with local and state game regulations.

COMBATTING DISEASES

Plants don't die for no reason. They get diseases, just as people do. These diseases have names and specific remedies that will cure them or stop their spread. If you can identify the disease, you can usually cure it.

Plant diseases are often frustrating to gardeners because they can't see the microscopic agents that are causing the problem. The sudden wilting of a tomato plant or the appearance of mildew on rose leaves can be quite a surprise. But there is really nothing so mysterious about plant diseases. The treatment of most plant diseases is relatively simple. The information in this section can be used to help you control the plant diseases you are most likely to encounter in the home garden.

Conditions necessary for infectious plant disease

Infectious plant diseases require at least three conditions: a susceptible host plant must be available, a virulent *pathogen* (causative agent) of some sort must be present, and a favorable environment must encourage the disease. Disease control strategies focus on disrupting at least one of these conditions.

Susceptible hosts vary according to the disease. Some diseases flourish on only a certain kind of plant, such as Dutch elm disease on elm trees. Though this disease infects only one species, it remains one of

Powdery mildew is one of the most widespread plant diseases. It attacks roses wherever they are grown.

the most serious plant diseases in the country because it kills thousands of elms each year. Other diseases, such as powdery mildew, affect a wide range of host plants and are not restricted to a single species.

Virulent pathogens include bacteria, fungi, viruses, and nematodes. *Fungi* cause the largest group of plant diseases. Some 8000 fungus species cause plant diseases. Since fungi lack chlorophyll, the green pigment that enables plants to make their own food in the presence of light, these organisms depend on living and dead plant (or animal) tissue for nourishment. Most fungi aren't active when temperatures become colder than 25°F or hotter than 110°F. Fungi reproduce primarily by spores. Sometimes fruiting bodies that form the spores are noticeable, such as those of mushrooms. Spores are usually carried to new plants by wind or water. Most spores must remain in a drop of water for 6 to 8 hours before they germinate and infect a leaf. Powdery mildew is one exception; it can spread without any free water in which to germinate. Fungi can penetrate through plant tissue (bacterial diseases require a natural opening or wound on the plant to become established in the host).

You can control fungus disease by keeping plant leaves dry, choosing disease-resistant plants, and

applying fungicides. (Be sure the fungicide label indicates it is both effective against the fungus and safe for your plant.)

About 200 species of *bacteria* also parasitize plants. Some bacteria secrete toxins that poison and kill the cells of the host plant. Others manufacture enzymes that break down resistant plant material. A few exude growth-stimulating substances that result in cancerlike cell growth. Major symptoms of bacterial plant diseases are soft rot of tissue, leaf spots that don't cross the veins, as well as wilt (although most wilts are fungal), blight, and swelling (such as galls). Bacteria often reach the potential host plant when splashed onto it by rainwater. Bacteria also spread in seed or when transported by people on cultivating tools, pruning shears, or plant material. They enter the plant through natural openings or through wounds. The devastating bacterial disease called fire blight enters through small nectar holes at the ends of flowers as bees and other insects pollinate the plant. Bacteria often live within a protective ooze that they create in the infected plant.

The main controls against bacteria are preventive measures, such as good sanitation and choosing resistant plants. Chemicals, such as antibiotics or basic copper sulfate, assist in control if they supplement careful sanitation. Remove all the affected parts.

Viruses are submicroscopic particles composed of proteins and nucleic acids. The few viruses that are serious or fatal to plants usually reach the plant through hand and tool contact or are carried by insects. Most viruses only slightly impair plant growth and manifest symptoms only under certain conditions. Infected cuttings and infected graftings are a common source of viruses. If the infection spreads rapidly, viruses can decrease the plant's ability to manufacture and store food by reducing chlorophyll manufacture. Mosaic viruses mottle or streak leaves; ring-spot viruses form pale rings on leaves; and stunt viruses cause stunting of foliage. In some hosts, viruses thicken, curl, or distort leaves. Yields of vegetables, fruits, and flowers are reduced.

Chemicals can't cure viral infections because the virus lives inside the host cells. Control of insect vectors transmitting the disease helps restrict the damage. Aphids and leafhoppers are major virus carriers. Remove and destroy infected plants to reduce the spread of viruses. Buy seeds, bulbs, cuttings, and young plants only from certified nurseries and seed companies with disease-free propagating techniques. Control weeds that may be hosts to the viruses.

Nematodes, also known as eelworms or roundworms, are microscopic worms. Some types live in the soil and feed on root hairs and root tips. Other types live within the roots themselves. Nematodes are a major problem in some soils in the South, especially those that are moist and sandy. *Root* nematodes, attracted to root juices or sap, either feed on the outside of the root or burrow inside. The main damage is from nematode "saliva," which causes cells to collapse and disintegrate, resulting in dark lesions and dead areas along the roots. In some cases, toxins from the nematode stimulate rapid gall-like growths on the roots. Nematode damage limits the roots' ability to supply aboveground parts of the plant with water and nutrients, causing wilting, discoloration,

These tomatoes are suffering from tobacco mosaic virus, which can be transmitted from cigarette tobacco on the hands of the gardener.

stunting, and sometimes death. *Foliar* nematodes feed on plant stems and leaves, swimming on wet plant surfaces. They can cause stunting, distortion, and blotches on foliage. Hawaiian soil has many nematodes and other diseases, which is why quarantine restrictions on plants from that region are so strict.

Don't attempt control measures for nematodes unless positive identification has been made by a lab. The first step is to remove affected plants. If nematodes are a problem in your area, your Cooperative Extension Agent can give you a list of plants resistant to nematodes. Confine your planting choices to that list to avoid problems. To kill nematodes, you will have to fumigate the soil before planting.

Favorable environments for most plant diseases include water, partly because most fungal and bacterial infections spread under moist conditions. For instance, roses in the shade will have mildew, but the same roses in the sun, where the sun can dry the leaves, will be less susceptible. Good air circulation and adequate spacing of plants also reduce the environmental conditions favorable to many diseases.

Environmental plant diseases
It is important to distinguish between infectious plant diseases and physiological disorders, which also retard normal plant development. Physiological disorders result from a physical condition instead of from microbes. Collectively, these physiological disorders are called *environmental diseases.* The symptoms are similar to those of infectious diseases, but the causes are different. It has been estimated that 90 percent of plant disorders in the home garden are caused or aided by environmental factors.

When diagnosing plant disorders, begin by eliminating environmental factors before concluding that your plant has an infectious disease. To prevent or control environmental disorders, first alter the plant's environment and the care you give it. However, plant stress due to environmental factors can encourage any infectious diseases that may be present.

Classifications of plant diseases

Plant diseases fall into orderly classifications in various ways. Some gardeners classify by symptoms, such as chlorosis (the yellowing of a leaf), regardless of the reason.

Others classify by the type of plant affected, such as diseases of roses. Still others organize by the part of the plant infected, such as petal, stem, or root diseases.

Diseases also can be classified by type of pathogen (fungus, bacteria, virus) or by the way they spread (wind, water, soil). For our purposes, we'll divide diseases into two groups, those that are borne by the soil and attack roots (see page 174), and those that affect leaves, stems, and petals (see page 176). When you know what the disease is, you can project what similar plants may harbor it, whether it poses a serious threat to your plant, and how you can control it.

Controlling plant diseases: breaking the disease cycle

Every disease has a cycle or set of conditions that must be met for the disease to begin and then to flourish. A home gardener who breaks the cycle can disrupt the disease. Here are some strategies for disrupting the disease cycle.

Exclude the disease by inspecting plants brought into your garden. Make sure the soil is free of nematodes. Buy only certified disease-free plants, cuttings, and seeds. Nurseries propagate strawberries, for instance, from "mother blocks" of certified disease-free plants. These plants remain in a screened environment that aphids, which transmit viruses to strawberries, can't penetrate.

Eradicate the disease with good sanitation practices and winter cleanup. Remove fallen fruit, dead flowers, and debris throughout the year. Be particularly thorough in the fall, since neglected vegetation is a favorite winter home for many pathogens. Reduce alternate hosts among nearby weeds.

Decrease the rate of disease infection with appropriate dormant sprays and seasonal plantings. Plant peas, for instance, when cold, rainy weather favorable to powdery mildew and damping off has passed. Reduce insect vectors, such as aphids and leafhoppers.

The streaking on these gladiolus petals is caused by a virus that is passed from one generation to the next in the corm.

Sterilize pruning tools to prevent the spread of disease. Avoid importing disease-contaminated soil to your garden.

Use cultural controls to prevent disease. For diseases that are plant-specific, remove or rotate plants to control the disease. Allow the soil to dry up slightly between irrigations. Constantly soaked soil invites a multitude of disease organisms. Keep water off leaves that are susceptible to diseases that thrive in a moist environment.

Select disease-resistant plants, such as VF tomatoes, which resist verticillium and fusarium wilt. If certain diseases plague your region, grow nonsusceptible plants.

Use chemical controls. Fungicides, the main chemical control against plant disease, act in various ways. Labels on the products will alert you to these nuances. Some fungicides kill established fungi. Others protect against future fungal attack but don't kill established fungi. Some remain on the exterior of plants, and others travel systemically through the plant with the sap after the plant absorbs the chemical. Some are safe for use on food plants; others should be used only on ornamentals. Several products combine fungicides with insecticides. As with all garden chemicals, read and follow the label directions carefully (see page 158) and observe appropriate safety precautions when storing or applying (see page 146) the chemicals.

SOILBORNE DISEASES

These diseases attack plants from the soil. Some of the most troublesome soilborne diseases you're likely to find in a home garden are described here. The symptoms of each disease are described, and some methods of control are suggested for each.

Armillaria root rot

This disease—also known as **mushroom root rot, honey mushroom,** and **oak root fungus**—is caused by the fungus *Armillaria mellea*, which attacks the roots of a wide range of plants. Diseased ornamentals or fruit trees die over a period of years. The fungus appears as a white, fan-shaped mat in the lower part of a tree, between the bark and the wood, causing decay in the roots and lower trunk. Leaves may become yellow and stunted. As the roots die, the plant slowly starves. If the fungus girdles the crown of the plant, the plant wilts quickly. In autumn, mushrooms may appear at the base of the plant.

Control the disease by removing badly infected trees, including the stump and roots if possible. Save partially infected plants by removing soil, cutting out diseased tissue, and exposing the fungus to the air. Reduce summer irrigation whenever possible.

Bacterial wilts

Plants with these diseases exhibit wilted leaf and stem tissue. Typical hosts include vegetables, flowers, and tropical plants. Several kinds of bacteria cause wilts.

Infected plants will die. Remove and destroy them to avoid spreading disease. Keep the garden clean by removing plant debris. Use resistant varieties in infected soil.

Damping off

Damping-off disease kills seedlings, either before they break through

Armillaria root rot

Bacterial wilt

Damping off

the surface of the soil or shortly thereafter. Developing seedlings suddenly fall over and die. Dark lesions may appear on their lower stems and roots.

The problem is caused by one of several soilborne fungi (*Pythium, Phytophthera,* and *Rhizoctonia*). They can affect seeds and seedlings at any stage of germination before the plant matures.

Start seeds in a sterile medium (see page 22). Sterilize pots before reuse. If you plant outside, or in a soil-based potting mix indoors, avoid conditions that encourage succulent plant growth until the seedling has begun to harden. Wait to add fertilizer until plants develop at least one pair of true leaves. Let the soil surface dry slightly between waterings. Encourage rapid seedling growth by planting when the soil temperature is optimum (70° to 75°F is good for most

vegetables, but cooler soils are satisfactory for peas, for instance). Coat seeds with fungicide before planting them.

Nematodes

These tiny worms, also known as **eelworms** and **roundworms,** cause wilting, discoloration, stunting, and sometimes death. Knots or nodules may form on the roots. Nematodes are most troublesome in the South in damp, warm, sandy soils. The tiny worms move only a short distance per year under their own power, but irrigation water or transport on soil and tools can carry them about rapidly.

Send a soil sample to a lab (see page 14) to get a definitive answer that the problem is nematodes. There are no chemicals available to the home gardener that will kill nematodes without killing the plants too. Remove infected

Nematode damage

Sclerotium root rot

Crown rot caused by water mold

Verticillium wilt

plants and replace them with nematode-resistant varieties. Your local Cooperative Extension Agent can supply you with a list for your region. In some areas, it may be necessary to fumigate the soil before planting.

Sclerotium root rot

This root rot (also known as **southern wilt, southern blight,** and **crown rot**) causes infected plants to wilt, turn yellow, and decay. Roots and crowns of plants rot, stems develop cankers, and bulbs or tubers rot. Infection occurs at soil level and below. White fungal threads surround and cover the infected plant, secreting oxalic acid that kills healthy plant cells and allows the fungus to enter.

The disease is caused by a soil-borne fungus (*Sclerotium rolfsii*) that feeds on vegetables, flowers, and some woody shrubs. Spores survive as pellets in soil or plant debris; they remain most active in warm, moist, sandy soil that is low in nitrogen.

Infected plants will die. Remove the plant and 6 inches of surrounding soil. Add a balanced fertilizer and liberal amounts of organic matter to improve the soil. Clean up plant debris to eliminate fungal pellets.

Verticillium or fusarium wilt

Plants with this disease wilt, their leaves and stems discolor, and eventually the plants die. The wilts can affect annual vegetables, flowers, and herbaceous perennials. Verticillium wilt also affects many woody shrubs and trees.

The two types of fungi causing these diseases are *Verticillium* and *Fusarium*. Both can thrive in the soil for years after the host plant has died. *Fusarium* likes warm soil and is a major problem in the South. *Verticillium* is more prominent in the North. Fungal strands penetrate the roots of the plant and expand through its water-conducting vessels. If the disease is present in your soil, plant resistant varieties. Look for seed packets that indicate resistance with the notation "VF-resistant." Once the diseases are in the soil, they will remain there until they are killed by fumigation.

Water mold

Water mold causes the leaves of plants in soggy, poorly drained soil to become dull and individual branches or entire plants to wilt, turn yellow, and die.

The disease is caused by either *Pythium* or *Phytophthora*, fungi that thrive in wet, poorly drained soils, especially in constantly watered lawns and flower beds. The disease is most active in warm (55° to 80°F) soils. Gardeners often mistake the leaf symptoms of water mold disease for those of drought and increase watering in an attempt to correct it, but increasing the water supply only worsens the problem.

Remove thoroughly infected plants, but save partially infected plants by drying out the soil. Begin a program of improving the drainage (see page 18). The more you can dry the soil, the further you will reduce the mold. Water thoroughly but infrequently. To reduce the plant's water needs during the drying period, shade it, cover it with a plastic wrap (if it is in the shade), or apply an anti-transpirant, available at nurseries. Where excess soil moisture is likely, plant *Phytophthora*-resistant plants, such as some species of camellia, rhododendron, chamaecyparis, and juniper.

LEAF, STEM, AND FLOWER DISEASES

Most plant diseases attack plants from spores or bacteria that are carried by wind, insects, or splashing rainwater. Several of the most common diseases, and some possible controls, are described here.

Botrytis blight

This disease is also known by several other names: *gray mold, blossom blight, flower blight,* and *bud blight*. Brown spots and blotches appear and grow on plant leaves, flowers, or fruits. Brown or gray fuzzy mold often appears on affected tissue.

Affected plants typically live in an environment of high humidity and cool temperatures. The disease is caused by a fungus (*Botrytis*). It infects a wide range of plants, especially soft fruits such as strawberries and grapes. *Botrytis* spores are present in most soils.

Clean up dead leaves and flowers. Keep foliage dry and improve air circulation around the plant. Water at the soil level rather than on the leaves. Spray plants with fungicides.

Fire blight

When twigs or branches appear scorched and wilt suddenly, fire blight may be the culprit. Blossoms turn black and die, leaves curl and hang down, and bark turns black. This disease attacks only plants in the rose family, such as pear, apple, quince, pyracantha, hawthorn, and crabapple.

The disease is caused by the bacterium *Erwinia amylovora,* which spreads rapidly during warm, wet weather. In dry areas, it is a spring disease. In regions with humid summers, it is active all summer. Rainwater and overhead sprinkling splash disease-carrying spores to plant parts, and bees carry bacteria from plant to plant as they pollinate.

Prune the affected parts 6 inches below visible infection and destroy them. Sterilize pruning tools in

Botrytis blight

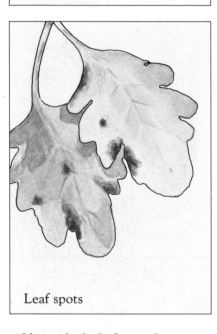

Leaf spots

rubbing alcohol after each cut. Spray with streptomycin or a fixed copper spray weekly as buds open and flower. Reduce nitrogen fertilizing because succulent growth is particularly vulnerable.

Leaf spots

These can be caused by bacteria or fungi. Leaf spots appear as spots and blotches. They may affect all the plant's leaves.

Most leaf spot diseases are caused by fungi; a few are caused by bacteria. Bacteria are carried in drops of water; they may be carried from plant to plant in splashing raindrops or by insects or gardeners working among wet plants. Fungal spores are carried in drops of water or by the wind. The

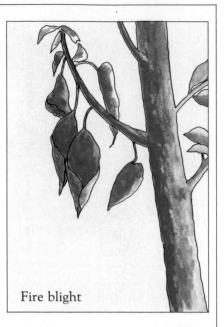

Fire blight

bacteria or fungi infect the leaf where they contact it. Each spot is made by a new infection.

Spray with a fungicide. The fungicide puts a protective coating on the leaves to prevent the disease from spreading. Repeat the application as the fungicide is washed off by weather or when new growth needs to be coated. Remove and destroy severely infected leaves. Keep the leaves as dry as possible. Don't mist or water the plants from overhead.

Mosaic virus

Leaves of the plant show blotches or mottles of yellow and green, and leaves may curl. Diseased plants grow slowly.

Beans, corn, cucumbers, peppers, dahlias, delphiniums, and petunias are typical hosts among outdoor plants. Aphids spread some viruses, and handling wet plants encourages virus spread. Smokers spread tobacco virus on their hands unless they wash them thoroughly before handling plants.

There is no cure for mosaic virus. Control aphids and weeds in the garden to prevent infestation and spread of the virus. Many plants can tolerate the disease and are not severely injured by it. Destroy badly infected plants.

Mosaic virus

Peach leaf curl

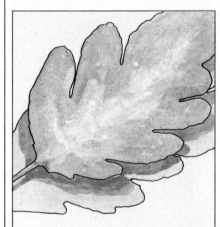

Powdery mildew

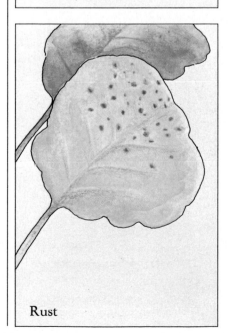

Rust

Peach leaf curl

Leaves of peach, nectarine, and almond deform by thickening, curling, and blistering. The foliage turns orange or red and falls prematurely.

The fungus *Taphrina deformans* causes peach leaf curl. The disease occurs in the spring as new leaves appear on the tree. Fungal spores live through the winter on the bark and buds of trees.

Once damaged leaves appear in the spring, it's too late to do anything about the disease that season. The following autumn, spray with a lime-sulphur, chlorothalonil, or a fixed copper dormant spray as soon as the leaves fall. If leaf curl has been severe, spray again just before the buds open in spring.

Powdery mildew

A white or grayish powdery material appears as a thin layer or irregular patches on leaves, stems, or flowers. Infected leaves may turn yellowish or reddish and drop. A wide range of outdoor and indoor plants can become infected.

Powdery mildew can be caused by several different fungi. It is the only leaf disease that is active in dry weather, although it is more severe in damp weather. Plants growing in shady areas may become severely infected. Mildew is spread by spores carried from place to place on air currents.

Use fungicides to control powdery mildew. Provide for adequate sunlight and ventilation when spacing plants that are susceptible to mildew, such as roses. Water on the leaves also encourages mildew, so avoid sprinkling the leaves of vulnerable vegetables such as squash and cucumber.

Rust

Rust-colored or brown powdery pustules appear on the leaves, fruits, or stems. Spots may spread, and leaves and fruits may fall prematurely.

Rusts are caused by fungi (*Puccinia* species and others). They infect a number of plants, including lawn grasses, snapdragons, and roses. Wind and splashing water spread the spores.

Apply fungicides to control rusts. Be sure the label lists your plant. Prune off badly damaged plant parts, if pruning won't destroy the beauty of the plant. Keep foliage dry to reduce the chance of infection. Fertilize to help plants overcome rust damage. Fertilize lawns so that the affected leaves will grow up and be removed when the grass is mowed.

SUREFIRE PLANTS

What are some of the favorite plants of American gardeners? If you are planning a garden, you may want to know the plants that have proven satisfactory to gardeners throughout the country. Here are recommendations for plants that can be successfully grown in varying climates and garden sites. Most of these plants grow best in particular areas of the country, although some are so adaptable that they can be grown almost anywhere. Your local Cooperative Extension Agent or nursery can expand on this beginning list and verify whether or not the plant will grow well in your region.

Surefire flowers

(A=annual, Bi=biennial, Bu=bulb, P=perennial, Rh=rhizome, Tp=tender perennial, Tu=tuber)

Spring flowers
Anemone (*Tu*)
Astilbe (*P*)
Calendula (*A*)
Columbine (*P*)
Crocus (*corm*)
Daffodil (*Bu*)
Forget-me-not/*Myosotis* (*A*)
Freesia (*corm*)
Grape hyacinth/*Muscari* (*Bu*)
Hellebore (*P*)
Hyacinth (*Bu*)
Iris (*Rh*)
Lily-of-the-valley (*P*)
Pansy (*A, Tp*)
Phlox (*A, P*)
Poppy (*A, P*)
Primrose (*A, P*)
Ranunculus (*Tu*)
Snapdragon (*A*)
Stock (*A*)
Sweet pea (*A*)
Tulip (*Bu*)
Viola (*Tp*)

Summer flowers
Ageratum (*A*)
Amaranthus (*A*)
Aster (*A, P*)
Astilbe (*P*)
Bearded iris (*Rh*)
Begonia (*A, Tp*)
Black-eyed Susan/*Rudbeckia* (*A, P*)
Browallia (*A*)
Campanula (*P*)
Candytuft/*Iberis* (*A, P*)
Canna (*Tp*)
Carnation (*A, P*)
Chrysanthemum (*A, P*)
Cineraria (*A*)
Cleome (*A*)
Cockscomb/*Celosia* (*A*)
Columbine (*P*)
Coral bells (*P*)
Coreopsis (*A, P*)
Cosmos (*A*)
Dahlia (*Tu*)
Delphinium (*A, P*)
Dimorphotheca (*A*)
Foxglove (*Bi, P*)
Gaillardia (*A, P*)
Geranium/*Pelargonium* (*P*)
Gerbera (*Tp*)
Gladiolus (*corm*)

Hemerocallis (*Tu*)
Hollyhock (*Bi*)
Hosta (*P*)
Impatiens (*A, P*)
Lily (*Bu*)
Marigold (*A*)
Nasturtium (*A*)
Petunia (*A*)
Pinks/*Dianthus* (*A, P*)
Portulaca (*A*)
Ranunculus (*Tu*)
Salpiglossis (*A*)
Salvia (*A, P*)
Snapdragon (*A*)
Stock (*A*)
Sunflower (*A*)
Sweet alyssum (*A, P*)
Verbena (*A, P*)
Yarrow/*Achillea* (*P*)
Zinnia (*A*)

Fall flowers
Black-eyed Susan/*Rudbeckia* (*A, P*)
Calendula (*A*)
Canna (*Tu*)
Chrysanthemum (*A, P*)
Cosmos (*A*)
Dahlia (*Tu*)
Gaillardia (*A, P*)
Gladiolus (*corm*)
Lobelia (*A*)
Marigold (*A*)
Nasturtium (*A*)
Petunia (*A*)
Phlox (*A, P*)
Portulaca (*A*)
Verbena (*A*)
Yarrow (*P*)
Zinnia (*A*)

Winter flowers (in warm climates)
Calendula (*A*)
Cineraria (*A*)
Pansy (*A, Tp*)
Primrose (*A, P*)
Snapdragon (*A*)
Stock (*A*)
Sweet alyssum (*A*)
Viola (*A, P*)

Perennial flowers that make the best cut flowers
Anemone
Aster
Baby's breath/*Gypsophila*
Black-eyed Susan
Blazing star/*Liatris*
Carnation

Daffodils are a favorite bulb for spring bloom.

Chrysanthemum
Coneflower
Coral bells
Coreopsis
Daylily
Delphinium
Foxglove
Gaillardia
Geum
Globe thistle
Golden marguerite/*Anthemis*
Goldenrod

Heliopsis
Hosta
Lupine
Peony
Pincushion flower/*Scabiosa*
Pinks
Poppy
Stokes' aster/*Stokesia*
Sunflower
Torch lily/*Kniphofia*
Veronica
Yarrow

Roses especially good for cutting

Hybrid Tea
'Blue Moon'
'Charlotte Armstrong'
'Chicago Peace'
'Chrysler Imperial'
'Double Delight'
'First Prize'
'Fragrant Cloud'
'Friendship'
'Garden Party'
'Honor'
'Miss All-American Beauty'
'Oklahoma'
'Pascali'
'Peace'
'Perfume Delight'
'Red Masterpiece'
'Tiffany'
'Tropicana'
'White Masterpiece'

Floribunda and Polyantha
'Angel Face'
'Cecile Brunner'
'Charisma'
'Cherish'
'Europeana'
'Marina'
'Orangeade'

Grandiflora
'Aquarius'
'Arizona'
'Love'
'Mount Shasta'
'Pink Parfait'
'Prominent'
'Scarlet Knight'
'Sonia'
'White Lightnin'

Roses that are especially fragrant

Hybrid Tea
'Bewitched'
'Blue Moon'
'Candy Stripe'
'Chrysler Imperial'
'Crimson Glory'
'Fragrant Cloud'
'Granada'
'Helen Traubel'
'Mister Lincoln'
'Papa Meilland'
'Perfume Delight'
'Proud Land'
'Rubaiyat'
'Seashell'
'Sutter's Gold'
'Sweet Surrender'
'Tiffany'

Floribunda
'Angel Face'
'Iceberg'
'Spartan'

Viburnum dilitatum.

Grandiflora
'Arizona'
'Sonia'
'Sundowner'
'White Lightnin'

Climbers, Ramblers, and Pillar Roses
'Climbing Crimson Glory'
'Climbing Shot Silk'
'Don Juan'
'Viking Queen'

Surefire trees

Trees essentially pest-free
American hop hornbeam/*Ostrya*
Amur oak/*Phellodendron*
Bald cypress
Cedar/*Cedrus*
Chinese pistache
Dawn redwood
Fringe tree/*Chionanthus*
Gingko
Goldenrain tree/*Koelreuteria*
Hackberry
Japanese pagoda tree
Katsura/*Cercidiphyllum*
Liquidambar
Magnolia
Olive
Russian olive/*Elaeagnus*
Sweet bay/*Laurus nobilis*
Zelkova

Trees for fall color
Ash
Birch
Callery pear
Chinese pistache
Chinese tallow tree/*Sapium*
Dogwood
Franklinia
Ginkgo
Katsura/*Cercidiphyllum*
Larch
Liquidambar
Maple
Nyssa
Oak
Persimmon
Poplar
Sassafras
Serviceberry/*Amelanchier*
Smoke tree/*Cotinus*
Tulip tree/*Liriodendron*
Sourwood/*Oxydendrum*
Zelkova

Trees good for areas with restricted root space
Amur maple/*Acer ginnala*
Black haw/*Viburnum prunifolium*
Chinese pistache
Crabapple
Dogwood
Flowering peach, plum, cherry
Goldenrain tree/*Koelreuteria*
Hawthorn
Hedge maple/*Acer campestre*
Holly
Hornbeam/*Carpinus*
Japanese maple
Redbud
Saucer magnolia/*Magnolia soulangiana*
Siebold viburnum
Silk tree/*Albizia julibrissin*
Snowbell/*Styrax*
Star magnolia/*Magnolia stellata*

Trees that grow quickly
Acacia
Alder
Beefwood/*Casuarina*
Birch
Black locust/*Robinia*
Catalpa
Eucalyptus
Poplar
Silver maple
Sycamore/*Platanus*
Willow

Trees that attract birds
Cherry
Cherry laurel
Crabapple
Dogwood
Eastern red cedar/*Juniperus virginiana*
Hawthorn
Holly
Loquat
Madrone
Mountain ash/*Sorbus*
Oak
Plum
Russian olive/*Elaeagnus*
Serviceberry/*Amelanchier*
Sweet bay/*Laurus nobilis*

Surefire shrubs

Shrub favorites for basic landscapes
Abelia
Azalea
Barberry
Boxwood
Camellia
Cotoneaster
Daphne
Escallonia
Euonymus
Flowering quince
Forsythia
Heather
Heavenly bamboo/*Nandina*
Holly
Honeysuckle
Hydrangea
India hawthorn/*Raphiolepis*
Juniper
Lilac
Oregon grape
Photinia
Pieris
Pittosporum
Podocarpus
Privet
Pyracantha
Rhododendron
Rose
Viburnum
Yew

Lilacs are available not only in their namesake color, but in white, pink, blue and purple.

Shrubs with showy flowers
Azalea
Broom/*Cytisus*
Bush cinquefoil/*Potentilla*
Butterfly bush/*Buddleia*
Camellia
Cornelian cherry/*Cornus mas*
Daphne
Flowering quince
Forsythia
Fuchsia
Heather/*Calluna*
Hibiscus
Hydrangea
India hawthorn/*Raphiolepis*
Lilac
Mock orange/*Philadelphus*
Mountain laurel/*Kalmia*
Oleander
Rhododendron
Rose
Spirea
Viburnum
Weigela
Witch hazel/*Hamamelis*

Shrubs with showy fruit
Barberry
Beach plum/*Prunus maritima*
Cotoneaster
Elaeagnus
Father Hugo rose

Flowering quince/*Chaenomeles*
Heavenly bamboo/*Nandina*
Highbush blueberry/*Vaccinium*
Holly
Honeysuckle
Manzanita
Nanking cherry/*Prunus tomentosa*
Oregon grape/*Mahonia*
Pomegranate
Pyracantha
Red chokeberry/*Aronia*
Sapphireberry/*Symplocos paniculata*
Shining sumac/*Rhus copallina*
Viburnum
Virginia rose

Shrubs for containers
Aucuba
Box honeysuckle/*Lonicera nitida*
Boxwood
Camellia
English laurel/*Prunus laurocerasus*
Fuchsia
Gardenia
Heavenly bamboo/*Nandina*
Holly
Hydrangea
India hawthorn/*Raphiolepis*
Juniper

Leucothoe
Mountain laurel/*Kalmia*
Mugo pine
Myrtle
Oleander
Osmanthus
Pittosporum
Podocarpus
Pomegranate
Privet
Pyracantha
Rhododendron
Rose
Viburnum
Winter creeper/*Euonymus fortunei*
Yew

Surefire ground covers

Ground covers easiest to grow
Ajuga
Campanula
Cotoneaster
Dwarf coyote bush/*Baccharis pilularis*
Dwarf rosemary
English ivy
Iberis
Juniper
Liriope
Mondo grass

Pachysandra
Potentilla
St. John's wort/*Hypericum*
Star jasmine
Stonecrop/*Sedum*
Vinca
Wintercreeper/*Euonymus fortunei*

Ground covers for dry sunny areas
Bearberry/*Arctostaphylos uva-ursi*
Cotoneaster
Dwarf coyote bush/*Baccharis pilularis*
Dwarf rosemary
Gazania
Iceplant
Santolina
Stonecrop/*Sedum*
Thyme

Ground covers for shady areas
Ajuga
Baby's tears/*Soleirolia soleirolii*
English ivy
Epimedium
Mock strawberry/*Duchesnea*
Pachysandra
St. John's wort/*Hypericum*
Vinca
Winter creeper/*Euonymus fortunei*

Surefire lawns

Lawn grasses especially good for:

The cool North
Bentgrass
Kentucky bluegrass
Red fescue
Tall fescue

The warm South
Bahiagrass
Bermudagrass
Carpetgrass
Centipedegrass
Dichondra
St. Augustine grass
Zoysia

For shady lawns
Bentgrass
Red fescue
Tall fescue
St. Augustinegrass
Zoysia

Lawn grasses that will withstand wear: most to least
Zoysia
Improved Bermudagrass
Bahiagrass
Common Bermudagrass
Tall fescue
Kentucky bluegrass
Perennial ryegrass
Red fescue
St. Augustinegrass
Centipedegrass
Paspalum
Colonial bentgrass
Creeping bentgrass
Dichondra

Surefire food plants

Herbs for basic culinary purposes
Basil
Bay
Chives
Dill
Garlic
Marjoram
Mint
Oregano
Parsley
Rosemary
Sage
Sorrel
Tarragon
Thyme

'Springset' tomato produces a high yield of medium-sized fruit.

Vegetables for the warm season
Bean
Cantaloupe
Corn
Cucumber
Eggplant
Pepper
Squash
Tomato
Watermelon

Vegetables for the cool season
Beets
Broccoli
Cabbage
Carrots
Cauliflower
Lettuce
Peas
Spinach

Tomato varieties widely adapted to varying climates
'Better Boy'
'Big Set'
'Bonus'
'Burpee's Big Boy'
'Burpee's Big Girl'
'Burpee's Early Girl'
'Burpee's VF'
'Early Cascade'
'Early Girl'
'Fantastic'
'Floramerica'
'Marglobe'
'Monte Carlo'
'Rutgers'
'Springset'
'Super Sioux'
'Terrific'
'Vineripe'
'Wonderboy'

Vegetable varieties for containers
Beets: 'Detroit Dark Red', 'Spinel'
Cabbage: 'Dwarf Morden', 'Baby Head'
Cantaloupe: 'Minnesota Midget', 'Short 'n Sweet'
Carrots: 'Royal Chantenay', 'Tiny Sweet'
Corn: 'Golden Midget'
Cucumber: 'Pot Luck', 'Patio Pik'
Eggplant: 'Dusky', 'Ichiban'
Lettuce: 'Tom Thumb'
Peas: 'Little Marvel'
Potatoes: 'Irish Cobbler', 'Norgold Russet'
Pumpkin: 'Cinderella', 'Spirit'
Squash: 'Creamy', 'Bush Acorn', 'Table King'
Tomatoes: 'Tiny Tim', 'Salad Top'

Surefire houseplants

Houseplants grown for their foliage
Asparagus fern
Bloodleaf/*Iresine*
Boston fern
Caladium
Cast-iron plant/*Aspidistra*
Chinese evergreen/ *Aglaonema*
Coleus
Croton/*Codiaeum*
Dieffenbachia
Dracaena
English ivy
False aralia/*Dizygotheca*
Grape ivy/*Cissus*
Japanese aralia/*Fatsia*

Mother-in-law's tongue/ *Sansevieria*
Nerve plant/*Fittonia*
Norfolk Island pine/ *Araucaria*
Palm
Peperomia
Philodendron
Piggyback plant/*Tolmiea menziesii*
Pilea
Pothos
Prayer plant/*Maranta*
Rex begonia
Schefflera/*Brassaia*
Spathiphyllum
Spider plant/*Chlorophytum*
Swedish ivy/*Plectranthus*
Syngonium
Wandering Jew/ *Tradescantia*
Weeping fig/*Ficus benjamina*

Houseplants that produce showy flowers
Achimenes
African violet
Anthurium
Cape primrose/ *Streptocarpus*
Christmas cactus/*Zygocactus*
Chrysanthemum
Columnea
Cyclamen
Dracaena
Flame violet/*Episcia*
Geranium
Gloxinia
Hoya
Kalanchoe
Lipstick plant/ *Aeschynanthus*
Orchid
Poinsettia
Spathiphyllum

GLOSSARY

Acid soil: Technically, soil with a pH lower than 7. In practice, it is usually used to mean a pH lower than 5.5. Acid soil is needed by acid-loving plants, such as azaleas and blueberries.

Acid-reacting fertilizer: Fertilizer, such as ammonium sulfate, that lowers the pH of the soil, making it more acid.

Aeration: The exchange of air in the soil with the air in the atmosphere. Soil with good aeration allows air to penetrate easily. Plant roots need oxygen in the soil to survive.

Alkaline soil: Soil with a pH higher than 7. Common in areas of low rainfall or where the underlying rock is limestone.

Amendments: Any bulk materials incorporated into the soil, usually to improve drainage, soil structure, or soil aeration.

Annuals: Plants that go through their life cycle, producing seeds and dying, within a year. Many perennials that die with the first frost are treated as annuals.

Auxins: Plant hormones that influence and regulate plant growth. Auxins are used to assist in rooting some cuttings.

Available nutrient: The part of the supply of plant nutrient in the soil that can actually be taken up by the plant to affect plant growth. Plant nutrients may be present but not available because of their chemical form or because of the pH of the soil.

Bagasse: A sugar cane processing by-product that is sold as a soil amendment.

Balled and burlapped: A method of selling plants at nurseries in which the root ball is dug from the ground and covered with burlap or plastic.

Bare-root plants: A method of selling plants with the roots bare of soil. Deciduous plants are frequently sold this way during their dormant period, but evergreens are sold bare-root only when young plants are sent through the mail.

Biennials: Plants that develop vegetatively in the first year, and make flowers and set seeds in the second year. They die after setting seed.

Blend of grass seed: A combination of seed that contains two or more varieties of the same species of grass, such as Kentucky bluegrass. A *mixture* has two or more species, such as ryegrass and Kentucky bluegrass.

Bolting: The tendency of some food plants, such as spinach or lettuce, to go to seed prematurely, triggered by heat, day length, drought, or nutrient deficiency.

Bone meal: A fertilizer, high in phosphorus, made from steamed and ground animal bones.

Bonsai: Dwarfed, containerized trees, carefully shaped. The art was developed in China and Japan.

Budding: A form of grafting in which a small piece of bark with a bud, rather than a whole stem, forms the scion.

Bulbs: The dormant form of some perennial plants. The word is used casually to mean the underground resting form of any herbaceous perennial flower. True bulbs, such as tulips, are tiny, fully formed plants surrounded by fleshy scales that are modified leaves.

Capillary watering: Watering plants from below with wicks or with direct contact at the base of a container between container soil and a moist medium. Capillary watering makes use of capillary action, drawing water against gravity through wicks or porous soil.

Chlorophyll: Green pigment in plant leaves, necessary for the process of photosynthesis.

Chlorosis: Yellowing of plant leaves due to the breakdown of chlorophyll, which may be caused by environmental stress, disease, insect infestation, or a nutrient deficiency.

Clay soil: Soil whose particle size is extremely small. Clay soils sometimes have drainage problems. They have a large capacity for water and plant nutrients.

Cloches: Protective tunnels made from plastic or glass, used as mini-greenhouses to warm plants in the garden.

Cold frames: Unheated glazed boxes used outdoors to trap solar heat. They are usually used to extend the growing season by starting seedlings early and protecting plants from early frosts.

Complete fertilizers: Fertilizers that contain each of the three primary plant nutrients: nitrogen, phosphorus, and potassium.

Compost: Partially decomposed organic matter used to amend the soil. Compost is often made from grass clippings, leaves, and manure.

Corms: Bulblike underground dormant structures composed of a modified stem.

Cultivation: The process of stirring the soil with a hand tool or rotary tiller, for any of several purposes, such as weeding, improving aeration, improving drainage, or mixing in soil amendments.

Damping-off fungus: A soil-borne fungus that attacks germinating seeds or seedlings, causing them to rot and die.

Deadheading: Removing spent flowers on ornamental plants to stimulate further flower production and to improve the appearance of the plant.

Deciduous: A plant that drops all or most of its leaves for the dormant season, usually in the fall.

Decurrent: A pattern of tree growth that is rounded and spreading, without a central trunk that dominates the pattern.

Determinate: Plant growth with a distinct ending. Determinate tomatoes set all their fruit at once, then die. Determinate conifers grow in distinct waves, causing their branches to radiate from the trunk in whorls (spruce, fir, and most pines).

Division: A method of vegetative plant propagation in which the whole plant is separated into two or more plants, each with the essential root, stem, and foliage parts.

Dormancy: A state of rest and reduced metabolic activity in which plant tissues remain alive but don't grow.

Double digging: A technique of soil cultivation in which soil is dug consistently to two spade depths.

Double potting: The practice of putting a draining pot within a larger but nondraining pot. Double potting often encloses a utilitarian plant container within an ornamental plant container.

Drainage: A quality of soil describing how quickly water will pass through the soil.

Drip irrigation: A watering technique using low-flow emitters that deliver a small amount of water for an extended period next to the plant.

Dry well: An excavated area, filled with rock or gravel, used as a drainage destination for downspouts or other water sources.

EC: Electrical conductivity, a measure of the amount of salts in soil.

Espalier: To train a plant, such as an apple or pear, in a fixed pattern, usually symmetrical, and usually flat against a wall or fence.

Evergreen: A plant that retains all or most of its foliage throughout the year.

Excurrent: A pattern of tree growth in which a strong central trunk remains in control of growth development.

Fertilizers: Substances that contain one or more of the necessary plant nutrients. Legally, the amount of nutrients must total at least 5 percent of the fertilizer.

Field capacity: The amount of water held in soil after drainage has stopped.

Forcing: Stimulating a plant to bloom out of season, often by manipulating the temperature or periods of light and darkness.

Fungicide: A chemical that kills fungi or protects leaves from fungus diseases.

Galls: Plant tumors stimulated by infections or insect activity. Most are harmless and none are fatal.

Grafting: A method of vegetative propagation in which a stem or bud of one plant is joined to a stem or root of another plant to form a new plant.

Green manure: Cover crops, such as legumes or grasses, grown to be tilled into the soil to increase soil organic matter and nutrients.

Greenhouse effect: A phenomenon that occurs under clear glass or plastic when the short-ray light waves from the sun, which pass easily through glass, strike an object and become longer heat waves. The longer waves are unable to pass back through the glass, so the area is warmed.

Gypsum: Calcium sulfate. A soil amendment that improves drainage in sodic (salty) soils by replacing the sodium in the soil with calcium, without raising the pH.

Hardening off: A process of accustoming seedlings germinated indoors to the harsher outdoor climate by gradually lengthening their exposure to the outdoor environment.

Hardpan: A cementlike soil layer, usually a foot or so under the surface, and usually only a couple of inches thick. Hardpan stops water drainage and root penetration.

Hardware cloth: A galvanized welded wire mesh, usually with ¼-inch squares, used for durable plant coverings aboveground or for gopher protection underground.

Hardwood cuttings: Cuttings, for rooting, made late in the season from woody growth of the past season.

Hardy: A quality of plants able to withstand cold temperatures or frost. The term is relative; it can mean that a plant is able to withstand a couple of degrees of frost or that it is able to survive the winter in a given location.

Heading back: In pruning, the removal of the end of a branch, but not all of the branch.

Heavy soil: A soil with a high percentage of clay. The word does not refer to its weight but to the impression it gives when it is worked. Because the soil is sticky, it feels heavy when shoveled or plowed.

Herbaceous: Plants that are mainly soft and succulent, without a woody stem.

Herbicide: A chemical that kills plants.

Horizon: A layer of soil in the soil profile.

Hotbed: A cold frame whose sun heat is supplemented by electric heater cables or other nonsolar heat.

Humus: A complex of organic chemicals, the relatively stable end product of organic decay in soil.

Hybrids: The offspring of two different plant varieties or species, bred to produce a plant with the best qualities of each parent.

Indeterminate: A pattern of plant growth that is continuous. Indeterminate tomatoes bear fruit continuously until killed by frost. The branches of indeterminate conifers radiate from the trunk in a random fashion (arborvitae, hemlock, juniper, and yew).

Insecticide: A chemical that kills insects.

Internode: The section of stem between two nodes.

Iron chelate: Iron molecules bound to a molecule of an organic acid. A chelating agent keeps iron from being *fixed*, or made unavailable to plants, by alkaline soil.

Iron sulfate: A chemical compound added to the soil to make it more acid or less alkaline and to increase available iron. It is also sprayed on plant leaves as a source of iron.

Latent buds: Buds within the bark that can be stimulated to grow if provoked by pruning or plant injury.

Lateral bud: Buds along the stem, contrasted with the terminal bud at the end of the stem.

Layering: A method of vegetative propagation in which roots form along a stem while it remains attached to the mother plant.

Leader: The central, highest branch on a tree or shrub from which side branches are produced. The main trunk.

Leaf mold: Decomposed leaves, used as a soil amendment or an ingredient in potting mixes.

Lime: Calcium carbonate. Used to make soil less acid.

Loam soil: Soil with a mixture of particle sizes.

Micronutrients: Nutrients needed by plants in small quantities. Also called *trace elements*, the micronutrients are zinc, iron, manganese, copper, boron, molybdenum, cobalt, and chlorine.

Mulch: A layer of material placed on the surface of the soil. The most commonly used mulches are loose organic material, such as bark chunks, sawdust, and leaves; rocks and gravel; and synthetic films, such as black plastic.

Mushroom compost: A by-product of the mushroom-raising business, consisting of composted manure and straw, used as a soil amendment.

Naturalizing: Establishment of bulbs, such as daffodils, in the ground for perennial flowering without further human attention.

Nematodes: Microscopic worms, some species of which damage plants by feeding on roots, stems, or leaves.

Nitrogen: The plant nutrient most often needed in garden soils. Nitrogen is essential for vigorous green vegetative growth of plants.

Node: The part of a stem where leaves and buds are attached.

NPK: Nitrogen, phosphorus, and potassium, the primary nutrients that plants need. Numbers on a fertilizer label refer to the percentage of nutrients contained, always in the sequence N-P-K, with a 0 if the primary nutrient is missing.

Organic matter: A substance derived from plant or animal material.

Pathogen: An organism, such as a fungus, bacterium, or virus, capable of causing a disease.

Peat moss: Partially decayed sphagnum moss mined from swamps. Used as a soil amendment, peat moss retains moisture and nutrients well, drains well, and is quite acidic.

Perennials: Plants that live for more than two years, contrasted with annuals (which live for one year) and biennials (which live for two years).

Perlite: A mineral of volcanic origin that is mined, crushed, and then heat-treated, causing it to expand into a lightweight, white soil amendment. Perlite drains well and is stable in potting mix. It does not retain nutrients or water well.

Permanent wilting point: The point of soil dryness at which plants can no longer obtain water from the soil.

Pesticides: Chemicals that function as herbicides, insecticides, or fungicides.

pH: Potential hydrogen (H is the chemical symbol for hydrogen). Relative acidity or alkalinity, as measured on a scale of 1 to 14, with 1 representing the most acid, 7 the neutral point, and 14 the most alkaline. Garden soils range from about 4.5 (very acid) to 9 (very alkaline). Most plants grow best at a pH of from 6 to 7.

Phloem: Vessels found throughout the plant that transport plant food produced in the leaves to the rest of the plant.

Phosphorus: One of the major plant nutrients, essential for seedling development and for flower and fruit formation.

Photosynthesis: The process by which plants use the sun's light to produce sugars.

Pinching: In pruning, the removal of the stem tip to produce dense, stocky plants and more blossoms.

Pleaching: The decorative interweaving of branches of adjacent trees to produce a canopy or wall.

Plugging: A method of starting a lawn, suitable for certain grasses, in which pieces cut from grass sod are planted and allowed to grow together to form a lawn.

Polarity: The direction of growth of a plant stem or root. When grafting, it is important to match polarity of the stock and scion.

Pollarding: Cutting a tree back to the same place each year. London plane trees are frequently pruned this way.

Postemergence herbicide: Herbicide that kills plants after they have emerged from the ground. It is applied to growing weeds.

Potassium: One of the three primary plant nutrients, essential for overall plant health.

Potting mix: A mixture of ingredients used for growing plants in containers. A good potting mix retains water and nutrients well and drains quickly.

Preemergence herbicide: Herbicide that kills weed seeds as they germinate. It is applied to clean soil to prevent weed growth.

Profile: The appearance of a vertical cross section of soil.

Propagating: Act of reproducing plants either sexually (through seeds) or asexually through one of several vegetative propagation techniques.

Pruning: The removal of part of a plant.

psi: Pounds per square inch. A measure of pressure. Most sprinkler heads and drip emitters are made to operate within a set pressure range. Check household water pressure with a *pressure gauge*, which screws onto an outdoor faucet.

Raised beds: A gardening style in which soil is mounded and may be enclosed with boards or masonry. Raised beds offer good drainage, rapid warming of soil in spring, and a defined garden space that is never walked on and compacted.

Reaction of soil: The relative acidity and alkalinity of the soil, which may affect, among other things, whether nutrients are available to plants. See *pH*.

Rhizomes: Underground stems of certain plants from which new plants can grow.

Rooting cuttings: A method of vegetative propagation in which a stem, leaf, or root part is used to grow a new plant.

Runners: Aboveground, trailing stems of some plants, such as strawberries or spider plants, that form plantlets at their nodes and root when the plantlet makes contact with moist soil.

Sandy soil: A soil with large particles that usually drains quickly and holds nutrients poorly.

Scaffold branches: The major side branches of a tree.

Scaling: A method of propagating certain bulbs in which the outer scales of the bulb are removed and rooted.

Scion: In grafting, the upper or stem part of the graft. The scion will become the top of the new plant.

Scooping: A method of propagating certain bulbs in which the base of a bulb is cut off to stimulate production of bulblets in the remaining bulb.

Scoring: A method of propagating certain bulbs by cutting a cross on the base of the bulb to stimulate bulblet production at the cuts.

Secondary nutrients: Plant nutrients needed in large quantities, but which are usually present in soils, and seldom need to be added as fertilizer. The secondary nutrients are calcium, magnesium, and sulfur.

Selective herbicide: Herbicide that kills one form of plant but not others. For example, 2,4-D kills broadleaf weeds in a lawn without harming the lawn grasses.

Shearing: In pruning, cutting back all stems of a plant on a single plane, usually with hedge shears.

Silty soil: A soil with intermediate particle sizes.

Sodic soil: Soil with a high sodium content, usually found in desert areas. Also called *alkali* soils, sodic soils frequently will not support plant growth.

Softwood cuttings: Cuttings made in spring from the current season's growth.

Soil: A mixture of solids, liquids, and gases that serves as a growing medium for plants.

Soil conditioner: A name commonly used in the nursery trade for composted ground bark or sawdust, usually fortified with nitrogen, ready to be incorporated into the garden soil.

Sprigging: A method of starting a lawn, suitable for certain grasses, in which pieces of grass stem are planted.

Spurs: Short twigs or branchlets on some trees that bear flowers and fruit.

Standard: A "tree" shape, with a single trunk. A tree rose is a standard.

Stock: The lower part of a graft, which will provide the root system of the new plant.

Stolons: Aboveground trailing stems. Also called *runners.*

Stomates: Microscopic pores located mainly on the undersides of leaves. Oxygen, carbon dioxide, water vapor, and other gases move in and out of the leaf through these pores.

Stooling: A variation on layering as a propagation technique. The parent plant is cut back to its crown and new shoots develop in the crown area.

Structure: The way soil particles adhere. Clay has a strong structure; clods can be as hard as rocks. Sand has a weak structure; clods fall apart at a touch. The structure has a pronounced effect on soil drainage. Soil structure can be improved by adding organic soil amendments.

Suckers: Shoots that sprout from a tree's roots or the base of its trunk.

Systemic: Herbicide, insecticide, or fungicide that is absorbed by a plant and travels throughout the plant.

Tender: Plants that die when the temperature drops below freezing.

Tensiometer: An instrument that measures the amount of water in the soil.

Terminal bud: The bud at the end of a stem or branch.

Texture: A quality of soil that is determined by the size of the soil particles. *Sand, silt, clay,* and *loam* are used to describe soil texture.

Thatch: A mass of dead grass roots and stems that may build up between living grass and soil. Excessive thatch (over ¼ inch) should be removed to allow water and nutrients to reach the grass roots.

Thinning: Removal of entire branches, back to the trunk or a larger branch.

Topiary: Plants trained into geometric shapes or statues. Often whimsical, topiary most often is done on boxwood and yew.

Topsoil: The soil of the top inches of the ground, where most plant roots get their nutrients and water.

Transpiration: The evaporation of water from a plant through stomates on the plant's leaves.

Vectors: Insects or other animals that spread disease from one plant to another. Leafhoppers and aphids are vectors of many plant diseases.

Vegetative propagation: Forming new plants from parts of old ones without sexual reproduction. Vegetative propagation produces *clones,* plants that are genetically identical. Rooting, dividing, grafting, and layering are all vegetative propagation techniques.

Vermiculite: A mica mineral that has been heated to about 3000°F. The high temperature causes it to pop like popcorn. Vermiculite holds moisture and nutrients well and drains well, but it is fragile and eventually breaks down.

Water sprouts: Vigorous, vertical shoots from tree branches. If allowed to remain, they clutter the center of a tree.

Weed: A plant that is growing in the wrong place.

Xylem: Microscopic tubes that carry water and dissolved nutrients from the roots to other plant parts.

INDEX

U.S. MEASURE AND METRIC MEASURE CONVERSION CHART

Formulas for Exact Measures

Rounded Measures for Quick Reference

	Symbol	When you know:	Multiply by:	To find:			
Mass (Weight)	oz	ounces	28.35	grams	1 oz		= 30 g
	lb	pounds	0.45	kilograms	4 oz		= 115 g
	g	grams	0.035	ounces	8 oz		= 225 g
	kg	kilograms	2.2	pounds	16 oz	= 1 lb	= 450 kg
					32 oz	= 2 lb	= 900 kg
					36 oz	= 2 1/4 lb	= 1000g (a kg)
Volume	tsp	teaspoons	5.0	milliliters	1/4 tsp	= 1/24 oz	= 1 ml
	tbsp	tablespoons	15.0	milliliters	1/2 tsp	= 1/12 oz	= 2 ml
	fl oz	fluid ounces	29.57	milliliters	1 tsp	= 1/6 oz	= 5 ml
	c	cups	0.24	liters	1 tbsp	= 1/2 oz	= 15 ml
	pt	pints	0.47	liters	1 c	= 8 oz	= 250 ml
	qt	quarts	0.95	liters	2 c (1 pt)	= 16 oz	= 500 ml
	gal	gallons	3.785	liters	4 c (1 qt)	= 32 oz	= 1 l
	ml	milliliters	0.034	fluid ounces	4 qt (1 gal)	= 128 oz	= 3 3/4- l
Length	in.	inches	2.54	centimeters	3/8 in.	= 1 cm	
	ft	feet	30.48	centimeters	1 in.	= 2.5 cm	
	yd	yards	0.9144	meters	2 in.	= 5 cm	
	mi	miles	1.609	kilometers	2-1/2 in.	= 6.5 cm	
	km	kilometers	0.621	miles	12 in. (1 ft)	= 30 cm	
	m	meters	1.094	yards	1 yd	= 90 cm	
	cm	centimeters	0.39	inches	100 ft	= 30 m	
					1 mi	= 1.6 km	
Temperature	°F	Fahrenheit	5/9 (after subtracting 32)		Celsius	32°F	= 0°C
					68°F	= 20°C	
	°C	Celsius	9/5 (then add 32)	Fahrenheit	212°F	= 100°C	
Area	in.^{2}	square inches	6.452	square centimeters	1 in.^{2}	= 6.5 cm^2	
	ft^2	square feet	929.0	square centimeters	1 ft^2	= 930 cm^2	
	yd^2	square yards	8361.0	square centimeters	1 yd^2	= 8360 cm^2	
	a	acres	0.4047	hectares	1 a	= 4050 m^2	